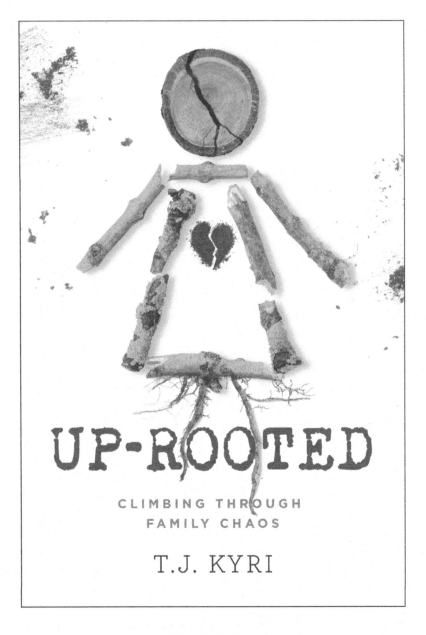

UP-ROOTED

CLIMBING THROUGH FAMILY CHAOS

T.J. KYRI

Woodhall Press
Norwalk, CT

UP-ROOTED

T.J. KYRI

Woodhall Press
Norwalk, CT

woodhall press

Woodhall Press, 81 Old Saugatuck Road, Norwalk, CT 06855
WoodhallPress.com

Cover design: Asha Hossain
Layout artist: Wendy Bowes

Library of Congress Cataloging-in-Publication Data available

ISBN 978-1-954907-54-6 (paper: alk paper)
ISBN 978-1-954907-55-3 (electronic)

First Edition

Distributed by Independent Publishers Group
(800) 888-4741

Printed in the United States of America

Dedicated to all the children who deserve more chances, and all the families who find sunshine in the clouds.

CONTENTS

PART III: THE DIVORCE

INTRODUCTION

I wrote *Up-Rooted* for the opportunity to tell my story in my voice, which had previously been silenced. The events and characters in this book are all based on my perspective and memory, however faulty that may be. Most names and places have been changed to protect my family, whom I cherish.

I hope that other families can benefit from reading about my experience and that it can pave the way for those connected to adoption or divorce. May they come to see that no matter how bad things get, they can get better. I believe that everyone deserves to have joy in their life. Finding it starts with believing you are worthy and choosing to see the positives around you.

May those who are Up-Rooted find themselves replanted in a better place.

PROLOGUE

"The court said Mommy has to leave. I don't want to—they are making me. I'll be at a hotel nearby, just for a little while, while we sort this out." I hugged Charlie's slender body so tight, he could have gone through me.

He looked at me, joining in my tears, and said, "But there's a silver lining."

Meekly, I looked at him and asked, "Really? What is it?"

He innocently responded, "I don't know, but you do. You always do."

And there it was. The mirror of my parenting, being held up to me by my ten-year-old son. I cried even harder, if that were possible. I had no answers. This was one time I couldn't see any sunshine through the thick, black clouds that engulfed me. Somehow, I had to make it okay, but it wasn't.

My children's father, Richard, whom I was trying to divorce, was coming to pick up the kids soon. I had to relay the information to the other children and make sure they were packed for their weekend in the city with him—all while trying not to collapse from the enormity of what was happening on this Friday, the thirteenth of November, 2015.

Niki, age eleven, had also been in the car while I some-how held it together for the five-minute drive from their middle school. I couldn't hide the fact that I had been crying nonstop for the past three hours. I didn't even try. Of course, they de-manded to know what was wrong as soon as they saw me. I kept repeating "I'll explain when we get home" like a mantra, so I wouldn't lose it and crash the car into a tree, which I thought about doing as I drove home from court that day.

As we opened the outer door and then unlocked the front door, I motioned for Charlie and Niki to join me on the stairs just inside. I couldn't go any further or try to get comfortable on one of the three couches in the living room. This was more than uncomfortable. This was death during life.

They knew we'd had court that day—the first time Mommy and Daddy were seeing the judge. All of the other times were with the court referee. Their lawyer, Don Brunt, made this happen. Not understanding issues of international adoption, reactive attachment disorder, cutting, or anything else directly affecting my family, he had listened to the ringleader, my oldest daughter, Paulina, and followed her lead, painting me as the Devil.

Paulina had threatened weeks ago to have me removed from the house. I foolishly scoffed, thinking courts would understand the natural order of parents being in charge, not children. I was wrong. She held more power than a fifteen-year-old ever should.

People mistakenly think that children who are adopted should be grateful for being "saved" from their former life. Not my daughter. She resented it. She resented me. Resented having left everything she knew back in Ukraine, just three years earlier. Resented being forced to care for her newborn sister, Niki, at the tender age of five, back in Ukraine. Resented having to figure out that if she put sugar on Niki's pacifier, she'd stop crying and no one would get beat up. Resented her bio-mother for choosing alcohol over food—so much so that she convinced the court it was me, this Jewish mother, who had no food in the house. So good was Paulina at manipulation and pulling others in that she'd had our current au pair take a picture of our third refrigerator—the empty one in the basement, mostly used for entertaining—and submitted it to the court as proof.

As a trained, non-practicing attorney, I was taught to believe in justice. Justice died that day as I was silenced in the courtroom while the family I'd worked so hard to build was ripped away from me. No one asked or let me explain the circumstances. No one checked the other two refrigerators or pantries. No one wanted to hear that cutting is not usually a suicide attempt, which I'd learned two years earlier when

6

Paulina tried it and we rushed to get her help. They looked at the photo that Paulina had taken and Richard had produced in court and determined that it was my fault that Niki had tried cutting herself that week. She must have been so unhappy living with me, they reasoned, that she'd decided to cut herself. The implications of a vindictive child held more weight than the word of a grown adult.

In the blink of an eye, the judge had ordered me to leave my home, immediately, not even waiting until after the Thanksgiving holiday, when I'd been set to host thirty-five family members from five states. No one cared.

Courts are designed to move people through and have those in authority make decisions when the people involved seemingly can't. My simultaneous training in law and mediation had shown me early on that giving the parties voice usually leads to better, longer-lasting results. But my attempts at my craft failed. Even hiring the president of a major mediation organization had not been enough to give me a voice. She couldn't manage Richard. She couldn't get him to stop talking over me. His booming voice silenced everyone around him. Nothing she did could get him to stop being deceitful. It wouldn't un-buy the $1.45 million apartment in Manhattan that he never mentioned. It wouldn't undo the affair he had had with our first au pair. Even bringing attorneys to the mediation didn't bring back the confident voice I'd once had.

Now, I had to steady my meek voice to tell Charlie and Niki that Mommy wouldn't be living with them for a while. Niki reacted as I could have predicted, bounding up the stairs before I'd even finished explaining. She never learned how to manage her big emotions, flipping them on and off like a light switch, self-protectively. I'm sure she was conflicted.

It was how Niki's actions were represented, one-sidedly in court, that had nailed my coffin shut. From my perspective, Paulina had brainwashed her and my son Eric

7

to think I was the cause of their problems. Niki was probably partly happy that I was leaving. The other part of her was probably sad because she was losing another mommy. First, the one in Ukraine, and now, me. Although abandonment issues were the more obvious ones, no one seemed to understand how they played out with reactive attachment disorder (R.A.D.), and no one wanted to learn.

I couldn't tell Paulina directly, since she still wasn't speaking to me, but I knew Niki would as she ran up to the room they shared. I expected that Paulina would be outwardly jubilant. Her walls were too thick to reveal any sadness she might have felt about the effect of her actions, on her or anyone else.

Eric would be returning on the school bus from Fusion Academy shortly. As a child with special needs, there was no telling how he would respond. I walked the same tightrope with him that I did with Richard, never knowing what his mood would be or what might set him off.

When Eric got home, I started by saying, "Dad's coming to pick you up soon. You'll spend the weekend in the city. Let's pack a bathing suit so you can swim in the pool in his building."

I watched for his reaction before telling him the rest, trying to ease him into the enormity of the situation. He didn't look at me, but he didn't flip out, either.

I continued, "The court said I have to move out and Dad will move back in. I'll be nearby and we'll get everything figured out soon."

He didn't cry. He didn't scream.

I followed behind as he went upstairs to his room and slammed his door.

I was left to stare at the white paint of the door, chipped from the countless times it had previously been slammed in my face.

I prayed for the strength to manage just a little longer, until Richard came and took them away. Somehow, I had to pack up the life I knew and leave it behind by Monday, 2:00 p.m. sharp! Then I would be left. Alone.

PART I:

RELATIONSHIP DEVELOPMENT

CHAPTER 1
Spark!

Although we didn't know each other yet, independently we both knew that we wanted to have children. Boys and girls. Biological and adopted. How and when that would unfold was still a mystery. Our lives were fresh, waiting to be uncovered, discovered, created.

Richard and I met the same way in 1990 and again in 1991. We had a mutual friend, Jared Vines, who did amateur comedy, and we each went with friends to see him perform. Daniella was the tie between the two sets of friends. I've known her since first grade, when we went to children's services together at B'nai Israel in Brooklyn. Every week, it was her and her mom, plus three sisters and one brother and then me. My sister, Robyn, hated services and never really felt a connection to the Jewish religion, so she never joined me.

Daniella knew Jared and told me and the girls about him performing. We were always up for something fun to do on a Saturday night, so it was an easy decision to go.

The first time, in 1990, it was just an introduction around the table. My friends Daniella, Michelle, Susan, and me, plus Richard and a few other college-age guys. There were hi's and nods and not much conversation. I noticed Richard's handsome, clean-shaven face and caught his smile, but between the distance of our seats and the raucous environment, I couldn't yet know that he was an intelligent guy with sense of humor as dry as yesterday's toast. As a mix of old friends and new acquaintances, we all laughed at Jared's jokes about school and life, and we enjoyed the other comedians, too. After the show, we all left Manhattan and headed home to Brooklyn.

A year later, I had graduated from SUNY Brockport and was back in Brooklyn for the summer before heading off to law school. Once again, we found ourselves seated around a rectangular table in a prime location at the comedy club, right in front of the small, slightly raised stage, perfectly positioned to watch Jared perform. We could see the reflection of the stage lights in the darkened room as we again listened to his somewhat lame jokes. (A little alcohol can make anything seem funny!) We drank and chuckled at him and the other comedians until the show ended around eleven p.m.

This time, rather than going straight home, someone suggested we all go out for a bite and more drinks at a nearby restaurant called Mumbles. It was the perfect casual place for our young adult crowd, with burgers, pizza, and no shortage of alcohol. With the change in atmosphere and the slightly quieter environment, we were able to have some real conversation.

As someone who is good at getting a conversation started, I kicked things off by saying "I'm looking forward to this summer, now that I've finally graduated!"

Seated to my left, a guy named Ben asked, "What are you doing this summer?"

"Not much," I said. "I finally get a break before going to law school."

"You're going to law school?!" he exclaimed. "Wow! Where?"

"Franklin Pierce Law Center, in New Hampshire."

"That sounds far."

Susan chimed in with a friendly smirk, "Yeah, she wants to get as far away from us as possible!"

I proudly said, "It is far, but it's closer than SUNY Brockport, and much prettier. The school is across the street from a park. I could've gone to Seton Hall in New Jersey, but I decided I'd rather look at a park than a parking lot! What are you up to?"

"I'll be local," Ben said. "Just working for my dad."

Noticing Richard in his button-down shirt, I turned to him and asked what he did for a living.

"I own a collectibles business," he replied.

Intrigued, I inquired further, "Really? What do you sell?"

"Rare coins."

Jared piped in with, "Yeah, he has some high-end Morgan silver dollars and the 1943 Lincoln Head Copper Penny, plus so many rare international coins!"

Daniella clarified that Jared worked for Richard, so he should know.

Wanting to extend the conversation with Richard, I continued, "That sounds cool. Where did you go to school?"

"NYU. Majored in business."

Our dialogue was abruptly cut short by Ben protesting that he was hungry, urging us to order. We ordered some pizzas to share and I got my typical girly, fruity drink, a piña colada.

I wanted to keep the conversation going with Richard, but it was tough, since I was seated closest to Ben. Plus, it was getting noisier as more intoxicated people piled in. Ben and I seemed to get along, though, so when he asked for my number, I was happy to oblige.

Richard did get my attention again at the end. We had each started to take out our wallets as we tried to figure out how much to pay.

Suddenly, Richard grabbed the check and said, "I've got it."

We looked at him incredulously.

"What do you mean, you've got it? For all of us?" Daniella questioned.

"Yes," he replied, handing the waiter a hundred-dollar bill and some twenties.

Wow, I thought. Who does that at twenty-four years old? I wondered what his coin-collecting business was really all about.

I lamented that the night was coming to an end before I could find out more about the cute, rich guy in the button-down, but was flattered that my banter with Ben had resulted in him asking for my number. At least I'd left with the prospect of a date, which was more than the others could say at the end of the evening. I resolved that even though my interest was piqued, one guy asking for my number was enough for one night.

Ben called me the next day and asked me out. Our date later that week proved that this relationship wasn't going anywhere. We went to a diner and the conversation just didn't flow. Without the alcohol, he really wasn't that cute or interesting, so I was thrilled to be invited to a small party with a similar group of friends, including Richard, a week later, without Ben.

I drove and picked up Daniella, Michelle, and Susan and off we went to someone's apartment in Brooklyn. The elevator had that "old people" smell, which matched the decor of the building. We searched the dimly lit hall until we found the right apartment.

While the dated furnishings seemed to fit the building, the small crowd was anything but old. There was a quiet hum of recent college grads as we entered and said our hellos.

I spotted Richard on the lime-green couch and he got up to greet me.

With a beer in hand, he asked what I'd like to drink.

"A wine cooler, please."

With that, we reclaimed his spot on the couch and started chatting.

"So, you're going to law school?" he began, remembering our conversation from the prior week.

"Yup."

"What kind of law?"

"I want to work with kids. At Brockport, I designed my own major in children's studies."

"That's cool," he replied. "When do you start school?"

"August. What are you up to this summer?"

"I work."

"Right. You have a business with rare coins?"

"Yeah."

"How did you get into that?"

"My brother and I collected coins. I started selling them in school when I was young. Now it's my business."

"What's it called?"

"ReliCoin. I have an office in the city."

Wow—he must be pretty rich to have his own office in Manhattan, I thought.

"That's amazing!" I said. "I'd love to see it sometime."

With a flirtatious lilt in his voice and a lifted eyebrow, he replied, "That can be arranged. So, what do you like to do when you're off for the summer?"

"Not much. Shop. See my friends. Movies. That kind of thing."

"I like to go out to eat," he said. "What's your favorite food?"

"Lobster! How about you?"

"I love lobster! We should go out for some."

"That would be fun!"

At this point, we were totally flirting. I put my feet on his lap and he started tickling them, making me giggle. The rest of the room ceased to exist as I was completely captivated by this charming, handsome, rich guy.

As the night progressed, I don't think I said two words to anyone else. When Richard motioned for me to follow him to the back bedroom, I didn't think twice. He started kissing me as his hands cupped my neck and my tongue found its way in circles around his.

The spell was briefly broken when I heard my friends calling for me. I went out to see what they wanted and Richard followed. Apparently, time had evaporated and my friends were ready to leave. I wasn't. Fortunately (this is before Uber), they were able to get another ride home, so I could have more time with this sexy guy.

Eventually, I drove him home and we parted ways, though just for a few hours. He asked to see me the following day, and I excitedly said yes.

The next afternoon he arrived at my house, once again wearing a dashing, button-down shirt, and he immediately met my parents, Loretta and Lance, and my younger sister, Robyn.

My mother was one of four sisters, all of whom were in the field of education. My mom went back to school when I was in third grade and became a teacher for children who were significantly disabled. I have always been close to her, though we fought quite a bit when I was a teen. She balanced work and family and always had dinner on the table by 5:45 p.m., when my dad came home from work.

My dad was a branch librarian for the Brooklyn Public Library and spent much of his career running the branch across from my high school. I could leave South Shore High, drop off my books, and go to my job at a different library a few bus stops away. I wasn't aware of it at the time, but this was one of the ways I was privileged, to have an in to get a job in the same field as my parents.

I started working at the library when they got their first computer, so I knew the card system as well. My dad would always have an old file card and at least one pen and one pencil in his shirt pocket. He also taught me early on, at least subliminally, to make lists. Those cards in his pocket always contained a list of some kind, neatly printed in pencil.

I was close to my dad, as well. He taught me to fight for what I believed in with words. He could be counted on to write a letter to the head of whatever company had done something wrong, and virtually always got results—and still does.

When my sister Robyn and I were kids, we used to play together all the time, though we fought on occasion, as most siblings tend to do. Under the dining room table was a favorite place to play as young children. I would pretend to be Barkley the dog, and this spot served as my dog house. She played the role of my owner, despite the fact that I was the older sister.

As we grew up, our different personalities—I was outgoing, and she was private—did not foster closeness, to my great disappointment. We remain generally nice to each other, just not close.

At the time I met Richard, Robyn was about twenty and was used to going out with her group of friends, so when I asked for a suggestion of where I could go for my first date with Richard, she suggested Randazzo's in Sheepshead Bay.

Richard did all the right things with the handshakes and "nice to meet you's." My parents were polite and didn't grill him much. After suggesting where we should go, my sister let us be and disappeared back up to her room. We didn't stay long, as we were eager to be alone for our date.

We drove about twenty minutes to get to Randazzo's and circled around, looking for a parking spot, as is to be expected in Brooklyn. When he found one, we got out and he awkwardly held my hand as we walked to the restaurant.

Randazzo's is a typical bustling, noisy Italian restaurant with durable red leather chairs and wooden tables. On the right, you can watch them make pizzas, or you can get a distorted view by watching them in the mirror, across from them. Wait staff and customers alike squeeze between the tables to get around.

Our waiter directed us to the second table from the front door, where Richard had a view of the busy street and the piers beyond. I sat facing him, looking deep into the crowds of people gabbing, drinking, and eating throughout the narrow restaurant.

"I think I'll have the linguine with clam sauce," I told him. "What? I thought you loved lobster? That's what I'm getting."

We should both get it."

"Well, lobster is expensive. It's, like, the most expensive thing on the menu," I protested.

"That's fine." he insisted. "I don't care what it costs. Let's both enjoy our lobster!"

Still uncertain, I tried again. "Really? I don't know. It's so messy."

"I don't care. We can be messy together."

One last attempt. "You sure?"

"Absolutely!"

As the waiter approached, Richard spoke for both of us. "We'll each have a one-and-a-half-pound lobster, steamed."

I thanked him as we noshed on the bread and sipped our drinks. I probably got a rum and Diet Coke, after imbibing the night before. The lobster bibs and nutcrackers appeared ahead of our meal. We put on our plastic, matching bibs and didn't have to wait long for our feast to arrive. They placed the giant red creatures in front of us and we went to work.

Being the type of person who saves the best for last, I usually approach my lobster by carefully sucking out the meat of each tiny tentacle. Next, I pick out the bits of meat from the crevices of the belly, enjoying the green tomalley that people either love or hate. Next, I move on to the knuckles, then the claws, cracking them and drawing out the succulent meat with the tiny forks they provide. Saving calories, I usually only dip the tail in butter, as the final morsel to savor. Most meals, I eat very quickly, but lobster requires meticulous work to ensure that you don't miss anything. The time it takes to eat allows for lots of conversation, especially if you get dinged with juice when someone cracks a claw!

We ate, chatted, and made each other laugh. My face hurt from smiling all night, or maybe that was from all the lobster? When the check came, Richard refused my offer while placing his Gold AmEx card in the little black check pouch. I thanked him and got up to wash my fishy hands.

Not wanting the night to end, we walked along the marina a bit before finding our way back to our car. It must have been a three-hour meter, because we didn't get a ticket.

He drove me home and we made out in the car before I went inside. I knew I would see him again, and soon!

One night, a few dates later, we sat in his station wagon outside his apartment, waiting for a spot to open up.

Richard looked at me and said, "I think you're a really special person and I would really like it if we could be boyfriend and girlfriend."

Things were going well, but I knew I'd be heading off to law school at the end of the summer.

"Look, I really like you," I said, "but you know I'm leaving in just a couple of months. I don't want to be in New

Hampshire and have you get jealous if I go for a drink with someone else. I don't want there to be strings attached while I spend three years in another state."

He persisted. "I understand that you'll be leaving, but for right now, you're here, and I'd really like to be exclusive with you. How about just for the summer? Then when you go off to law school, you can be free to do what you want to."

I couldn't see a strong argument against this plan, so I agreed. Smiling, we kissed, sealing the new status of our relationship.

A week or so later, Richard went on a business trip to California while I went up to Canada to see Niagara Falls with my old college roommates, Arya and Bonnie.

"So, there's this guy, Richard . . ."

Arya and Bonnie's eyes widened. They turned toward me, all ears, hearing the excitement in my voice.

"It's probably just a summer fling," I prefaced, "given that I'm heading to law school soon. But he's really cute, and he's taken me out for some nice dinners."

They pressed for more details.

"Where did you meet him?" "What does he do?"

I filled them in on everything, ending with, "We agreed to be exclusive, just for the summer."

"Wow, you move quick, girl!" Bonnie exclaimed.

I nodded and laughed as we walked into one of the tourist shops near Niagara Falls. I remembered Richard telling me that he loved apple butter, so when I saw some for $5, I thought it would be a nice gesture, to show I was thinking of him.

When Richard and I returned from our trips, we were happy to see each other. It turned out that I wasn't the only one who had picked up a little something. Richard thanked me for the apple butter and said he'd bought something for me as well. He pulled out a small jewelry box and I gasped upon opening it. Inside was the most beautiful and expensive thing any man had ever bought for me: a necklace with a heart-shaped charm, graduated-size rubies around the "V" and diamond chips around the curves at the top. It lay neatly in the box with the gold chain carefully tucked behind it.

I could not conceal my shock.

"Uh, it's . . . it's beautiful! And really expensive. And there is no way I can accept it," I protested, thinking *We've only been dating three weeks!*

"I thought of you a lot while I was gone. I picked it out just for you. It's not like I can go back to California and return it. Please, I really want you to have it."

Looking from him to the sparkling necklace in my hand, I relented and somewhat guiltily accepted the lavish gift.

How flattering it was that this tall, handsome, intelligent man, of some means, found me to be interesting and desirable. Even then, I was fairly self-confident; I was going off to law school, after all. Yet, to have a man, whom I was definitely attracted to, express the same, was quite an ego boost. While I was proud of my accomplishments so far in my young life, to have a man who was attractive and successful be smitten with me made me blush, on the inside.

The dating seemed almost surreal. Fancy dinners, all paid for by him. Gifts, both big and small, were romantic, showing that he cared for me. Care, before love, because we couldn't know that yet. We shared plenty of physical affection— his hand on my bottom, or resting easily around my waist, despite our height difference (his six-foot-one stature compared to my five-foot-one-and-a-half inches).

How long did it take us to get the hand link just right?

When you hold a man's hand, sometimes it works, your hands fitting easily one inside the other. But sometimes it doesn't, and then there's a certain awkwardness involved. Do you break the uncomfortable link to fix what doesn't feel right? Do you bear it, because you don't want to insult his manhood with a correction? I had mastered the simple act of interlocking fingers, but he had yet to do so. I opted not to risk insulting him, instead saying nothing while our hands stayed twisted together. Perhaps the struggle began there—learning my place, when to adjust, correct or bear with discomfort; learning how well he handled suggestions, or didn't.

Perhaps that is where I first learned to keep my mouth shut, or should have. I know now, years later, that he would rather ignore discomfort than to have me gently suggest a simple improvement that would make both of us more comfortable. Now it's too late for me to suggest and too late for him to learn. Our hands will never again be intertwined.

That summer, we continued seeing each other quite a bit, and it wasn't long before I was staying over at his apartment in Bensonhurst, not yet having sex, but getting intimate. I even grew to like his all-white male cat, Ditsy. At first, Ditsy objected to me taking his place on Richard's bed, but eventually, he learned that I would feed and pet and play with him, so he allowed me to share the bed.

Richard's mother, Elaine, was a slender, frail-looking woman whose lifestyle never maximized her five-foot-nine-inch frame. In her youth, she had briefly worked as a model for a bridal company, but her beauty and vitality faded. When I met her for the first time, she seemed like a shell of a woman, coming down the hall to Richard's apartment to feed Ditsy. Her purpose in life had been taking care of Richard and her husband, Lionel. I would learn later on that Richard resented the fact that she hadn't worked for most of her adult life.

As we grew more serious, it was time to meet Lionel, too. We went out for Chinese food locally in Bensonhurst and ordered up a storm. In contrast to Elaine, Lionel was a robust man with a hearty appetite. At six-foot-four, his height was compatible with Elaine's, and as I came to learn, so was their lack of taking care of their physical health. Lionel's friendly smile was disproportionate to his obese frame. As a smoker with diabetes, Elaine was always trying to get him to be healthier, but it never worked. She didn't exactly lead by example, refusing to go to the dentist, even as her teeth started to fall out. Lionel worked as a restaurant distributor and spent most of his days driving to visit different clients. He made enough to support his family and mostly seemed to like his job.

As we enjoyed our meal, it became apparent where Richard got his sense of humor. His parents joked around with each other and with us, putting me at ease. We all seemed to be getting along, and they seemed thrilled that their son had found someone special, as he hadn't dated much before me.

In August, Richard needed to return to Los Angeles on business, and this time, he invited me to join him, all expenses paid. Again, I was conflicted. Of course, it was exciting to be treated so lavishly, but coming from a modest background, I wasn't sure what to make of it. I was fortunate to grow up having everything I needed. We had family vacations, but they were on a budget. I was used to motels and two-star hotels, not five-star extravagance.

I also didn't know Richard well enough to know whether he would have any expectations of me, sexual or otherwise, and I didn't want to feel like I "owed him" for treating me. As with the lobster on our first date and the necklace, he persisted, and my resistance faded to acceptance.

At twenty-two years old, I was excited for the trip and impressed with the fancy hotel we stayed in. I even called my mother from the phone in the bathroom!

One of the people we met on the trip was Bill Mumy from *Lost in Space, Twilight Zone,* and *Babylon 5,* a client and personal friend of Richard's. We went out to dinner with Bill and his children. His three-year-old daughter Liliana was the cutest thing you've ever seen; with her red curls and freckles, she looked like an actual doll. (She later went on to act as well, in movies such as *Parent Trap,* with Steve Martin.)

23

She and her five-year-old brother, Seth, were well-behaved in the tiny sushi restaurant. The place was so small you could almost touch both walls with outstretched arms. Bill knew that these hole-in-the-wall places were truly the best! We enjoyed some of the freshest California fish and pleasant conversation.

It was strange for me to be having dinner with someone who was famous, and their family. Bill Mumy turned out to be the first of several famous people I'd meet over the years, including Mark Hamill, Miguel Ferrer, Nick Cage, and Leonardo DiCaprio. It always seemed bizarre to have casual conversation with these people who seemed larger than life, though I tried to remember that they are people, too.

One night in the hotel—it was August 3, 1991—Richard seemed quiet and sad. When I asked what was wrong, he admitted that it was the tenth anniversary of his brother, Andrew's, death. Until then, I'd had no idea he'd even had a brother. We sat up in bed and he tearfully told me some of the details.

"I had a brother, Andrew," he began. "He was older than me, eighteen, when he died."

I listened attentively as he continued.

"He was going to go to Buffalo University to be an architect. My dad got him an apprenticeship with an architect friend he knew in Brooklyn. He and another boy were working in the basement when an electrical fire broke out. Andrew tried to break the little basement window, but there were bars on the windows and he couldn't escape. The other boy must have stayed low. He lived. But Andrew . . ."

Richard's voice cracked as it trailed off.

I hugged him, knowing my gesture could hardly console him after such a momentous loss.

After a while, he continued.

"Andrew was the one who first started collecting coins. I was fourteen when he died. I continued what he had start-

24

ed. At first, I would just trade with friends in middle school, but soon, I was going to coin conventions with my parents. I learned quickly that if I bought a coin and promoted its value, I could sell it for more money. I started doing that more and more, and by high school, ReliCoin was born."

I later witnessed his mother, Elaine, unable to even speak Andrew's name without crying. His father, Lionel, blamed himself for getting him the apprenticeship in the Brooklyn house in the first place.

One time, when Lionel was driving me home and I was directing him where to go, I unknowingly had him drive down the street where the tragedy had occurred. I could see the tears forming in his eyes as he told me. I apologized for having him go that way, even though there was no way I could have known which street it happened on.

Lionel told me that he had been so distraught in the months following Andrew's death that he would absentmindedly find himself yelling out the car window as he drove.

The family never recovered from his death, and I think that event confirmed their lack of belief in G-d.

CHAPTER 2
Long-Distance Relationship

A few days later, Richard and I returned from our trip and spent our last few weeks together.

Before we knew it, it was time for me to head up to New Hampshire for law school. Richard had offered to drive me, so we packed up his station wagon and shared the six-hour drive, staying at the Comfort Inn, because the place I was renting wasn't ready yet.

When we arrived, we decided to pay a surprise visit to the place I was renting, since the landlord had seemed reluctant to provide details about the status of the place. When we arrived, we could see why. Electrical wires hanging from the ceiling and half-painted walls immediately told us their renovations were far from complete. Ultimately, they decided not to rent to me. Since I needed a place to stay immediately, I felt simultaneously furious, betrayed, and very concerned. How could they do that? We had a deal, and they were the ones who clearly weren't ready for a tenant.

As sometimes happens in the Northeast at this time of year, there was a hurricane approaching. Working quickly, we contacted a realtor who found me a furnished two-bedroom apartment. The only problem was that unlike the original place, it was much too far to walk to school.

The storm caught up to us and Richard was unable to leave. He decided to stay longer, until the storm passed, and help me settle in before my family came to visit a few days later.

Thankfully, my father gave me his car and drove back with Richard. I stayed in that apartment, with that car, throughout law school.

Over the next three years, Richard and I maintained a long-distance relationship. Though he hated driving, he would make the six-hour trip to visit me in New Hampshire. Sometimes he would take a train into Boston and I would drive to meet him there. We enjoyed nice dinners in the North End, and he always picked up the check.

Having gone to law school with the rare, express intent of never planning to practice law, I found my niche early on when I took an Intro to ADR (Alternative Dispute Resolution) class as a 1L. It is rare in law schools for first-year students to be allowed to take an elective, but that was one of many things that had attracted me to this progressive school.

I always pictured myself working with children, not in a law office or courthouse. My first training as a mediator in law school was in CHINS (Child in Need of Services) mediation. Parents can bring a CHINS petition to the court for help when their children are either a runaway, habitual school offender, truant or a stubborn child. If the court finds in the parents' favor, the child may have a parole officer to report to. I learned to mediate with these parents and their children, listening to each of them express their concerns to each other and supporting them in coming up with agreements that worked for their families. This felt like a natural progression from my self-designed college major of children's studies, where I took courses in child welfare, education, psychology, and more.

I found my groove through the challenging course work and made some friends. I enjoyed cooking for them in my two-bedroom apartment or going out to Tio's for margaritas and dinner. Sushi was still a novelty back then, and we would occasionally make the forty-five-minute drive to Nashua for our sushi fix.

Pizza was from one place in downtown Concord, which didn't serve individual slices. If you called up and asked for a pie, they would sarcastically ask, "Apple or cherry?" The correct terminology in Concord was, "I'd like one pizza, please, and also some pop." "Soda" was not something you said in New Hampshire. It was one of many adjustments for this Brooklyn girl. Another big one was stopping at crosswalks while driving, which was expected in New Hampshire. In Brooklyn, you would be angrily honked at for daring to give a pedestrian the right-of-way. It was a constant cultural shift each time I went home!

Not being much of a TV watcher, I was content with the thirteen-inch black-and-white TV I picked up at a tag sale in New Hampshire one weekend, for about $10. It wasn't long before a giant package arrived at my door. Richard felt I should have a proper TV and had sent me a twenty-six-inch color set. That TV stayed with us through having our children, more than ten years later.

Our visits continued and law school progressed. On one trip home, I told my paternal grandmother, Zissel, about Richard and showed her his picture. She thought he was very handsome and cooed approvingly. Coyly, she raised her eyebrows and declared in her Yiddish accent, "If only I were a little younger, I'd like him for myself!" She actually slept with his picture under her pillow.

After a few months of scoping out the guys in New Hampshire, I decided I liked what I had way better than anything I found there. The guys in New Hampshire and in my law school class seemed ordinary compared to Richard. Though my peers were generally planning to be lawyers, none were as polished as he was. The locals? In my eyes they had nothing to offer in their plaid flannel shirts, compared to the buttoned-down man waiting at home. I soon decided that I loved Richard and planned a romantic way to tell him.

He came up one weekend and I had made hearts and bought signs that said "I love you!" I put them all over my apartment, leading into the bedroom and onto the bed. When Richard arrived, I watched his face as he took in the message. He smiled with his whole face and confirmed that he loved me, too. We enjoyed another nice weekend together, although we still hadn't consummated our relationship. At twenty-two years old, I was still a virgin. I had had a few boyfriends and wasn't a prude, but sex was something I was saving for the right time, place, and person.

Growing up, sex was not really talked about in my family, but I certainly got the message that it should not be done casually. When I was sixteen, a friend came to the house for our block party with her baby. I'll never forget my mother's eyes, narrowed like darts, as she firmly warned, "Don't you ever!" I didn't need her to tell me she disapproved of teenage pregnancy, but I wasn't about to discuss it with her.

At first, Richard was patient and didn't push the issue. But by the time we took our first major trip together to Cancun, in December of 1991, it seemed reasonable to try to discover what "making love" really meant.

Before our trip, I ran around, bundled up in the cold of winter, running errands, on and off with the scarf, hat, and gloves throughout the day. When I returned to the apartment, I was devastated to discover that I had lost the necklace Richard had given me! I clutched my neck where the necklace used to be and tears flowed, knowing I'd lost something that was very precious to me.

I frantically called around to every place I had been, trying to retrace my steps, but it was never found. A couple of years later, Richard attempted to replace it with an even prettier necklace. This one had a heart shape that alternated full-sized rubies and diamonds on a thick, gold chain. I loved that necklace and have it still, though I will always regret losing the original one.

We spent winter break climbing the ruins in Cancun and were there for New Year's Eve. I still have a sweet picture of Richard bringing me a whole trail of balloons at the party we went to at the hotel. It made me laugh and glow with joy at his silliness.

We had planned to have sex that night, and Richard thought I would relax more if I drank, so he wanted me to have extra champagne. I didn't like it, and it didn't work. We tried to have sex, but it was so painful that we stopped before we had barely begun. Richard was clearly disappoint-

29

ed, but stopped when I asked him to. This was the beginning of a lifetime of painful sex and many unsuccessful attempts to overcome it. Through lots of therapy, I came to understand that part of the problem was a fear of penetration and lack of control. It also seemed strangely linked to my needle phobia.

I believe I started to be afraid of needles when I was about six years old. I distinctly recall needing a shot and being chased around the waiting room, in nothing but my pink-flowered underwear. The people in authority, the doctors, nurses, and my parents, had all the control in that situation. As a helpless child, all I could do was try to run, but they were bigger and smarter than me and soon cornered me behind a dark brown, wooden chair, stabbing me with the needle, despite my fear-induced tears.

I have come to learn that it is the lack of control I have a hard time with, so now when I need an injection, I practice calm breathing, use stress balls, look away, and tell the person when I am ready. This way the injection is on my terms, not forced on me.

It sort of works.

Despite our sexual frustration, we enjoyed the rest of our vacation before returning to his apartment in Brooklyn for a few more weeks, prior to the start of my second semester of law school.

Once I was back at school, I realized I missed Ditsy, Richard's cat. Richard suggested I get a cat of my own, and came up one weekend to pick one out with me. When I told my parents of my plans to get a cat, my father was worried about the responsibility. I assured him that it would be fine, and that a cat would be a good companion for me.

As planned, Richard and I went to a local shelter and picked out a kitten. They grilled me as to where I lived and what kind of life this kitten would have. I told them honestly that I was in law school and that when I came home on breaks, the cat and I would be with Richard and Ditsy.

They ended up rejecting me, saying that it would not be good for the cat to be with another cat part-time. I was devastated! Knowing I wanted to adopt children someday, I sobbed in the parking lot; my first attempt at adoption had failed. Someone thought I wouldn't be a good mother—to a cat!

As a way of cheering me up, Richard suggested we go to the mall and look at the pet store. I protested; I was aware that animals from pet stores are often from puppy and kitten mills, where they are mass-bred and not well cared for. Richard assured me that we would just look, so I reluctantly agreed.

Well, what do you think happened? I saw an adorable black kitten with a crooked white mustache. He was barely seven weeks old and mewed softly as I held him close against my chest. We bought him on the spot. Confirming my original hesitation about getting animals from pet stores, when I took him to the vet the next day, I learned he had fleas and ear mites! Not one to go back on my commitment, I got the medicine and treated him until he received a clean bill of health.

Shadow remained my sweet kitty for the next sixteen and a half years. He and Ditsy didn't like each other much at first. They would hiss and swipe and chase each other through the apartment. When we moved into our first house in Green-burgh, New York, in 1998, it seemed like they looked at each other and said, "It's just you and me and this big house with stairs! We're in this together." From then on, they were friends.

My relationship with Richard continued, and we had our share of ups and downs. I began to get a taste of Richard's temper, which was intermixed with loving moments and lots of generosity. We would be having a conversation and suddenly he would become short with me and raise his voice. Whether we disagreed about politics—which happened regularly, with Richard a staunch Republican and me a liberal Democrat—or about where to go, or when we would see each other, there was never room for my opinion if it differed from his.

Looking back now, it would seem I overlooked much of the fighting and focused on the positives. As a grateful person who always looks for the silver lining, it was better for me to focus on what I did have and not on what I didn't. I was in a relationship with a handsome, successful, generous man. I willingly committed to the relationship, focusing on the positives and pushing aside the growing list of negatives, believing that "all relationships take work," and we just had to keep working on ours. I wouldn't realize until much too late that Richard's booming, relentless voice would always overshadow mine, until it became pointless to argue with him. Later, I tried to pick only the most important battles to try to express my opinion, but even then, my voice was drowned by his.

Richard's coin business, ReliCoin, had its own 1-800 number. I would use the pay phone at school and call him during the day. Most days, we would speak first thing in the morning, last thing at night, and at least one to two times during the day. This was before cell phones!

Our conversations were rarely long, but they were punctuated with sweet words for each other as I tried to drag them out a few minutes longer. We developed our own language of love, as many couples do. We would represent smoochy kisses to each other with the word "Schwoop" and describe how much we loved each other with comments like, "I love you more than ice cream with hot fudge, whipped cream, and a double back flip cherry on top!" With Richard not being one to write, I treasured the cards I received from him on special occasions, like my birthday, where he would at least sign it Schwoop XXX-OOO. He found other ways to show his affection, which enabled me to gloss over many of the challenges in our relationship.

CHAPTER 3
Religion

Like most couples, there were things we had in common and areas where we differed, especially around religion. Both of us were Jewish and had celebrated bar/bas mitzvahs, but I grew up more religious than he did. My family celebrated every major Jewish holiday and we loved to entertain. We are still close to all of our extended family from my mom's three sisters, Judith, Rhona, and Rina. Both sets of my grandparents were Orthodox, and I attended the Orthodox shul across the street from my house, where I enjoyed the weekly children's services with Daniella.

I grew up generally practicing Conservative Judaism, with my parents keeping kosher in our home, meaning we didn't mix milk and meat products (no cheeseburgers), and we didn't eat pork or shellfish, among other dietary customs. As is commonly practiced among Conservative Jews, when we went out to restaurants, we were allowed to order anything we wanted, but we could not bring leftovers home. For Passover, we were even stricter, not having any bread, pasta, rice, crackers, corn—or anything else from a long list of restrictions—even visible in the house, a practice I continue today.

In my Orthodox shul, I recall being admonished for carrying an umbrella in the rain, because it is forbidden to carry anything on Shabbat. Men and women were physically separated to pray, and women were not allowed to touch or do anything sacred with the Torah. My parents did not follow such strict practices, but since this shul was right across the street from our home, it's where I went to Hebrew School and to shul until I became a bas mitzvah. While bar and bas mitzvahs are known in some places for big parties, it is the coming of age that marks the achievement of this milestone, not the way the event is celebrated.

I enjoyed Hebrew School and services, but I was the only girl to continue my studies long enough to become a bas mitzvah. My Hebrew School told my parents that they only did B'nai Mitzvot (bar/bas mitzvah for multiple people, together) for girls, and since there were no other girls, they would not do one just for me.

Frustrated, my parents pulled me out and sent me to East Midwood Jewish Center to be privately tutored by a cantor who taught me to sing a passage in Hebrew for my ceremony. The ceremony had to be on a Sunday, as was tradition for girls. At nearly twelve years old, I didn't know enough about the world to further challenge the patriarchal system. I gladly accepted the situation, as it meant that I would be allowed to complete my studies and achieve this milestone in my life.

On the day of my bas mitzvah, I wore a simple white dress that I got from a Joyce Leslie clothing store. Since it was not Shabbat, pictures were allowed to be taken, which I now treasure. To the audience's delight, my vocal training enabled me to sweetly sing my Hebrew passage. I gave my well-rehearsed speech, called a D'var Torah, where I thanked everyone, and then drew connections between what I had sung in Hebrew and my life. I spoke about the matriarchs in my passage and connected them to the people in my family who were their namesakes.

After the service, which was attended by family and friends, we had a party back at my house, with lots of food and sweets. Nothing too elaborate, as these affairs often are now. It was just right for me and my family in 1981, to mark the occasion of being recognized as a woman of the Jewish people.

Richard's family didn't seem to celebrate holidays, and I had never been invited into his parents' apartment down the hall to even say hello, much less for a meal. This confounded me; since I thought they liked me, I couldn't understand why they would never invite me over. It would be years before I understood why no one was ever allowed to visit.

In preparation for keeping kosher for Passover, my family always has an annual "eat down" where we limit what we buy in the weeks before Passover and try to finish as much as we can before the holiday. This idea was foreign to Richard. When I protested him buying frozen meals that were not kosher for Passover, he became so enraged that he threw one down the aisle of the supermarket! I was mortified and a bit scared. The outburst shocked me into silence as tears streamed down my face. I had never been involved in such a public display of anger. This was the beginning of me learning to try to keep my mouth shut so as not to set him off, which was quite hard for me as an outspoken, independent woman.

Growing up, it was rare for me to see my parents express anger, and it would never happen in public. My only frame of reference was my high school boyfriend, Neil, who also angered easily. Our mutual friend, Jerry, used to counsel me to stay quiet and let his moods pass.

I tried to apply this advice in my relationship with Richard, as well. Since he wouldn't listen to rational thought in the heat of the moment, it seemed the best way to keep the peace was to not continue to engage in the conversation, at least until he'd had time to calm down. Sometimes we could have a reasonable conversation about our fights later on; at other times we just ignored them until they bubbled up again. Conflict avoidance has a nasty way of doing that.

That day in the supermarket I cautiously followed behind Richard as he paid for the groceries. It wasn't until much later that night that I even tried to broach the subject of what had happened. Still new at my conflict resolution skills, I tried to explain my point of view before listening to his. When his rant started to heat up again, I stopped and asked him an open-ended question.

"Can you help me understand what happened earlier today?"

"If I want to buy a G-d damn frozen meal, I will!" he retorted.

I tried to stay calm, and paraphrased. "So, it seems you were upset that I didn't want you to buy frozen meals?"

"You can't tell me what I can and can't buy!"

"So, it was important to you to buy what you wanted without my input?"

"Yes. I don't give a s**t about Passover. It's not even for another two weeks!"

"I understand that you may not care about it, but it's important to me. My family and I have always celebrated Passover, and we prepare for it weeks ahead by using up food that we can't have that week."

Calming down a bit after being heard, he continued. "Well, that's not what I'm used to."

"I guess we will both have to learn to do things a bit differently."

"Maybe."

After that, we let it go and went to bed.

CHAPTER 4
Relationship Battleground

I learned to pick my battles and tried not to challenge him, especially in public. When I would relay some of these incidents to my friends, I found myself making excuses for his behavior, downplaying what had happened or following it up by recounting a moment of sweetness, lest they think he was not a good choice for me. My friends were supportive, and didn't challenge his behavior too much. If I said I was happy, then they let it be so. On balance, I thought I was happy, so I stayed in the relationship.

One day, as I sat on an Amtrak train heading back from seeing my old roommate, Arya, in Buffalo, I pondered my relationship with Richard. I was twenty-three years old and thinking about my life goals and my future. As I stared at the world going by from my window seat, I took out a pen and paper and wrote a list of pros and cons to staying in this relationship with Richard.

PROs
Smart
Owns his own business
Handsome
Loves me
Affectionate (privately)
Loves kids

CONs
Has a temper
Fighting
Republican
Works a lot
Public displays of affection

The list continued, and when I read through it, I decided the pros outweighed the cons and I would stay.

I may not have seen the extent of the negative issues, but some people on the outside did.

One night, Richard and I went to Tony Roma's for ribs. Shortly after ordering, Richard got up to watch a sports game on the TV at the bar. He normally was not one to be interested in sports, so I questioned why he was getting up in the middle of our date. He snapped that I couldn't control him, and if he wanted to watch a game, he would.

I sat there momentarily stunned at his overreaction as he stalked away. A woman at a table nearby had apparently witnessed the situation. She approached me knowingly and said, "No one deserves to be treated like that. You shouldn't be with someone who would act that way."

I was speechless at her boldness—a perfect stranger! In hindsight, I should have heeded her warning, but I became adept at making excuses for how Richard acted. Was it really so bad for him to watch something for ten minutes during our date?

Our emotions hung silently over the table when he returned. His annoyance at my protest was evident, and my confusion over what this woman had just said was spinning around in my head, unbeknownst to him. We stayed quiet for a bit, but when the food came, we ignored the incident and went on to other topics.

While I rarely believed his reactions were my fault, I also felt that I had made a well-reasoned, intentional decision to stay, so I continued our relationship, feeling he was a good catch overall. This ongoing precarious and painful walk across eggshells became more frequent as we began to build a life together.

The following summer we mostly lived together in Richard's apartment. We fought over who would feed the cats, over dishes in the sink, and even the proverbial cap on or off the toothpaste.

Often, though, we would enjoy coming back to the apartment after work with Chinese food and watching a rented movie. We'd sleep in on the weekends and hang out with each other's friends. We loved to go out to dinner, and since I was an unpaid intern at Legal Aid, Juvenile Rights in Brooklyn, Richard most often picked up the bill, despite my always offering.

As we grew more serious, it was time for our parents to meet. We took them out to Bamonte's in Brooklyn. We were all a bit nervous at first, but soon we were all appreciating each other's sense of humor. We ate and laughed and began cultivating our deepening, long-term relationship. When we each spoke to our parents afterward, they said they'd enjoyed the evening. I wonder if they thought then about the possibility of becoming in-laws?

The highs and lows continued as time went on.

Another area we differed in was music. I liked classic rock, like Billy Joel and Elton John. Richard liked heavy metal, like Metallica and Guns N' Roses. We both liked light rock, like Neil Diamond and the Bee Gees. One day, while doing some errands, tensions started to rise over the music playing in Richard's car. He insisted on blaring his heavy metal music; I wanted to find something we both liked or to simply shut it off. At the time, he had a station wagon he used for business, which had a Benzi box type of stereo system. As was common practice in Brooklyn at the time, you would remove the face of it and either lock it in the glove box or take it with you so no one would break in to steal it.

The conflict reached its peak in the parking lot of the very same supermarket where Richard had delivered his earlier tirade. As he parked the car, he pulled off the front of the Benzi box in a huff and threw it at the windshield from the inside, breaking it.

I jumped in disbelief and started crying in fear. I couldn't believe he was so incapable of controlling his rage that he would damage his own car—over our choice in music! He didn't throw it at me, I later reasoned; he was just so angry that he'd snapped and reacted without thinking. This seemed to be my barometer: If I wasn't the direct target, or physically harmed by his actions, then I could handle it.

The day ended in silence as we drove back to the apartment.

A couple of days later, we were planning to take a long drive for a vacation. He had to work the next day and I didn't. He asked me to take his car in to fix the windshield so we would have it for our trip. Initially, I didn't want to, feeling that since he was the one who'd broken it, he should get it fixed. However, Richard was very skilled at turning things around.

He became upset that I wouldn't do this for us, since I had the time and he didn't.

Giving in to the guilt trip, I begrudgingly took the car in to be fixed. In hindsight, that was one key time that I should have had him take full responsibility for his actions. He broke it. He should fix it. End of story.

Except it wasn't. The story continued, with him writing the rules, for many years to come.

CHAPTER 5
Graduation and Moving In

Despite our challenges, we had wonderful, loving moments, and it became obvious that my cat, Shadow and I would permanently move into his Bensonhurst apartment with his cat, Ditsy, after my law school graduation. After three long years in law school, I finally graduated in May of 1994.

It was a beautiful, sunny day in New Hampshire and my parents, Richard and his parents, and my two college roommates, Arya and Bonnie, all joined me in White Park, across the street from the school, to celebrate this momentous occasion. We listened to White House correspondent Helen Thomas, our keynote speaker, and posed for pictures near the small bridge in the park. We all went to dinner and then packed up our cars to take all of my things back to Richard's apartment in Brooklyn. (Mom and Dad did keep my cartons of books in their basement.)

I moved in and Richard made room for my clothes and belongings. It took some adjusting for all of us, to have me around all the time, especially while I was studying for the Bar and not yet working. Richard's mother, Elaine, was often in the apartment, taking care of things for Richard. She was used to feeding Ditsy, bringing Richard food, buying him clothes, and generally making herself at home. One day I came home from the store and found her in the kitchen, in her underwear and shirt, peeling a cantaloupe at the sink. (Awkward!)

Despite having gone to law school intentionally never planning to practice law, Richard convinced me to take the New York and New Jersey Bar exams. I studied day and night and took the Marino Bar Review class at Fashion Institute of Technology (FIT) in Manhattan while he worked. When I finally sat for the Bar exam at the cavernous Javits Center,

I could help but think, "Oh my G-d! This is it. This is the Bar exam." I nearly psyched myself out of taking it.

Months later, while looking for a job, the envelope arrived in the mail. I had failed. I missed New York by three points and New Jersey by just one. I was devastated! All that work for nothing, and I wasn't even planning to practice law.

Once again, Richard convinced me I had to try again, since I was so close. So, I did. This time, instead of studying at the apartment, I was able to use the library at SUNY Optometry, where my best friend, Susan, was enrolled. It was perfect: It was quiet; the people were really nice, and let me leave my heavy books there; and it was within walking distance to FIT.

One night in 1995, after taking a practice test at Marino, the timing was perfect and we got to see a rare performance of Barbara Streisand in concert. Richard paid a fortune to get us seats so close to the stage that I could even see her French manicure!

I sat for the exam again, and this time, I passed New Jersey and failed New York by one point! Happy and frustrated, I gave it one more try and finally passed New York. In the meantime, my loans were coming due, and the only job I could find was temping as a soon-to-be lawyer at the Dewey Ballantine Law Firm. It paid okay, but they would keep me there long hours as a glorified assistant, mostly making copies. If we stayed past seven p.m., they bought us dinner; past nine p.m., they paid for a black car home. (There was no Uber in those days; this was a higher-end version of car service.) My salary was still not enough to cover my loan payments, so Richard paid the difference and I kept a handwritten running tab of what I owed him.

Eventually, in February of 1996, I got my first real job in my chosen field of ADR, (Alternative/Appropriate Dispute Resolution) as deputy director of Project S.T.O.P. (Schools Teaching Options for Peace) at Victim Services, which later became Safe Horizon. I was thrilled to be working in schools with educators, training students to be peer mediators and teaching parenting workshops. Finally, I was able to begin to fulfill my life plan of working with children, and I got the top of my salary range ($35,000), due to my law degree.

Richard was quite used to taking the New York City subway, which was new and a bit scary for me, since we usually drove to the city when we went there together. Growing up, there was no subway near my home in Brooklyn. On the rare times I went to Manhattan, I would take the Command bus.

On my first day of work, Richard rode with me to my stop, showing me where to get off. I was terrified that I wouldn't know where to get back on! Uptown, downtown, which line, which stop to get off—fortunately, my fear and confusion were short-lived, as I quickly learned to navigate the subway system along with the responsibilities of my new job.

Over the next couple of years, Richard and I fell into our new routine. We'd run to the train in the morning (literally running down the block to make it, as we heard it coming). We'd work, then usually arrive home separately, within about an hour of each other. At night, we'd eat, feed the cats, and snuggle in bed before falling asleep. Snuggling was my favorite part of the day, morning and night. I always felt my head fit perfectly in the crook of his shoulder. In the morning, before getting out of bed, we would both agree to a one- or two-minute snuggle. Though sex remained a problem, we were quite affectionate with each other.

We were getting more serious and started looking at houses to buy. We spent many months looking in New Jersey. We finally found one we liked, then tried the commute. By then, Victim Services had moved to Brooklyn Heights. It took me over two hours to commute from New Jersey by public transportation. Richard's commute to the city wasn't much better. We wondered what we were thinking all this time, house-hunting in New Jersey; how could we have been so stupid, wasting so much time looking in an area with an unreasonable commute?

I happened to be at a family gathering, lamenting about our housing quandary, when my cousin, Linda, suggested Westchester County. In my naiveté, I didn't understand the difference between Westbury, Long Island, and Westchester, New York. Fortunately, Richard had a client friend in Edgemont, who connected us with a broker, so we started looking there.

We went out to Edgemont one weekend and saw seven houses in a single day. We both liked the first house best and felt we had something to compare it to, having looked for so long in New Jersey. It was a beautiful four-bedroom house with a pool. We took his parents to see it and they liked it, too. We talked about bidding on it, but since we were heading out to San Diego, our decision would have to wait.

For many years, I accompanied Richard to the San Diego Coinarama, helping out in the booth for ten-hour days, coming back to the hotel, quickly changing, and then running back out with him for three-hour client dinners in fancy restaurants. At first, I didn't understand the expectations and bemoaned my exhaustion over the long hours, constantly smiling and being on my feet. Eventually, though, I adjusted, and despite the challenges, I enjoyed the customer service and entertaining aspects of the trip.

In July of 1998, we had arrived home from San Diego late at night and had fallen into bed.

Around three a.m., we were awoken by Richard's mother, frantically ringing the doorbell. We jumped to our feet and rushed to the hallway to see Richard's father, Lionel, collapsed, facedown, outside his apartment door.

I had recently learned basic CPR through my job at Victim Services, but I needed Richard to turn him over, as Lionel was six-foot-four and obese, at about three hundred pounds. Richard immediately called 911, and the operator was trying to calm him down and give instructions.

Fortunately, EMS showed up quickly and I did not have to perform CPR. I felt guilty that I wasn't able to do it right away, but was comforted when they told me he was already gone, and there was nothing I could have done.

It seemed that Lionel had gotten up in the middle of the night, as he often did, evidently not feeling well. He had diabetes, which was not well controlled. We think he'd gone out for a smoke and was coming back when he apparently had a heart attack, though we'll never know for sure, since they opted not to do an autopsy. Nonetheless, since he technically died in a public place—the hallway—rather than his apartment, I was the one who went down to the coroner the next day to identify the body, since neither Richard nor Elaine could manage it. Seeing a dead person's pale body is not something I ever want to do again. To this day, I can't shake the haunting images of him in the hallway and on that cold metal table.

After they took his body away that night, I suggested to Elaine, understandably distraught, that she spend the night in our apartment, on our foldout couch, which she did. I could not have known then that my moment of kindness would be the start of a dramatic change for us. She ended up essentially moving in with us, into our one-bedroom apartment.

Suddenly, the life we were building together had a third person in it, all the time. Lionel's death sent Elaine into a tailspin of depression. Already a hoarder, her apartment became barely habitable, although I didn't know this at the time, since I was never allowed to go down the hall to her place. She spent virtually all her time either in our apartment or wandering the neighborhood, toting her shopping cart, filled with assorted bags.

I felt suffocated. With her around all the time, I had no privacy. We had no privacy. No one could return to any kind of normalcy.

I recall retreating to our tiny bathroom one night, crying in frustration. I lay down on the seafoam-green bath mat and contemplated sleeping there, rather than having to leave the bathroom and face the chaos of Richard and his mother. They had always had a tumultuous relationship. There was always lots of yelling, threatening, and aggravation. Finally, I emerged from the bathroom and told Richard, either she goes or I do!

Ultimately, we put a bid on that very first house we'd seen in Westchester. It was technically in Greenburgh, one block from Edgemont, but it had the coveted "Edgemont" address used by houses in close proximity from multiple towns. Richard felt it was vital to bid on that house, since it was the only one his father had ever seen.

I remember us practically hyperventilating on the way home, thinking, "Oh my G-d! We just bid on a house!" It took a bit of negotiating, but we got the house.

We started packing up the amazing number of things we had crammed into that little apartment. The house needed some work, so it was several months before we actually moved in. Elaine moving in with us was not even a consideration, considering how volatile her relationship could be with Richard, and how suffocated I felt, having her around constantly.

Each day, we tried to get Elaine closer to moving back into her apartment and out of ours. Her famous words for everything were, "I'm not ready." She was never ready to deal with her son's death, let alone Lionel's. Never ready to consider getting a job. Never ready to let me see her apartment. Never ready to go to the dentist. Never ready to have an answering machine or cell phone, lest people be able to reach her. Sadly, Elaine was never ready to allow joy into her life.

46

CHAPTER 6

Our First House

Finally, moving day arrived. The movers took our furniture, our boxes and everything we had, leaving the apartment empty, except for Elaine. She was the very last one to leave, putting off until the last possible moment having to face the rest of her life without her place to escape. She had to return to her apartment down the hall and to what the next phase of her life would bring.

That life was a very lonely one, largely of her own making. She filled the void with things. At the time, I was still hurt and perplexed as to why I'd never been invited to her apartment, mere steps from ours. It wasn't until years later that I learned the truth. The landlord called me about gaining access to her apartment. He was concerned that she was living in hazardous conditions that could put other tenants at risk, including him and his family, who lived on the premises.

Elaine was a hoarder. If you've ever watched any of the hoarding TV shows, you've seen how bad it can get. We needed to assess the situation and arranged for her to stay with us in Westchester for a few days. Richard made a copy of the key to her apartment so he could see the extent of the problem. It was beyond comprehension! There was no electricity—it had been disconnected long ago—so there was no working refrigerator or microwave. Piles of clothing, newspapers, and junk covered every surface.

We hoped that Elaine would see the severity of the situation and be willing to accept help. We tried desperately to stage an intervention, hiring Leslie Josel of Order Out of Chaos to at least speak with her. We lured Elaine to our home for a visit and arranged for Leslie to be there. Leslie got no further than an initial conversation at our home.

"I'm not ready" was all we would hear Elaine repeatedly protest.

We tried again a few years later when I was pregnant with her first grandchild. We hoped to appeal to her common sense, for her grandchild's sake, to no avail. Like many hoarders, she didn't have the ability to accept help for the way she'd found to cope with the profound loss of her son and her husband.

Over the years we continued to try to intervene periodically. As time went on, it got so bad that Richard had to clear ten garbage bags of just newspapers so he could open the front door! It seems she slept on one side of the bed, since the other side, where Lionel had been, was now piled with papers and clothes.

She held a lot of anger toward everyone she perceived had wronged her for decades. There were years where she refused communication with us or even her grandchildren. She wouldn't get an answering machine or cell phone. The best we could do was provide her with a calling card that she rarely used. It would be more than ten years of her living in filth before she was forced to leave that apartment.

Finally, we got a call from a hospital that she had fallen and had been in the hospital for two weeks, denying she had any family. Out of desperation as her release grew closer, she had the hospital call me on the kids' last day of summer break. Suddenly, I had twenty-four hours to find a nursing home for the mother-in-law who hadn't spoken to me in a year and a half. After canceling plans to spend the day out with the kids, by some miracle I found Port Chester Rehab and Nursing, located near us, and they agreed to accept her the following day.

We made the arrangements, and she moved in. She was never able to return to her apartment, leaving Richard and Leslie Josel's crew, a few months later, to sort everything and disinfect it. For the first and last time, I finally saw her apartment. I went with Richard to go through some of the things they had sorted. The sadness was in the walls, the carpet, and every item that remained. I hoped that when we were done, the landlord's renovation could give the next tenant the hope and joy Elaine was never able to find.

CHAPTER 7
Vows

We had been dating since 1991. Although I did not want to give any ultimatums, by the end of 1998 I needed some idea of where this relationship was heading. We discussed it and Richard promised me that he would propose before the new millennium.

On New Year's Eve, 1999, I called Arya. As my old college roommate, Arya could always be counted on for sage advice and a good laugh. We discussed how the night ahead would either be wonderful or awful. I believed there was a strong chance that he had forgotten the promise he'd made. She tried to reassure me, and I said I'd call her at the New Year's Eve event she was attending at a hotel in Buffalo, New York, if I had any news.

Richard and I made lobsters at the house, for the two of us. Earlier in the day, we'd had a fight, so when he handed me a typewritten note as we sat down, professing his love (a rarity), I took it as an apology and accepted it.

For T.J.

There is nothing that I like better than to go to sleep at night with you and wake up in the morning with you. To feel your warm body. To stroke your hair. To see your cute nose and even your boo faces.

You fill my life with meaning. You are the reason that I am able to face the world. You pick me up when I am down. You make me laugh even when I do not want to.

To hear about your accomplishments fills me with pride even though I have trouble expressing it to you.

I think that together that we can overcome the problems that face us. You are my partner and I am yours. We are a team.

I look forward to meeting life's challenges with you. Beside you. I also look forward to spending the rest of my life with you and growing old with you. I look forward to the children that we will have and to the grandchildren that we will have.

My only regret is that I don't say I love you enough.

T. J., I love you.

I went to put the note in a safe place, and when I returned, there was a ring box in the claw of my lobster! I was thrilled that he had remembered, and of course, I said yes! We popped some champagne and I excitedly called everyone and told them the wonderful news.

My parents were with my aunts and uncles in New Jersey and they shrieked with delight, talking over each other. Next, I called Arya, as promised, and the front desk paged her to come to the phone (again, this was before we all had cell phones). I made the rounds, calling my sister and my friends to share what a happy new year this had turned out to be.

We soon set a date to get married about a year later, since I needed time to plan the event of my dreams. After looking in Manhattan and Westchester, New York, for the perfect venue, we ended up choosing the place where my friend Susan had married her husband, Jason—Oceanside Jewish Center in Long Island, New York. It was the comfortable feeling I got in speaking to the coordinators, that they would manage everything well and I could relax and enjoy myself, that sealed the deal.

I knew exactly what I wanted my dress to look like and was shocked that it wasn't easy to find. I am persistent when I set my mind on something, and eventually, I found the perfect gown—lots of lace, with a long, elaborate train. Being a lifetime member of Weight Watchers, since my college days in 1988, I set out to lose the weight I'd gained while studying for the Bar exam. Focused on how I would look in pictures for eternity, I got down to my lowest weight, 112 pounds on my five-foot-one frame, requiring the dress to be taken in again just before the wedding.

About two weeks before the big day, Richard came to me and said, "I need you to sign a prenuptial agreement."

"What? How can you say that now? That will take time, and the wedding is in two weeks! I have a million things left to do and you want to throw this at me now? What are you worried about—do you think I'm in this for your money?"

We talked and fought about it, and ultimately, I called a mediator/attorney friend to see what we should do. We met in my friend's office and he discussed possible terms. It seemed that Richard wanted to protect his assets in case we didn't have children. He agreed that if we did have children, as we planned, then it wouldn't be an issue. In the end, we never signed anything, both because we knew we planned to have children, and because there wasn't enough time to figure out terms we could both agree on.

We had an amazing wedding on January 20, 2001, despite an ice storm at the end. My cousin Jared and his family, coming from New Jersey, were practically the only ones out of the two hundred people who had RSVP'd that couldn't get there in the storm. We signed the ketubah (Jewish marriage document) in advance of the ceremony. There was an elaborate cocktail hour which I couldn't be part of (since the bride couldn't be seen prior to the ceremony), including a vodka luge, kosher sushi and caviar, and top-shelf liquor.

Most things went smoothly, except that Richard's one aunt, Frieda, never got picked up by the car we'd arranged for her. As they were cueing us to start to walk down the aisle, Richard was on his flip phone with the car service, trying to figure it out. At seventy-seven years old, she was dressed and waiting downstairs in her apartment building on this cold January night. The car never came. Richard was furious, since she was one of the very few family members he had left.

I tried to be understanding, since I wanted her there, too, but he was on his cell phone as they were playing our song, the theme from the film Somewhere in Time, as we'd planned.

Finally, the wedding coordinator convinced him to end the call so we could begin the walk of our lives, down the aisle.

"If you fucking think I will ever use your car service again, you have another thing coming." He snapped his phone closed, put it in his pocket, and followed the coordinator to his assigned place.

Sadly, Aunt Frieda never made it to the event.

Thankfully, virtually everything else went well. The band was great and kept us dancing, from the hora to popular music like Billy Joel and Meatloaf. The awesome sit-down dinner after the ceremony started around nine p.m. There was a choice of prime rib, chicken, fish, or a vegetarian tower (so I knew Arya would have something yummy).

After the meal was a Viennese table, in addition to the multitiered wedding cake. Everyone took pictures with the disposable cameras on each table, which was the thing to do at the time. My boss, Tony Durrant, complimented the event, saying it had my detail-oriented thumbprint all over it!

As the wonderful evening drew to a close around midnight, I felt bad for the valets who had to de-ice every car just to bring it up for each guest. We tipped them very well. Guests marveled at the offerings as they left. There were brownies with our names individually written on them in a heart, black-and-white cookies, bagels and zeppole, bottles of water, and the Daily News, meaning everyone left with a smile as they departed into the storm.

The twenty-four-person limousine we had hired to take our guests to nearby hotels took forever to get back in the icy weather. The plan was to deliver all the guests who were staying at the hotels (different hotels at different price points), then us, and finally, our parents back to Brooklyn. My parents were originally going to stay in the hotel, but, preferring to sleep in their own bed, had canceled their reservation the week before.

By the time we'd wrapped everything up, the staff at the venue was trying to call a car service for us, since it had been more than an hour since we had heard from the limo driver, and the hotels were only ten minutes away on a normal day. Finally, at three a.m., the limo driver appeared, to our relief and dismay.

Wearily, he told us, "The bridges are all closed due to the storm, so sorry, folks, but no one is going back to Brooklyn tonight. I'll make one more round to get whoever is left to the hotel, and it looks like I'll have to stay there as well."

"Wow. Okay, let's get everyone together," I said, since we still had some cousins hanging out with us.

The wonderful event manager reassured us, saying, "We'll keep all the leftover food until tomorrow and you can pick it up when you are ready. Get home safe."

"You, too," I replied, and thanked them again.

We all piled into the limo and I grabbed my favorite, a black-and-white cookie, from my cousin Darren, since I hadn't gotten one in all the hubbub.

When we arrived at the hotel, fortunately they were able to find rooms for my parents, Elaine, and the limo driver. Elaine had brought tons of things with her in lots of shopping bags, just in case. My parents, on the other hand, had nothing. At nearly four a.m. on my wedding night, they knocked on my hotel-room door to borrow my toothpaste. How many newly married couples share toothpaste with their parents on their wedding night? No matter; between being exhausted and with the pain issues I experienced, it's not like we were going to have sex that night anyway. We were just happy to climb into bed and snuggle, relieved that we had pulled off an amazing wedding and that we were now husband and wife.

We'd been smart enough to plan to leave for our honeymoon two days later, leaving us time to recover and go back to Brooklyn to pack. Our honeymoon was a unique cruise up the Vietnam coast. I loved our long flight into Singapore, where my biggest decisions were whether to nap, snack, or read. After planning such an elaborate wedding, I craved the downtime.

What we didn't know was that we were landing in Singapore for two days during the Chinese New Year, when virtually everything was closed.

This was only the beginning of Richard's frustration. The one bus tour we took in the rain showed us that we were the youngest on this tour by several decades, which infuriated Richard.

Back at the hotel, I told him, "If you are really unhappy, let's go back to the airport and go somewhere else. I don't care where we go, as long as we're together." This was before 9/11, when it was easier to change plans while traveling. He yelled at the travel agent, long-distance, and I just sat there, trying to think of how to keep him happy on our honeymoon.

When the travel agent proved unhelpful, we decided to make the best of it and go down to the pool. The next day, we boarded the bus with the retired couples that took us to our small cruise ship.

There were around a hundred people total on this luxury cruise. I could easily understand why there was no one else our age there. Who else our age could afford such a trip? It was pretty unusual for a couple in their early thirties to be able to take a two-week international, luxury vacation. I appreciated every bit of it and didn't much mind the older company.

Richard remained resentful that our travel agent hadn't warned us about the age of our companions. He quickly grew tired of the cheek-pinching grandmotherly gestures of, "Oh, how sweet. You're on your honeymoon!" We did find a nice gay couple in their forties, also from Brooklyn, and spent some of our time with them.

We toured Ho Chi Minh City, Hanoi, and Da Nang, among others. I felt guilty sipping champagne at eleven a.m. on a river cruise while we watched fishermen in their tiny wooden boats, fishing for their family's dinner. Our tour guide told us that he was well paid in his job, at $1,000 per year. Most people made a fraction of that, which we could believe as we saw women toiling in the rice paddies, wearing their conical hats.

It was hard for us to understand a society that doesn't focus on capitalism. We were brought to people's homes and served tea and rice crackers, which we enjoyed. When we asked if we could buy some, they were confused by the idea of selling us something they had made.

In contrast, children would follow us, begging us to buy souvenirs from them, which we did as often as we could. After buying something from one child, Richard said no to another boy of about ten. As we boarded our tour bus, the boy pointed his finger at Richard, yelling, "You bad man. You very bad man!" We were surprised at the boy's reaction, and felt terrible.

While Richard still didn't much care for our travel companions, we did enjoy our unique, exotic honeymoon. After about ten days, our ship docked in Hong Kong, where we spent two days eating the local food and buying hand-tailored clothes.

Finally, we boarded our plane and headed home for our new married life together.

CHAPTER 8
Becoming a Mom

While sex remained painful, we did have it on occasion, especially on our honeymoon. It continued to be a source of conflict, as we were both frustrated that we couldn't seem to find a way to enjoy it comfortably and more frequently, no matter what we tried. Yet, just a few months after our wedding, I became pregnant. We were overjoyed, and told everyone immediately! I remember the reality setting in for both Richard and me, as I discussed the need for maternity clothes.

"Just the tops, right?" Richard inquired, naively.

I laughed and shook my head, thinking, "it's a good thing it's the women who are pregnant!"

As someone whose main goal in life was to be a mother, I loved almost everything about being pregnant. The anticipation of what was to be, filled me with joy. I dreamed about how I would teach my child to read and write, to play and grow, and ultimately, to love and be a good person in the world. I loved filling in my pregnancy journal daily, picturing what the life inside me looked like and was feeling. I read with rapt attention about what day the toes were forming, when the ears would appear, how it would get its nutrition from me. It was all enthralling, to know that my body was nurturing and sustaining another life!

The parts of pregnancy I didn't like were the food aversions and heartburn. I did not have morning sickness, but the heartburn was so bad that it was often hard to sleep, especially toward the end. Anything with tomatoes would make it worse. As someone who loves sushi, I was only allowed to eat cooked sushi while pregnant, but the idea of eel, which I normally loved, was repulsive. I couldn't stand the smell of eel or cooked meat. I was pescatarian at the time, but even being in a restaurant that served meat was difficult. Richard wondered if my taste for foods I used to love would return. (Fortunately, it did!)

I'll never forget having our twenty-week sonogram, the day after September 11, 2001.

That fateful day, Richard and I were driving to the city, expecting the usual routine. He would drop me off at the train to Brooklyn and then go to his office downtown, near Union Square. We were coming down the Henry Hudson on the west side when he turned on 1010 WINS news on the radio, as we often did. Instantly, we heard the breaking news: A plane had hit the World Trade Center!

I remember thinking, Wow! I wonder what happened to the pilot that would make him miscalculate so tragically? I didn't have time to process that thought, however, because moments later, the reporter was practically screaming that another plane had hit. We knew instantly that this was no accident.

Richard and I looked at each other, unable to comprehend the enormity of the situation.

Trying to be rational, he remarked, "You probably won't be able to go to your office, so you'll just come to mine."

I worriedly countered, "I don't think that's a good idea. I think we should both just go home."

We crawled along the highway, pulling over every few minutes for emergency vehicles to pass. Concerned, I wondered where my sister's fiancé, Patrick, was, since he was a police officer in Harlem. Pretty soon, we could see the smoke billowing from the Twin Towers in the distance.

The disagreement over our plan didn't last long. As we approached the 158th Street exit, we could see that police officers had blocked the rest of the highway and forced all nonemergency vehicles to get off and head out of the city. With no other option, we went back to the relative safety of our home in Greenburgh and turned on the TV.

I generally don't watch much television, and I particularly hate watching the news, but we were compelled to have it on all that day, trying to understand what was happening.

I called my sister, who said that thankfully, Patrick happened to have the day off. He was on his way to a lacrosse game in Orange County, New York, but he, like all other emergency workers, dropped everything and responded to the call. He was incredibly fortunate not to be a first responder that day. In the days and weeks to come, he and my sister attended funeral after funeral for his fallen comrades. The comfort we had taken for granted as Americans had been shaken forever.

Since the world, especially New York, was in chaos, I remember calling the sonogram place in Westchester the next day to see if they were even open. They said, "Sure, come on in." Televisions were on in the waiting room, replaying the previous day's events, while people tried to go about their day as best they could. It was a bittersweet time to experience such a momentous occasion, seeing our child in 3-D even as we realized the safety of the world as we'd known it had come to an end, just as we were bringing our child into it. The privilege of believing our freedom was protected from terrorism in America was shattered in an instant.

Thinking of how this new little life would be born into a world where people intentionally killed others made it scary, but I knew I could only do my best to keep my baby safe. What would be, would be.

Looking at the monitor for the sonogram, we learned that the baby was in a breech position, which was not optimal for a natural birth. The decision was made for the doctors to try externally to turn him (though we didn't know it was a "him" yet).

The following week we went into the hospital for the procedure, which was extremely painful. I had been working with my midwife, Maggie MacDonald, who I still see to this day. Maggie is a jovial Scottish woman whose smile and friendly manner instantly put me at ease. I trusted her with my life, and that of my unborn child. She worked for a medical practice that included herself and another midwife, Wendy, as well as several doctors. Since this was a medical procedure, one of the doctors, Dinesh Patel, attempted the rotation. He placed his hands on my protruding belly and gently but firmly tried to get the baby to face head down.

This was the first day we learned how stubborn our child would be. Dr. Patel pushed and pushed and got the baby three-quarters of the way down, but as soon as he released the pressure, which was intense, the baby went back to exactly where he'd started! Since the baby remained in breech position, I was told I would have to have a cesarean section. They suggested January 23, but that is my father's birthday and I wanted each of them to have their own day. We selected January 22, and given my needle phobia, we created an elaborate birth plan to help keep me calm for the IV needle I would need. At my insistence, we met with the anesthesiologist in advance to review the birth plan.

Needle phobia is no joke. I have gone through therapy, hypnosis, biofeedback, and desensitization to try to learn to handle a simple blood test. In therapy, psychologists tried to talk about the origin of my fear, but understanding it didn't help me deal with it. Hypnosis was interesting, but the therapists' attempts to put me in a relaxed state and suggest that I remain calm didn't resolve the issue either. For biofeedback therapy, I had a heart-rate monitor on my finger, which was connected to a computer. By controlling my breathing, I could successfully get the image on the screen to change from a woman to a mermaid, swimming calmly in the turquoise sea. When I am anxious about needles, I can still usually calm my breathing, so I don't hyperventilate, allowing me to stay in control of both myself and the situation.

The desensitization took time and patience, but it paid off. At first, I couldn't be in the same room with a needle. My therapist stood near the doorway of his office while I squirmed in my chair at the sight of the capped needle in his hand. Each week, he was able to get a bit closer, until finally, I was able to hold the needle in my own hand, calmly. The combination of biofeedback and desensitization enabled me to get blood drawn during my pregnancies, without getting hysterical.

On January 22, 2002, Richard drove me to the hospital and helped me get settled in the room. Then he went to the cafeteria for a bite to eat while we waited for the medical team. A nurse approached me while I was alone and tried to start the IV. I firmly insisted that she was not to touch me without my husband present. She did not know about my birth plan or my needle phobia, and there was no way I was letting anyone near me without support. She paged Richard in the cafeteria to return to the room. Concerned, he came up right away and I explained what was going on. I needed him to be my advocate, as we had discussed.

Since I was a bundle of emotions, he explained to the harried nurse that I was needle-phobic and that I had a birth plan that she needed to understand. The needle would be placed in my left arm, not my right (since I'm right-handed). He would be with me, holding my hand, while I tried to calm my breathing. Most importantly, I would tell her when I was ready. She was not to stick me until I said so.

Somewhat impatiently, she tried her best to follow our request. Finally, I gave the okay and she jabbed the needle in my arm. Richard tried to soothe me as I cried.

They wheeled me into the operating room, with Richard following the gurney in his blue hospital gown. They put up a screen so I couldn't see exactly what they were doing, and eventually, I heard the satisfying cry of my firstborn child. We chose not to learn the sex of our children until their birth, so we waited anxiously for the announcement.

"It's a boy!" Dr. Wolfe exclaimed, showing me the baby for just a second.

Right away we could tell something wasn't right. Our birth plan said I wanted him placed on my chest immediately and that I wanted to nurse him, but the doctors and nurses seemed to be scurrying and speaking in hushed tones.

Before we knew what was happening, they had whisked our newborn son away. Soon after, we learned that his Apgar scores were low. It appeared he had swallowed meconium (baby poop) that they had to suck out of his lungs with a machine. To our great relief, the procedure worked, and by the time they'd stitched me up, he had been cleaned up and brought to my room to nurse.

I've always wondered if we'd had him a day or two earlier, if he wouldn't have swallowed the meconium, and whether that impacted his disabilities later in life. We'll never know.

All I knew at that point was that my lifelong dream of becoming a mother had been fulfilled. Nothing could ever change that. I was overjoyed! We named him Eric Lionel, his middle name in honor of Richard's father.

Recovering from the C-section was challenging, since they'd cut the muscles in my abdomen, but after a few weeks, I could climb the stairs without pain. For a while, I lamented the scar across my stomach that could never be erased. Eventually, I changed my perspective and decided that the scar was my "Mommy Smile," serving as proof of when I became a mom! I truly believe that attitude strongly impacts outcome.

I cherished my three months of maternity leave, spending virtually all of my time in my new role as a mother. Eric was always on my hip, since I never wanted to put him down. He nursed well, though as he grew teeth, he would sometimes bite and I would yelp in pain! The biting habit unfortunately continued when we put him in a home daycare called Crayons and Cuddles. Joy, the owner, doted on the children she cared for, and she had a passion for cooking. When Richard and I went to meet her for the first time, she sent us home with one of the ten loaves of "monkey bread" (pull-apart bread) she had baked that day.

Joy and the other caregivers were patient with Eric as his quirks emerged. She always called him an "old soul," probably due to the spacey look he sometimes wore. We brought in red rubber "bite sticks" so he wouldn't bite the other children. When his face twisted up, we didn't yet know it was a tic, and we called it his "scrunchie face." Later, he would describe the process as being like a yawn that you just had to let run its course. It wasn't really something he could control.

When he was two, he started preschool half-days at Temple Israel, the shul we belonged to. The teachers would remark that Eric wandered the classroom and preferred to observe rather than engage in activities with other children. Being our first child, we didn't yet know that these were signs of developmental disabilities.

Eric met all his milestones at the tail end of normal. Our pediatrician told us that if he didn't walk by eighteen months, we could have him evaluated. He walked at eighteen months to the day! Since my sister was an occupational therapist, she noticed that he wasn't putting together multiword sentences and was having balance issues, so she suggested we have him evaluated for speech and occupational therapy. We did, and he caught up two weeks after the evaluation.

At the end of that year, we decided that in the fall of 2003, we would switch Eric to the preschool at the Jewish Community Center (JCC), before he turned three. By late fall, I was pregnant with our second child, due in June of 2004. Immediately, Eric's teachers at the JCC noticed issues and told us we should have him fully evaluated. We began the process with a letter requesting evaluation from the Greenburgh School District. The chair of the Committee on Preschool Special Education (CPSE) had me bring Eric for a "pre-evaluation." She had him play with puzzles and color while watching him and speaking to me. After thirty minutes, she determined he didn't qualify for services and needed no further evaluation. Naively, I left and informed the staff at the JCC of the outcome.

Thankfully, the JCC has a renowned program called "Toward Tomorrow" with a wonderful director, Naomi Goldstein. Incensed at their incompetence, she shepherded me through the process of insisting on a full evaluation. She informed me that there was no such thing as a "pre-evaluation," and that it was my right as a parent to have my child evaluated by the district. I wrote a stronger letter, being sure to include the rare attachment to my signature of "Esq.," and telling them that if they did not immediately begin the process of properly evaluating my son, we would take them to court.

It wasn't until he was four years old that Eric received the neurological, educational, psychological, psychosocial, physiatry, occupational, and speech evaluations through the district. Twelve of us sat at the CPSE meeting to discuss the results and determine what services were needed. I put a picture of Eric on the table to keep us focused on the person behind all the test scores, as I had been taught in my mediation training.

One by one, professionals reported on the findings of their evaluations and their recommendations for services. After more than two hours, the chair declared, "The committee will take this under advisement." Incredulously, I responded, "Committee? Committee of one? All the people in this room have shared their recommendations for significant services. This is the committee that makes those decisions, not you!" Eventually, with my strong advocacy, Eric began receiving services for social skills, speech therapy, occupational therapy for gross and fine motor skills, and a SEIT (Special Education Itinerant Teacher) who was the birdie on his shoulder to cue and encourage him in the classroom.

I had been cutting my hours at work after my maternity leave, since the commute from Greenburgh to Brooklyn was about ninety minutes each way. I would take the train to Richard's office and pump milk in the car from my bursting breasts while he drove us to pick up Eric and go home. Eventually, I quit my job as director of school mediation programs for Safe Horizon.

After receiving a request to do training privately at New York Technical Institute, I had decided to start my own business, T.J.'s Educational Training, in July of 2003, prior to my second pregnancy. This meant I was able to arrange my schedule around Eric's needs and still conduct workshops, which I enjoyed.

Starting my own business was challenging, especially when it came to finding clients and making the time to work. Richard hated when I put Eric in daycare or called a sitter, believing it to be a waste of money. He made a great living, so I didn't have too much pressure at first to bring in a big salary. Between starting the business, taking Eric to his various therapies, and becoming pregnant again, my hands were more than full.

Throughout my second pregnancy, everyone said it would be a girl. The people who did the sonograms kept repeating, "Oh, pretty baby, what a pretty baby!" Maggie, my midwife, said, "This one will be a girl." We didn't do any testing to find out for sure, but we were happy to think about having one of each. We decided to call her Veronica Sarah. We both liked the name Veronica, and we chose Sarah after my grandmother, since in the Jewish religion, we name after the deceased.

Since Eric was breech and had to be born via cesarean section, it was important to me to have my second child naturally, through a vaginal birth. Some in the medical community discourage this, as there is a slightly increased risk of re-tearing the original incisions. After doing research, I determined the risk was small and again wrote a detailed birth plan that included a VBAC (vaginal birth after cesarean) and no anesthesia.

I went into labor three weeks early, the evening of June 5, 2004. I called Maggie and she told me to try to get some sleep and to time the contractions in the morning. We alerted our parents and our next-door neighbors, Greg and Sharon, who had agreed in advance to watch Eric when I went to have the baby.

I tried my best to sleep, and we brought Eric over to Greg and Sharon's early the next morning, excitedly telling him he would soon be a big brother!

After twenty-six hours of labor without anesthesia, I was exhausted, and my water had not broken. Reluctantly, I allowed them to break my water, knowing that it would likely result in needing an IV and other medication. Too tired to fight it, I allowed them to give me a spinal for some relief. A spinal is a shot in the spinal column that provides temporary relief, as opposed to an epidural, which is an IV medication that provides for continuous numbing. Unfortunately, the spinal wore off before I actually gave birth, resulting in the most searing pain I could ever imagine! It was as if someone took a red-hot blade and sliced through layers of flesh while a dam that had been in place for nine months burst open and a dinosaur plowed through.

When the baby finally emerged, we were stunned when they said, "It's a boy!"

"A what?" we questioned.

"A boy!"

We were happy to have a healthy baby boy, even though we hadn't picked out a name for him. Finally, we settled on Charlie Scott Kyri. He continues to be my squishy, delicious boy who lets me give him hugs and kisses and wrap my arms around him as his "Mommy seat belt"!

Little did we know then that our Veronika Sarah (with a slight variation in spelling) had already been born, in a foreign land. She was about to turn a year old, but we would just have to be patient. It would be a while until we met. In the meantime, we'd have to wait and see what life brought.

CHAPTER 9
Pregnancy #3

On Father's Day, 2004, Richard and I took the kids to Rye Playland for the day. I was really tired walking around and suspected that I might be pregnant. Later that night, my suspicion was confirmed. Although we hadn't planned this pregnancy, we were happy to have a third child on the way.

As the pregnancy progressed, Richard thought that something might be wrong. I was utterly exhausted. One time, he came home to find our two toddlers in the enclosed play area, with me fast asleep on the floor. I attributed it to being pregnant while caring for two active toddlers. He suspected there might be more to it than that.

Unfortunately, it turned out that he was right. After doing a sonogram, we followed the high-risk doctor into her office and took the seats she pointed to, in front of her desk.

"I'm afraid I have some bad news," she said. "Your baby has a cystic hygroma, which means there is water on its brain and back, like this," she explained, as she drew a picture of a fetus with a sac on top of its head and back. "Generally, in these cases, it does not resolve. Your baby is going to die. Most people have an abortion in this situation."

Richard and I looked at each other, and suddenly, there was no controlling the tears. It was impossible to take in the enormity of what she had just said. Our other pregnancies were fairly normal. Now, not only was there an issue, but she was telling us that we should either end our baby's life or it would die on its own.

Then, she abruptly flipped the paper over and said, "But forget about that!"

We looked at her incredulously, trying to subdue both our tears and our rage.

"You just told us that our baby will die, and now, a minute later, you're telling us to forget that?"

Trying unsuccessfully to muster some emotion, the doctor continued. "Well, there is always a chance that it will resolve, maybe 5 percent, but that rarely happens for someone your age." I was thirty-six. "You could see another specialist," she added, "but as I said, most people abort right away. Otherwise, you will need to come for weekly checkups to see when the baby dies."

What she was saying seemed incomprehensible. We were reeling in shock over this unexpected and devastating news as we shuffled out of the office, feeling like we'd been punched in the gut. In a way, this was true for me. This life growing in my expanding belly was hurting in a way I could not fix.

The fifteen-minute drive home was mostly silent, lest Richard become too emotional to focus on the road. Eric and Charlie were still in daycare, so when we arrived home, we were able to sit on our couch and try to process what we'd been told. The soft cushions held no comfort for us.

"I don't want our baby to die," I cried.

With reddened eyes, Richard agreed. "But what can we do?"

"We can try more specialists. Maybe something can be done? If the baby is going to die, it should go when it's ready. I don't want to make that decision."

Richard nodded silently, and we agreed to see what we could find online about cystic hygromas, and possible treatments and specialists.

Most of what we found was even more depressing, as it confirmed the painfully small rates of resolution and survival our doctor had mentioned. We found a specialist in high-risk pregnancies, another for cystic hygroma, a third for older mothers. None provided much hope.

Each week, I would go to my appointment to see if the baby had died yet, but it hadn't. It was torture! I was starting to show and people would excitedly ask me about the baby. Sometimes I would fake it and just smile. Most of the time, I would bluntly say something like, "Thanks, but my baby is going to die." There is not much to say to that, so the topic was quickly dropped.

Then, when I was about eighteen weeks pregnant, I went for my weekly sonogram and learned that a miracle had happened. The cystic hygroma had resolved! Everyone was astonished. My theory was that doctors rarely see this outcome because most people abort right away. Amazed, but still concerned, they convinced me to do an amniocentesis, right then and there.

Being needle-phobic, and knowing they intended to shove a foot-long needle into my protruding belly, I tried to protest, but I had to relent; I knew we needed to understand as much as we could about the health of our baby. Unfortunately, the baby didn't cooperate. It kept moving, so the huge needle stayed jammed in my stomach as they moved it around for an actual five minutes, with me screaming and crying hysterically. None of the anti-phobia therapies were sufficient to keep me calm during that torturous procedure. The midwife and Richard kept telling me to breathe, so as not to hyperventilate. Eventually, they got the amniotic fluid they needed.

Once again, they sat us down for the results. This time, we were a bit more prepared for what they were about to tell us.

"The good news is, the hygroma has, in fact, resolved. The bad news is that your baby has Down syndrome. There is no way to know how severe it will be, if it lives at all, but given the issues it has already faced, it is not likely to be a good outcome. Do you want to know the sex?"

While we had reveled in the thrill of waiting until our other children were born to learn the sex, now it seemed important to know.

"Yes," we told them.

"It's a boy."

"Wow. Three boys," said Richard.

We left the office, our heads bowed with renewed shock and grief. Now we were faced with the awful dilemma about what to do next. Eric, probably understanding at age three that something was wrong, would not leave us alone for even a moment to discuss it. We finally had to have my parents come and watch Eric and Charlie while we went upstairs to my home office to try to talk.

Richard and I weighed the options.

"We could wait and see what happens," I began tentatively.

"But you heard what the doctor said. Most likely he won't survive the pregnancy anyway," Richard countered.

"I don't want to be the one to decide when he dies. I don't think I can do it."

"What if he does survive? He'll have such severe health issues. Think of how it will impact Eric and Charlie."

"I know. I'm also afraid that this will make it harder for us to move forward with our plans to adopt. Between the financial resources, the time and the emotional toll, I don't see how we could make it work. How can we have a child with such severe needs and then bring more children into the family? I also don't know if our marriage could handle that level of stress."

The tears were flowing steadily for both of us as we sat on the green and yellow duvet covering the daybed in my office. This was an impossible decision. There was no good answer. No good outcome. I've always believed that there is often not a right or wrong answer to big decisions, just the best decision you can make at the time with the information you have. I try not to look back and second-guess myself in those situations, even if other information becomes available later.

"If we do nothing, I'll have to keep going back every week to see if the baby has died yet. I hate that! It's so hard, and so sad. Plus, Dr. Wolfe said that if I'm past twenty weeks pregnant, he can't do the procedure. He said I'd have to go to

Kansas to have it done, and even then, it's only up to twenty-four weeks."

"Well, that's not happening," Richard snapped.

I nodded meekly, knowing I was not going to Kansas to have an abortion. It was amazing to think that even in 2005, terms for abortions could still be so antiquated and that politicians still got to decide what women did with their bodies, their lives, and the lives of their families. As hard as the decision was to make, there was no one more qualified to make it than the people enduring it—us.

Ultimately, I spoke to Arya, who was particularly well suited to give me advice in this situation. Her husband, Arjun, has an adult sister in India, Sonu, who has Down syndrome.

Arjun said to me, with complete honesty: "I love my sister, but my parents' entire lives, until they die, are devoted to caring for her. If they had known, they would not have brought her into this world."

I was a bit surprised to hear him speak so candidly. I have met his sister and she keeps a familiar smile on her face, yet when I see the quality of her life and the impact on her family, I knew that my existing family might not survive caring for such a child. While Sonu can feed and dress herself, she is completely nonverbal. They have developed a system to communicate on the most basic level. She will never read, write, speak, or be able to care for herself. Her parents will never be able to retire or even take a vacation without her. She fills up every aspect of their existence, and will forever.

As Arjun and Sonu's parents are growing older, the responsibility of her care will soon fall to Arya and Arjun. They are already starting to plan for the dramatic changes that will impact their lives once Sonu comes to the United States from India to live with them. I couldn't picture burdening Eric and Charlie with the care of their brother, once we were gone.

We had one more week before I would be twenty weeks pregnant. Ultimately, we both agreed that if our baby hadn't died by our next appointment, we would need to make the heartbreaking choice to end his life under the care of the doctors we knew and trusted.

The following week, we saw our baby alive for the last time through the sonogram. They printed pictures for us that I keep in the memory box I created. They had explained our choices about taking a pill that would induce labor versus having the doctor remove the baby with forceps. If I birthed the baby, I would have been able to hold him and bury him. We considered this, but decided that I did not want my body to go through labor to produce a dead child. I also did not want to have a grave that I would have felt guilty about visiting—or not visiting.

What was not clearly explained, and what I wouldn't understand until after the fact, was that in choosing to have our baby removed from my body, he would not be whole. It wouldn't be until several weeks after the procedure, when I requested my medical records, that I'd learn that no one knew where he actually was, because he was considered medical waste and had been disposed of. This was something that went against my usual mind-set of making the best decision I could with the information I had at the time. If I would have known that I couldn't find out where my baby's body was and how it would be treated, I likely would have opted for a birth and burial. Ultimately, there was nothing I could do to change it.

We made an appointment to return in a few days to start the procedure. They were to give me something to stop the baby's heartbeat. Then the next day, I would go to the hospital and they would remove him from my uterus.

I'll never forget that morning. I stood in the shower, with the hot water cascading over my protruding belly, obscuring my tears. As I touched my stomach, I spoke to him.

"I'm so sorry I could not keep you safe in this world. I could not fix you or heal your pain. I so wanted to touch you, to hold and rock you, but now that is not to be. Nothing will change the fact that you are my son and I am your mother. I hope that one day, we will be reunited, together in a place without pain or struggle. I love you."

No one heard my crying or saw my tears as they mixed with the flowing water. I couldn't believe that it was the last day I would have a life growing inside me. It was a moment shared just between my baby and me.

Eventually, I finished my shower and got dressed, and Richard drove us to the doctor's office. I was so hysterical that the doctor gave me a prescription to get Valium at the pharmacy downstairs, telling me to come back in a half-hour. I hated how drugged I felt and swore I would never take it again. It did what it was supposed to do, which was calm me down enough to allow the doctor to stop our baby's heart.

The next twelve hours were a blur. We went home and had to tend to Eric and Charlie while preparing for the procedure at the hospital the next day.

Sharing such news with others who know of your pregnancy can be challenging. I sent the following e-mail to most people who knew about it:

Dear Friends,

While I don't like to be the bearer of difficult news, I wanted to update you on our situation. As some of you know, these last few months have been difficult in my pregnancy. We were told that our baby would not survive the pregnancy, due to a "cystic hygroma," which is a buildup of fluid. We had a brief glimmer of hope when we were told that this terminal complication had miraculously resolved. This convinced us to do an amnio.

Ultimately, we learned that the baby had Down syndrome. Richard and I were faced with a gut-wrenching decision. After doing research, we came to the conclusion that we should not continue the pregnancy. Wednesday, September 14, 2005, was the last day of our child's brief existence, 19 weeks, 4 days.

We named him Collier Bradley Kyri. (I wanted a "C" name. We both love the movie, Somewhere in Time, a time-travel love story that has symbolic meaning for me. Richard and I also walked down the aisle to the theme song. Christopher Reeves played Richard Collier.) Bradley was the middle name of Richard's deceased brother.

We plan to donate to the National Down Syndrome Society in Collier Bradley's name. This organization helps improve the quality of life for those affected by Down syndrome.

We appreciate kind thoughts, but don't want to continue talking about the situation.

Thank you for your understanding.
T.J. & Richard

We went to a great support group through Good Samaritan Hospital in Rockland County, New York. The leader, Pam, was one of the most caring nurses I've ever met, and really helped the members of the group to connect. Most years, we still go to the "Walk to Remember" in October, which is a family event where we release blue, pink, and white balloons for our babies. Richard and I still go sometimes to the candle-lighting, which is done around the world to remember children who died.

Some years I write something to Collier in a special journal that I read to the group.

This is what I wrote on the eleventh anniversary of September 11:

Dear Collier,   *September 11, 2012*

Today is a day of mourning for much of the country. Remembering the fallen heroes of September 11, eleven years ago. As a mom, I always think of the children and their incomplete families. I am grateful that the children in the daycares of those buildings survived, but how many lost parents that awful day? I also think of all the pregnant women who had their babies without their husbands. Going through pregnancy and giving birth to a new life, while mourning one lost. Those children are now about ten years old, just like your older brother, Eric. I was pregnant with him, my firstborn, on that day.

Now we have added to our family: two sisters from Ukraine, Paulina and Niki. I was just thinking of Charlie. He had hoped he wouldn't be the youngest when we decided to adopt. You are our youngest child, but you are not here day to day. I can't imagine if you were. How would they treat you? They all fight so much. How would the girls react to you and the disabilities you would have had, if you'd survived? Would we even have been able to adopt them at all? Would we have been able to handle all those needs, emotionally and financially? We'll never know. Life is what it is, and what happens, happens. There isn't much to be done about it.

Eric asked me the other day about where you were buried. I don't know what made him think about it. He is old enough to try to explain one of the most difficult things for me. It still bothers me that I never got to see or hold you. We never got to bury you. Most disturbing is that the procedure did not leave you whole. I know it is a body that you never got to use, but thinking of you in pieces as "medical waste" seems to discount the person you were and the kicking I felt when you were inside me.

I will be away on the seventh anniversary of your death, though I will think of you, as I often do. I will always remember you, because you are my son and will always have a piece of my heart.

I love you.
Mom

That was in September 2012. The support group had helped us gain perspective on our situation. We learned that it was okay to feel however we felt, and that we had the support of others who had gone through similar experiences, even when people in the outside world made stupid comments or didn't understand. We worked through our grief and loss, and with time, Collier became part of our lives, part of our history forever. He was not the event in our lives that defined us. He was our child and would always be. In time, we were able to move forward, knowing we would never forget him.

In 2005, we still had plans for our future, and they included adoption. As the kids grew, we had to decide if we could expand our raised ranch house or if we would need to find a larger home. When Eric, at the age of five, taught two-year-old Charlie to climb out of his crib, we knew it was time to move.

Ultimately, we found a gorgeous 4,000-square-foot house in Greenburgh. It was built in 1911 and still retained remnants of what it must have been like back then. The arched stone carport was barely wide enough for our minivan, since it was built for horses and buggies. The coal oven had been sealed up and replaced with gas. In the basement was a wooden bar that epitomized the speakeasies of the 1920s. It still had the handles for iceboxes on either side behind the bar and the door had a square window set within the arched door, lending legitimacy to the rumor that our home had in fact been a speakeasy. We also knew that it had ironically also been a nunnery at one point.

When we took the kids to see the house, Eric actually got lost in it! Richard stayed with Charlie while the owner and I searched all four floors, including the basement. Eventually we found him hiding in the master bedroom.

We loved the house right away and were grateful to find a rare street with a sidewalk. When our bid was accepted, we were overjoyed! We moved in on August 25, 2007, right before Eric started kindergarten.

The first morning the kids were there, Eric came into our room. We asked him where Charlie was and he nonchalantly replied, "In the sister room." And so it became.

In 2008, we began what would be a three-year journey to find the sisters who would fill that room and complete our family.

PART II:

MISSION
ADOPTION

CHAPTER 10
The Adoption Process Begins

The following section consists mostly of posts taken direct-ly from my blog. I chose to craft it this way so you could understand the experience of it as we did, in real time. The blog contains contemporaneous entries about the numerous steps we took, as well as the highs and lows in our adoption process.

When we found our girls, we were advised not to use their names or identifying information in the blog until we brought them home, for fear that others would try to adopt them first. As a result, you will see references such as "older one" or "younger girl." I will give brief descriptions before the posts for context where needed.

January 16, 2011: The Journey Begins
Richard and I have wanted to adopt children since before we were married. I've always envisioned having two biological children and two adopted. We have both always wanted girls to join our family. Now that may be within our reach.

Richard and I began looking into adoption several years ago. We originally planned to adopt domestically, but learned that you can only adopt from your county in New York. We went to conferences, read books, did research, and learned that despite there being hundreds of thousands of children avail-able for adoption and probably hundreds of thousands of fam-ilies who want to adopt, the process is very complicated.

On December 20, 2010, I wrote this note to friends to up-date our progress, or lack thereof.

Yes, we are still trying to adopt. We went to another adoption conference in October. We went to the same one last year, and still no progress. Just more doors slammed, or so it seems. I still have the goal of picking an agency before Jan. 1.

Richard has greatly expanded his horizons on the parame-ters of who he would adopt, and still, it is so challenging.

We are too old or too Jewish for some countries. Oth-er countries are closed. Others only have teens or kids with significant issues. Some have wait times of five to six years from when your dossier is complete. Some you can't choose the sex. Some won't let you adopt if you've ever taken antidepressants. Some require three to four trips to the country. Some require you to stay in the country for three to six weeks (which leaves the very challenging question of what to do with Eric and Charlie).

We are currently considering India, Bulgaria, or Serbia as possibilities. It is incredibly frustrating, yet we are still hopeful. We saw a friend's six-month-old daughter yesterday and it's so sweet to watch Richard melt as he plays with her. Eric fed her a bottle. He is awesome with little kids and can't wait for a sister.

We set a goal of choosing an agency before December 31, 2010.

On the night of December 27, I spent about two and a half hours researching and taking notes (as I tend to do) on which countries we couldn't adopt from, and why, and then made a small list of possibilities. Once I had a list of about six possible countries, I noted which agencies served them and which were in New York. I shared this information with Richard at about 11:30 p.m.

He said, "Let me take a look at the computer."

We've looked at waiting children before and nothing ever clicked. This time, he half woke me and said, "What do you think of this?"

I looked at two beautiful sisters, read the limited informa-tion about them, and said, "I could do that!" He e-mailed their contact person. While I went to sleep, he didn't sleep all night, thinking we may have found our daughters!

The next day, we found out a little more information from their contact person. No apparent major issues. They are just older, and sisters (two strikes for them).

I was cautious. How likely was it that we could actually adopt those two girls? I rated it a 1 out of 10. Yet as we checked into it and spoke to references for the people we were to be working with, it began to seem like more of a reality.

Now I'm at about a 7 out of 10. There are still so many potential obstacles, but I think it could be pretty likely.

I printed out their pictures, which are all over the house, and started announcing our news.

This is what it said about them: *Niki and Paulina live at the Children's Center in Ukraine. Niki (age 6) is a healthy little girl.*

She studies at elementary school of the Children's Center. She is communicative and likes to spend time with her friends but sometimes she likes to be on her own and play with her toys. Very sweet and nice girl. Eagerly performs tasks of adults and usually obedient. Joyful and active, curious. Niki is a wonderful girl and is looking for a forever family to adopt her.

Paulina is happy, cheerful, smart, and communicative. She can cook. Paulina has a diagnosis of psoriasis. Paulina has a sister Niki, who is 6 y.o. and will be transferred to the same orphanage where Paulina is soon. (She is there now.)

Paulina is kind, active, curious and smart. She takes active part in all activities of the Children's Center. She studies with pleasure and is happy to see the results of her studies. Very nice, sweet girl who is looking to be adopted by a forever family. The Children's Center where she lives is wonderful, well-staffed, well-financed, nice furniture, lots of toys, has individual approach to children with possibilities to develop them well. We have excellent opportunity to send letters and packages to children in this center and establish a bond between child(ren) and prospective adoptive families before the families arrive to adopt.

We called the boys into the living room so they would be the first to know.

"Boys, we have something exciting to share with you," I began. "You know how we have been searching for a sister to join our family?"

"Yes," Eric said cautiously.

"Well, we think we may have found them," Richard said.

"Them?" Charlie questioned.

"Yes, them. There are two sisters, Paulina and Niki," he continued, showing them the pictures.

They stared, wide-eyed, trying to take in what we were saying.

"How old are they?" asked Charlie.

"Where are they from?" Eric wondered.

"We don't know for sure how old they are, but the younger one is about your age, Charlie, and Paulina is a bit older than you, Eric," I said. "They are from Eastern Europe, but we're not positive where yet. Dad e-mailed about them and we are waiting to hear more information."

"I only want a younger sister," Charlie protested.

"She may be younger. We're just not sure yet. They are both healthy, though."

"If we adopt two, then we will be the only family in the neighborhood with four kids. I don't want to be the only family with four."

I was a bit surprised to hear him say that, since Charlie rarely seems to care what other people think.

Eric tried to reassure him. "Then there will be more kids to play with."

"Yeah, but they're girls. They won't want to play boy stuff."

"Well, I can understand that," I empathized. "The reality is that we don't even know yet if they'll be able to join our family.

We hope so, but there are many steps before we know if it will be possible."

"Well, I think it'll be awesome!" Eric said. "Can I take their picture to school to show my class?"

"Sure, but remember, it's not a sure thing, and even if it happens, it probably won't be for at least five to twelve months," I estimated.

After a few days, we found out that Niki was, in fact, about a year older than Charlie, and that the girls were from Ukraine.

We checked in with the kids again and Charlie seemed to warm to the idea a bit, noting, "It will be a big change!"

How right he is! We're keeping an eye on him to help him adjust to the idea. When I asked him how much he wants them to come, on a scale of 1 to 10—1 being "Don't come," and 10 being "I can't wait until they get off the plane!"—he said a 3. For now, I'll take it! Eric said an 8 and I said a 9, since I'm still unsure of the obstacles we'll face.

Our contact told us to write a letter to the girls and send a small gift.

I woke up at four a.m. the following morning, writing the letter in my head for nearly an hour. The anticipation was making my mind race, so I had to get my thoughts down even before I was fully conscious.

At a more reasonable hour that morning, we all excitedly went to Target to get them some presents. Richard picked out a doll from the movie Tangled for the younger girl, after seeing her holding a Barbie doll. I didn't have a clue what would be age-appropriate for an eleven-year-old girl. Something not too babyish, but not too mature. Ultimately, I got the older one a "Color Explosion" kit so she could stencil outfits. We sent pictures of us, the boys, our cat Sparky, and our house. (I am purposely not using their names in the blog, as we were advised that other people could see this information and try to find the same kids.)

Here is the letter I wrote:

December 30, 2010

Dear Paulina and Niki,

Hi, I'm T.J., and my husband, Richard, is the one who found a picture of both of you with a little information about who you are. When we saw your pictures and read about you, we both said right away that we'd love to become a part of your lives! We'd like to tell you a little about our family and hope to learn more about you.

Our son, Eric, will be 9 years old in January, and our other son, Charlie, is 6 ½. We also have a gray cat named Sparky who is about 8 years old. Eric has a fish named Eric Jr.

We live in a big house in Westchester, New York. Our neighborhood is very friendly and there are lots of families with children whom we see often. We wait for the school bus in front of a friend's house across the street.

The picture we sent was taken in October when we went pumpkin picking. Charlie is holding the little pumpkin. He is in first grade at Highview Elementary School and loves to play Wii and Star Wars Legos. He also collects rocks. Eric is sitting next to him in the picture with his hands on his knees. He is in third grade and has recently started to play the piano. All four of us are taking lessons. Eric also loves to play the Wii and Legos. The boys and I also take martial arts.

Richard has a business selling rare coins. I work in different schools teaching both teachers and students how to get along better.

We all went together to pick out a special gift for each of you. We're not sure yet what you like or are interested in, but we hope you like what we chose. Niki, we saw the picture of you holding a Barbie doll, so we thought you might like a doll from the movie Tangled, which we all just saw. You can make her hair really long. Paulina, I thought you might like to draw. You can use the stencils to make outfits or just color with the special markers and see the different patterns underneath the paper.

We look forward to getting to know each other better and hope one day to meet you in person. We will write again soon. We hope this is a very Happy New Year for you both!

We sent in the application and the first check to the adoption agency with the gifts, then selected someone to do our home study. We knew from the adoption conferences that this was an important part of the process, so we needed someone who would not hold it against us that we already had two biological sons and that we were Jewish. While being Jewish doesn't technically disqualify us from adopting, far fewer Jewish people adopt compared to how often adoption is promoted in Christian churches. Some countries and individual families do not want their children to go to a family that practices a different religion, so it's one of those veiled challenges to overcome.

We also need our home study person to come quickly so we can move the process along. Since it's winter, we don't want bad weather to be a factor, so we chose someone in our county. We filled out her questionnaires and data form. We had to answer tons of questions about our background, our family makeup, our parenting styles, where the children would sleep, and more.

We will meet with her on January 19, the day before our tenth anniversary, and again on January 28. I also filled out most of the application for the New York agency connected to the social worker. The paperwork mountain is just beginning, but I am organized, with a pretty polka-dotted expandable file.

We found out the older child will celebrate her twelfth birthday this month. I went again to buy gifts and called my friend, Michelle, who has a twelve-year-old daughter. She suggested a journal for the birthday girl (which I agonized over for twenty minutes). We also bought pens, a purse, lip gloss, and chocolate hugs for them both to share with the other kids where they live. The card said something about hoping all her dreams come true this year. The birthday sister got a teddy bear, M&M-flavored lip gloss, and three heart-shaped ring stampers.

The crazy part is that we are so smitten with them and for the past two and a half weeks, they haven't even known we existed. We think they should have found out and received the first set of gifts TODAY. We are anxiously waiting to hear if we get any response. We'll keep you posted!

Next we were told to write to the director where they live to show we would be a good adoptive family. Here is the letter we wrote:

Dear Director of Novyy Dom,
(The Russian name of the Children's Center)

We fully appreciate your role in helping to find the best possible home for the children in your care. We wanted to write to you in order to express our genuine desire to adopt Paulina and Niki. We hope you will come to know us and trust that we would be able to give them a wonderful life in New York.

In our ten years of marriage, we have come to understand and appreciate the truly important things in life. At the very top of that list is the gift of making a difference in the life of a child, be it a biological child or an adopted child. For us, there is no distinction between the two. Our child is our child.

As you may know, we have two boys. Our oldest son, Eric, is 9 years old and our younger son, Charlie, is 6 ½. They are both active boys who have a variety of interests that they get to pursue after school and on weekends. Both boys, and T.J., take martial arts. All four of us have recently begun taking piano lessons on our newly acquired piano. Charlie loves sports and is taking "Super Sports" at our local community center. The center offers numerous activities for children, including swimming, dance, gymnastics, theater, and many other programs. T.J. also works there part-time running a fitness and nutrition program. Our children have gone to preschool and camp there and now attend different camps in the summer, based on their interests. Both of us have our own businesses. Richard created his business selling rare coins as a teen and has become renowned in his industry.

T.J.'s main job is providing training to children and adults in schools and organizations in conflict resolution, mediation, anger management, diversity, special needs, strategic planning, and numerous other subjects, which she has done for nearly twenty years, since graduating from law school.

Our family lives in a beautiful, fully restored 100-year-old, six-bedroom, five-bathroom Victorian home located in a wonderful section of Greenburgh called Pontico Hills. The neighborhood is simply amazing! There are lots of families with children right around Paulina's and Niki's ages, so we know they will have many friends. The top-notch, award-winning school system the girls would likely be a part of contains a diverse mix of children from around the world. That mix includes other families from Ukraine. We recognize that it will be a dramatic change in culture and surroundings to move from Ukraine to New York. By adopting both sisters, we hope they will find comfort and familiarity in being together in this new environment.

We have taken many great family vacations. Our most recent was to a place called Great Wolf Lodge, which has an indoor *water park and many activities for children. We went for Eric's birthday, and Eric suggested that we should go back again with Paulina and Niki. Last year, we took the kids on a Disney cruise and to Disney World with T.J.'s parents, Loretta and Lance. That is certainly a place we would love to return to with Paulina and Niki as well.*

T.J. also has a sister, Robyn, who is an occupational therapist for children. She lives about an hour away with her husband, Patrick, who is a police officer. They have four children, Kerri (age 7), Melissa (age 5), and twin boys Aiden and Ethan (age 4). All of the cousins get along well and look forward to seeing each other. Recently, we watched all the children overnight and it was wonderful to have girls at our home, making lip gloss and doing their hair. In a family of all boys, including our cat, Sparky, it will be nice to create more balance with two girls joining our family.

When we moved to our current home in 2007, Eric named the empty bedroom next to ours "the sister room." Our children have always been very excited about the idea of having sisters, so calling it the "sister room" just seemed natural. Nothing in this world would make us happier than to have that room become Paulina and Niki's room. We also have an additional bedroom upstairs, should the girls want to have their own rooms.

For us, the ability to adopt children from Ukraine is a dream come true. Richard's grandmother and aunt were born in Kamianets-Podilskyi. Maybe that is part of the reason we feel so drawn and connected to Paulina and Niki. The moment we saw their photos, we knew that we wanted Paulina and Niki to be part of our family.

We hope that as we all get to know each other, the girls will want to be adopted by us and that you will find us to be a

great family for them. We would be happy to speak with you or
answer any questions you might have. Richard's bookkeeper,
Tatiana, speaks Ukrainian and Russian and can assist with
translation, if necessary. Please feel free to e-mail us.
We look forward to speaking with you soon.

Sincerely,
Richard and T.J. Kyri

April 7, 2011: The Girls E-mailed Us!
We found out that our last package was received yesterday.

We had included our e-mail address in hopes that they might
try to contact us. IT WORKED! The older girl e-mailed us this
morning (our time)!

My heart pounded and my face flushed as I raced upstairs to
open their message on my computer. Richard had already left
for work and the kids were at school, so I was alone to relish
this amazing moment. Just yesterday, Eric was telling me all
about the translation program on Bing, so I tried it. Not perfect,
but good enough. Richard's bookkeeper helped with a better
translation.

They said they liked our gifts. (The Bing translation called
the jewelry boxes we sent "caskets"!) They are excited to meet
us. They told us their favorite colors (white for the older girl
and pink for the younger one). They love computer games
(so they'll get along great with the kids and every other kid
on the planet!). The older girl said that the younger one was
"overjoyed when she learned that someone wants to take the
family!" We also learned that they have Skype, so hopefully
we can arrange to speak with them. The older girl is learning
English! Apparently, she knows the alphabet and can translate
with a dictionary.

We are so thrilled to think about the reality of this happening.
I squealed and literally jumped up and down with delight to

think that the girls we have thought about adopting, nonstop, know we exist and seem to want to join our family!

I immediately called Richard and read the translation, then sent it to Tatiana for a better one. Overwhelmed with emotion, as he often is, he started crying at the increasing likelihood that this could become a reality. Hopefully we can communicate with them more regularly now!

Here is the best translation we have:

Good day.

We are very happy to meet you and have a relationship! I and Niki are very grateful for your presents. Last month I already sent you a letter to the address you gave but it seems you did not get one. All your packages are given to us by our guardians. Together we open them and are very pleased. Niki and I are very anxious to see you and are waiting for June to meet you.

I love very much white color, love playing on the computer, and also active games outside; also, I have many soft toys. Thank you very much for the boxes. We like them very much. Niki loves pink color; she enjoys playing with dolls and drawing. Niki was very happy when she found out that someone wants to take us in to their family! We both await your arrival. Incidentally, Niki's birthday is 9th of June; maybe you will be able to come to us for the holiday?

Here in the children's home we have Skype, if you also have we could communicate. Our log-in is Novyy Dom.

In school I am learning English and already know the alphabet, can translate with the help of a dictionary. Niki is not taking English yet but I think we will quickly learn it. Our friends who were adopted in America speak very well.

Until we meet! Anxiously awaiting your letters and call by Skype.

Paulina and Niki

April 13, 2011: We Skyped!
Sorry for the delay in posting. We did it! We were able to Skype with the girls—twice! On Sunday, we interacted with them for an HOUR! Then again on Tuesday for about twenty minutes (though the connection was really bad that day). Fortunately, our facilitator was also on to translate. It was AMAZING!!

We got to see them and speak to them and even said hi to some of their friends in the background. The older girl is blonde and looks much more like a girl than in her original picture. The younger one is very active, hopping in and out of view on the screen. We are starting to learn about their personalities. The older girl is very smart and asked good questions with a combination of Google Translate and the English she knows.

"Why you want adopt us?"

Not knowing any Russian, I typed everything into Google Translate and cut and pasted it into the chat bar.

"Well, we have always wanted to adopt and always wanted girls to expand our family. We have a 'sister room' waiting for both of you. We moved to a bigger house a few years ago so that we would have room to adopt sisters."

Eric added, "You are all we ever talk about in the car." (He's right!)

"How we go school? We go church?" she asked, trying her English. Translating for her sister, she added, "Are there parks near?"

"There is one we can walk to near our house, and look," I said, carrying the laptop to the window facing the back of the house, "this is the swing set you can play on in our back-yard!"

Smiles covered their faces as they clapped with excitement. I doubt they knew anyone in Ukraine who had their own swing set. Another point of privilege we held that would be new to them.

We pulled Charlie out of a friend's birthday party across the street, so he could speak to his soon-to-be (we hoped) sisters. He added and I translated, "We like to bake brownies. Maybe you can help us?"

The younger girl likes candy and makeup. She danced around when I asked if it would be okay for me to send her makeup. It looks like I got my girly-girl! I asked if there was anything they wanted or needed. The younger girl said she wanted a cell phone!

After less than a half-hour of talking to her future parents, at not even eight years old, she is already trying to get a cell phone. Well, the limits start now! I laughed and replied that Eric also wants a cell phone and that he would have to wait until he is at least twelve. (I guess in a few years those family plans will really pay off!)

Later in the call, she was sad at the thought of leaving her friends, but so excited about coming to New York and being adopted. She said, "Why can't you take me today?" Mixed emotions, I suppose, and perfectly understandable. I think it will be really hard for her to understand the amount of time until we can come (hopefully two months or less). I think it will be even harder when we go there and have to leave without them.

    When we were finishing the first conversation, I be-gan asking about speaking to them again in a week, on my birthday. The older girl got a look on her face and when I asked what was wrong, she said, "That's too long!" I said, "Oh, when would you like to speak again?" She said, "Tomorrow." I said, "Well, uh, I'm working then." I got my calendar out and we decided to speak again Tuesday.

When we spoke on Tuesday, the connection kept getting cut off. Richard teased the younger girl, who was eating a banana. He said, "Where is my banana?" She put the banana up to the screen and laughed. Comforting to know she gets his humor already!

After the screen blanked out, they came back on and the younger one said, "Hi, how are you?" in ENGLISH! Richard and I clapped, amazed. The older girl had already taught her younger sister one English phrase. Then the older one said to me, "You are beautiful!" in English.

Did you get that? My daughter told me I'm beautiful in English, after speaking to her a total of less than one and a half hours in her life! Do you believe in miracles? I do!

We will speak again on Friday and again on Sunday. I don't know how often we'll be able to get someone to translate, but it is so amazing to have the opportunity to do this, thanks to technology and the people who created Skype, and the people at the Center who enable them to speak to us and those helping to translate. We are a very lucky family!

April 20, 2011: Love!
As we continue to speak on Skype (we've done so five times now), our affection for each other grows exponentially. It has been wonderful to hear the older girl speak some English and teach her younger sister. I had decided that the first words I wanted to be able to say in Russian were, "I love you." I wasn't sure when or how that would happen and I didn't want to rush it or be presumptuous, although it is definitely how I have been feeling.

The other day, when we were on Skype, they showed me on the computer that they had written out, not typed, the word "Love" in English, with a heart. I think my heart skipped a beat when I saw it. I know it made me smile from ear to ear! We had Richard's bookkeeper on the phone, trying to get her hooked up to translate. I quickly asked her how to say, "I love you." She told me "Я люблю тебя" which read phonetically as Ya lyublyu tebya. I said it and they smiled big, beautiful smiles. Since then, they have been signing their messages on Skype with smiley faces and hearts. It is so sweet!

In other news, we overnighted our letter begging the US Citizenship and Immigration Services (USCIS) to expedite our I-171 (Notice of Approval of Relative Immigrant Visa Petition).

Ironically, I just discovered my old friend, Annie, from high school (that I haven't talked to in twenty-four years) is adopting a child with special needs from Ukraine and is within a week of our time frame. I spoke to her and we exchanged some info that may be helpful. She told me about a free place to stay (for a donation) in Kiev. I found out today that her congressperson was able to get the 171 for her due to the medical condition of the child she is adopting. I'm really happy for her!

We've also learned that the USCIS is a mess and is really backlogged. Apparently, they are well aware of the fact that Ukraine is closing their office for adoptions and are not planning to expedite anything on that basis. I'll call again tomorrow, but I am beginning to lose hope that this will happen any time soon. All prayers are helpful here!

We also got confirmation that our home study was submitted in Ukraine and they requested that our dossier be submitted on May 4. This would be really exciting, except that we probably won't be able to do it since we don't have the 171 yet. If we can't submit it when they request it, then it seems we will have to resubmit the home study and wait for a new date. Our paperwork is only good for six months. After five months we have to update virtually everything.

So, we may end up in a crazy loop of having to do everything over and waiting until the new Ukrainian agency creates all their new forms, then potentially doing it all over again, because documents may expire again. While we go on a paperwork chase, the girls sit waiting for us, and in the meantime, a new school year may begin. It's so crazy that this is currently contingent on US bureaucracy. I wish someone could help! (If you know anyone who knows anyone who can do anything to move this along, please tell me!) Thanks!

June 15, 2011: We Got Our Date!
After waiting for what seemed like an eternity, we finally got our date today: June 23rd! We were convinced that June was pretty much out of reach, and now we will be flying there just one week from tonight! Even our facilitator, when he informed us of the date, asked whether we could be there, given the short notice. We said, "Of course!"

Now I'm trying not to freak out about the number of things I have to do in such a short time: arranging things for work, the kids, the girls, plus the trip itself and what to bring.

Richard was great and booked the flights today. Golden Rule Travel seems to be the way to go. (We did check one other adoption travel agent, but they were a bit more expensive.)

We learned that after recently being reunited, the girls were just separated again as they were shipped off to different camps. The younger one is in a traditional sleep-away camp near the Black Sea, that has a certain number of slots allotted to orphans. The older one is several hours away at a medical camp where they treat her psoriasis. It will be a lot of traveling to see them both and they won't be together.

My friend is in Ukraine right now and keeps saying how much she loves Kiev and how beautiful it is. The people at the State Department for Adoptions (SDA) were very nice to her, and hopefully, everything will continue to go smoothly. It would be amazing to actually see her in Kiev after twenty-four years, and that may just happen!

We haven't been getting much sleep lately, and I still have to wake up early tomorrow for work, so I'll sign off for now, with much more to come.

CHAPTER 11

Meeting Our Daughters

June 23, 2011: What a Day!

At our SDA appointment today, we learned that the younger child's file was never registered, despite receiving both a letter and invitation stating that both children were available. They offered us files of other children that were available, but we refused. This means that the one-year time frame has not begun to tick and we cannot adopt her now. Yes. You read that right. We can't adopt the younger child for at least a year. We spent most of the day being upset about it—and then it got worse.

We just learned that there is a good chance the older girl will not want to be adopted without her sister. Even if she does, Child Protective Services or the guardianship committee may deny our request. Our facilitator told us that we could be here for three weeks and go home with nothing. We are devastated. I am trying not to think of the worst-case scenario. I am trying to keep Richard from blaming everyone and focus on the positive parts of this crazy situation.

At least we were told that we could see both girls. We may not have to make three trips now. We may be able to do this again more smoothly in a year. I am trying not to think about the girls staying here another year and us going back without them. I am trying not to contemplate having to redo the dossier and paying all the expenses all over again. This seems so unreal and so unfair.

As I've said before, it changes every minute. We are packed and ready to go first thing tomorrow. Maybe it will be a better day.

June 25, 2011: We Met the Older Child!

We met with the older girl for five hours! She is great! They called us in our hotel room, where I was napping, and said she

98

is downstairs right now. We quickly gathered our things and ran down to meet her. Richard and I had tears in our eyes and hugged her right away. I gave her the shirt that said "Love" with a picture of the United States in hearts and a white teddy bear with a heart that said, "I love you." She thanked us.

Then we went to Child Protective Services where we were officially supposed to meet for the first time. Again, they didn't ask us questions, only her. We tried to make it clear that we did not want to pressure her to decide now about whether or not to come to the United States, though it was one of the first things they asked her. They were nice, and asked her if she knew us and would like to spend more time with us. She was nervous, but said yes. They signed and stamped a bunch of papers saying that contact had been made and could continue for ten days.

After that we all went for pizza across the street. We learned that she had never gotten the phone we bought her to replace the one they gave her as a twelve-year-old, which broke. We found a place right next door to the pizza place and bought her a new, pink phone with a blue Hello Kitty case. She was very grateful. She played with the phone, programmed it, took pictures of us and her caregivers, and charged it.

After that, we went back with her to where she normally lives where we hung out for a while. She clearly felt right at home and took a quick shower and changed into the shirt I gave her. When we first saw her, she was wearing the Mickey and Minnie shirt I had sent earlier. In the pizza place she put on the earrings I'd brought for her from our family vacation at Beaches resort at Turks and Caicos (awesome place!). We went to both the old and new buildings where she lives, where the director, Yuri, gave us a tour. They are very nice facilities, compared to other traditional orphanages. She seems very well adjusted and had very comfortable relationships with her care-givers. We exchanged lots of hugs.

She was very excited to be allowed to stay in her regular place tonight and not have to go back to the camp. Apparently, the camp is more like a traditional orphanage, and she hates the food there. We showed her lots of pictures, including pictures of bed styles and bedding. She liked white beds and many patterns of comforters. It was so nice to hang out with her, and a bit surreal.

Tomorrow, we will go with her and a caregiver to shop for clothes. She was wearing a skirt she had received from the United States two years ago, when she was hosted by a family from Texas. They were supposed to adopt just her, but the adoption fell through. Her shoes are too tight. She is as tall as Eric and has a slightly smaller foot than I do, about a 6 ½. We will spend the morning together with the caregiver. Then, at the director's suggestion, we will spend the afternoon with her and our facilitator so we can bond more. We will see when and how to meet the younger child. We are not officially allowed to, but they are working out a way to do so, somehow. It will be torturous to explain to her that we can't take her now. Apparently, being adopted is even more important to the younger one than it is to the older one.

This has been such a roller-coaster ride, and there are more peaks, valleys, and turns ahead. Richard and I still can't believe this is all happening the way it is, and there's not much we can do about it. There are also a lot of politics concerning this one attorney who may be able to help. There are no others, and apparently, she is hated by many; if you don't work with her, she will intentionally muck things up. Because of things she has done, they have drastically cut the budget to the place where they live, so that they don't have money to buy the kids clothes. We are damned if we work with her and damned if we don't.

As Richard just said, as we sit in bed in our hotel room, it would be such a shame to miss another year of the older girl's life. He is totally smitten, which I expected. The director asked if we would take her shopping to buy some clothes, but asked us not to spoil her and buy her everything she asks for. After buying her the phone, Richard told our facilitator, "If she asked for a car right now, I'd say yes." He's such a mush!

The sweetest moment was when we drove from one building to the other. The older girl came with us and sat between us. At one point, she put her head on my shoulder. I got a tear in my eye and kissed the top of her head. A minute later, she put her head on Richard's shoulder, bringing a tear to his eye. She is sweet and smart and organized and pretty. We completely love her. Richard just texted her "Love you" and she texted back "I love you." Can't wait to see her tomorrow.

June 27, 2011: We Met Our Little Girl!

We drove about five hours, mostly in the rain, from Kiev to Elisavetgrad. Some of the roads are, uh, quite interesting. We chose the longer route that had a road, versus one with no actual road at all that our driver and facilitator had been on. When we arrived, there was a "welcoming committee" of children from where the younger child lives, who are also at the camp. They had called ahead to the older children to arrange for us to meet her.

The adults were extremely nice and I gave them small gifts when we left. Two older children and our young girl's counselor led us to where she sleeps. As they checked her room for her, she came with about five other kids, running from the other direction, straight into my arms! We were all so excited!

She ran to show us her room. She lives with one other child who is her best friend from where she normally lives. They asked us to go to another room with an administrator to hang out. She took to Richard immediately. It was amazing to watch. She kept wanting him to pick her up and he would hug and kiss her. She played with iPhones, iPads (she loved Angry

Birds), and three different cameras. She also loved gum and is now the owner of two of my lipsticks (light glosses).

After a while, we went to see the Black Sea. Richard and our little girl rolled up their pants and splashed around in the water. (It was too cold for me, plus I was videotaping.) She picked up shells to give to Charlie. We really think they will get along well. It seems like everything we thought about both girls was right on.

Next, we went to a playground. Nothing there has been painted in decades. We took turns pushing each other on a bench swing. She slid down one slide and walked up and down a smaller slide. She seems to have no fear. Richard pushed her on a swing that turns around. At one point, she jumped off and bent down in the middle. She picked dandelions and handed a fistful to me. Just like Charlie. I hugged her and tears rolled down my face. It was so sweet.

I forgot to mention that yesterday, when we were with the older child buying clothes, the people gave her two little bunny rabbit key chains. When she went back home to show the people there what she had bought, I joined them upstairs. She gave me one of the bunnies and I asked if it was for her sister. She said, "No, for you." She named it "Apple." It was so sweet to have this child, who has practically nothing, giving me something of hers. They are both very generous. The younger one shared the gum I gave her with all her friends.

Our younger girl is an active child who enjoys all the different things at the camp. She loves to swim, dance, sing, and read poetry. She is very sociable and everyone loves her. We do too!

We had been dreading the moment we would have to explain to her that we wouldn't be able to adopt her right now. We had discussed just coming out and saying it. We put the iPad to the side and told her she needed to listen. We calmly explained that we would have to say good-bye soon and that we would be able to come back to adopt both her and her older sister probably when the weather is cold.

Shockingly, she didn't have too much of a reaction. We had the translator, who was translating everything we said, make sure she understood. She seemed to. It was as if she wasn't expecting to go with us now anyway. We tried to explain that we hoped it would only be about four months, and that as soon as they let us, we would take her and her sister to America. She didn't cry. We tried not to. She just seemed to want the iPad back. Kids!

Shortly after that, she went to play with the other kids. Mostly, she wanted to show all her many friends the iPhone, iPad, and cameras. There were all enthralled. We were a bit like the Pied Piper. We told her to share and give her friends a turn, which she reluctantly did. We also taught her to pick up her garbage and not throw it on the floor. Three times, while we were there, she threw a wrapper on the ground. Each time, we made her pick it up. At first, she refused, but we wouldn't give her anything else unless she did. To prevent her from spitting her gum on the floor, Richard stuck out his hand and she promptly spit her gum into it. Twice. By the third time of making her pick things up, she understood that it was not okay and found a garbage can on her own. We were encouraged to see her figure it out, and feel she will do well with boundaries and guidance.

When it was finally time to leave, she had Richard sit in the car. She went around the other side, sat down, closed the door, and crossed her arms with a smile. She knew she couldn't leave with us, but made sure we knew she wished she could, in a totally playful way. It was so sweet. It was so hard to leave, knowing it will be months before we see her again, but at least in about six weeks, we will be able to Skype again, once camp is over. I also got contact information for the young administrator at her camp, who said I could contact her anytime to get in touch with our young girl.

After we left, we drove about an hour to Odessa where we met up with my childhood friend, Annie, and her new friends. We stayed in her huge apartment and one of her new friends cooked dinner for everyone. After they left, we did laundry (she actually had a washer and dryer in her apartment!) and stayed up until two a.m., chatting. I was able to give her a lot of the things I'd brought that I didn't need, like toiletries and snacks. We will only be here a few more days, but she will be here several more weeks, by herself.

Tomorrow, we will drive back to Elisavetgrad to see our older girl and meet her grandmother. Stay tuned!

June 29, 2011: She Said Yes!
Today has been such a long day; it feels like it couldn't possibly have been just one day. As I type this at ten p.m. in our apartment in Kiev, I am reminded of all the strange little things that are different here. One is the couches. There aren't really armrests at the end; they are actually pillows that are Velcroed on, so when you lean on them, they fall off! Another is that napkins are small, made of white paper and folded in a triangle, kept in the center of the table in a holder. They are too small to put in your lap and they are never under a fork. The toilet paper is tan and rough, rarely allowed to be put in the toilet. You put it in a garbage can next to the toilet, which is not quite as disgusting as it may seem. I even used a squat toilet for the first time today, and it was okay.

Nonetheless, I am fine with leaving, especially since we are going to stay for a bonus night in London. It is actually slightly cheaper to stay overnight than to try to make the connecting flight (they are in different fare classes). It will be strange to be in English-speaking London for most of one day before arriving home on Friday night.

Now, back to our day. After meeting for breakfast at 7:45 a.m., we went to Child Protective Services at 8:30. Our older girl was already there with the director. She was handwriting a statement saying that she would like to be adopted by us, with her sister. We were so happy! We had been told that she would do that, but it was great to watch her, especially when she signed her name!

She hugged us as she left and we stayed behind for our part of the paperwork. There was no computer on the "inspector's" desk (actually, the head caseworker). The only light was natural, from the window. At least it was sunny today. Our facilitator handwrote a statement saying that we will not go ahead with the adoption right away because the older girl wanted to wait for her sister. We spent about twenty minutes trying to reword it to make sure we made the point that it wasn't her idea for us to also adopt her sister, but that it was our intention from the beginning, as evidenced by the original SDA (State Department of Adoptions) invitation. The only reason we were waiting is because the younger one wasn't available yet, and we planned to come back "as soon as Ukrainian law allows."

Finally, we got it right and made copies. I had asked if it would be appropriate to give a small gift of a pad of paper. Apparently, the inspector had asked our facilitator if we could buy copier paper for them, so we bought two reams. In talking with our facilitator, we learned that our little girl will need to be registered locally for thirty days, after the mother receives notification of the termination of her rights and goes through the ten-day waiting period. The forty days should be while the SDA gets reorganized. Hopefully, as soon as they reopen, we can resubmit our dossier and get called for a new appointment to do this all over again. (With a bit less travel, but probably in the cold, snowy months.)

On the way back, I asked to stop for flowers. I bought our older girl five red roses (odd numbers are lucky, even for funerals) and a bouquet for the place where she lives. She was so excited to receive flowers! The only other person who had ever given her flowers was her brother, Nikolai. She touched them and smelled them and held them the whole ride back to camp. Her smile was priceless!

After Child Protective Services, we checked out of our hotel in Elisavetgrad, knowing we would be back in a few months. We drove to where our older girl was staying and had some quick tea (called chai), paid for the caregivers who stayed with her, and made a donation. Then the director asked if we could bring the children at her camp a few snacks and take her to lunch before driving her back. Sure!

We stopped at a supermarket where we bought bananas and treats for our older girl and her friends. I also bought her a neck pillow she liked with roses, and at my suggestion, nail polish and a couple of books. She asked to get a card for her friend as well. I bought a few things to bring home too.

Next, we returned to a place we ate at when we shopped. She did not order pizza. I tried borscht. It was very good, nothing like what we have in the States: It's a hot cabbage soup with meat and potatoes, with a dollop of sour cream. I also had a pancake with caviar (redfish roe) and a Ukrainian natural apple soda. Good lunch.

During lunch, I asked our older girl about her name, because there seems to be an official name and what people call her; same for her sister. Their middle name is their father's last name, and their last name is from their mother. I typed it out on my phone and added our last name. When I showed her the full name typed out, she got very excited and said "Yeah!," clapping her hands together. I told her how happy that made me!

During the drive to camp, we asked how the conversation went between her and her grandmother. She told us that the grandmother liked us and that she would think about it. I was relieved that she liked us. I think she will say yes.

After lunch, we drove one and a half hours on yet another bumpy road. Our facilitator told us, "There are no roads in Ukraine, only directions." I believe it. The roads are awful. For that reason alone, I don't think I'd take the boys on our next visit, since I wouldn't want them to get car-sick. Our girl used her new neck pillow and put it between us so we were leaning on each other with it. Her hand was resting on my arm. Then she lay down in my lap to try to rest during the crazy ride. It was such a sweet moment. I love my daughter, and she loves me.

After the bad roads turned worse and we had to stop for cows crossing in front of us, we finally arrived at her camp. Richard was crying, and at first I told him not to, but then I said, who am I to say, cry if you want to. We hugged her really tight and kissed her. We all said, "I love you." As she turned in her new pink outfit and walked away with our facilitator (who told us not to go in), I started crying too. It is so sad to think about the months of not seeing her. We will have virtually no contact while she is in camp, until mid-August. After that, we can resume sending gifts and Skyping.

We drove another three and a half hours on more bumpy roads before arriving in Kiev. In the past five days, we have driven more than 1,400 kilometers over the course of more than seventeen hours! Our driver made some interesting maneuvers to avoid some closed roads, including driving through a parking area on the sidewalk and coming down off the raised sidewalk to park close to our apartment.

After settling in, Richard and I went to the mall (I think it's called Dream Town Mall), a nice, high-end, indoor, multistory mall. I bought a couple of accessories. About 8:45 p.m., we went for sushi.

Now we are going to go to bed. I keep saying that I have to do the blog (spent about two hours on it yesterday), because so much happens in a day, that I forget.

Tomorrow, we can actually sleep in. Our facilitator will drop off our papers at SDA, and we don't need to be there. We need to check out of our apartment by noon. Our wonderful facilitator very graciously invited us to lunch at his place, before our four p.m. flight.

It's amazing to think that this portion of our adventure is coming to a close, yet there is so much more ahead. Stay tuned . . .

CHAPTER 12
She Called Me "Mom"

Here, we are back at home, and the girls are back from camp at Novyy Dom. We are trying to continue building our relationship from afar through Skype. We find out what we can, both from the girls and our facilitator, as we try to figure out the rules which we have no control over. We are pawns in both the adoption process and in the lives of our girls, having to trust strangers in everything we do.

August 1, 2011: Hospital
In Ukraine, orphans go to the hospital for everything. Doctors are not paid for, but hospitals are. There are no children's hospitals, at least not in Elisavetgrad, so children are mixed with adults. Today we found out that Paulina was in the hospital. While we were initially concerned, we later learned it was due to an ear infection. Ultimately, they kept her at the hospital and away from her sister, friends, and school for six days—for an ear infection! Poor girl.

August 18, 2011: Waiting Period Waived
Wonder of wonders, miracle of miracles, they actually waived the ten-day waiting period! We learned today that the court decision terminating the parental rights is effective immediately and has already been sent to Child Protective Services (CPS). The two thirty-day waiting periods have now begun. We were told that CPS will send everything to the State Department for Adoptions—or whatever it will be called when it reopens—no later than October 19. That means, if neither of the thirty-day waiting periods are waived (which we are still hoping for, but doesn't look too likely), shortly after October 19, the SDA should issue an invitation for us to return to Ukraine. That means we could be traveling at the end of October or early

November, and that we could probably bring the girls home in December.

Since a few people have asked about what the remaining trips will be, I'll recap them with the information we have, which we know by now is always subject to change. In all likelihood, we will still need to make three trips. It's almost like the first one didn't happen, because we have to do all of that over again, except, as far as they know, we only met the older girl, so we would be going back to meet the younger girl. So, here is how it should go (we think):

Step 1: a) Fly to Kiev for SDA appointment; b) get referral for younger girl the next day; c) travel to the region.

Step 2: a) Go to CPS in the region and get approval to spend time with the girls; b) spend a few days with them.

Step 3: a) Go back to CPS with them; b) the girls will sign something saying they want to be adopted by us, and we will fill out paperwork as well.

Step 4: (I'm not sure about the order of steps 3 and 4.) In this region, we need to get approval from a local board of trustees for the adoption; they only meet on Fridays.

Step 5: a) Go back to Kiev and file papers with the SDA saying we want to adopt both girls; b) the SDA sends everything to the court.

Step 6: We will fly home for approximately two weeks (many people stay for the duration) while we wait for the court date.

Step 7: Return for a one-day court hearing (Now we are hoping to take the boys on this trip, so they can see where there sisters came from). We will return home for the ten-day waiting period (many people stay). I'm wondering if there is a chance they will waive it again since it's the same region, though we hear it is rare to waive this waiting period.

Step 8: Return for the final time to Ukraine. At some point during this trip, the girls will say good-bye to everyone they know at the places where they are living; they will stay with us in the hotel while we run around getting medical checkups, new birth certificates, and passports. Some of this happens locally and some in Kiev.

Step 9: Fly home with our new family!

So that's what we know as of today.

Just want to give a shout-out here to my friend who has found two kids to adopt from Ghana. We wish her and her husband a speedy adoption journey.

September 21, 2011: She Called Me "Mom"!
I Skyped with our older girl today. We started with an average conversation about what we each did today. She told me again that she hates getting up early for school. Then, somehow, she grew concerned about us adopting her. She wrote something that didn't quite translate well, but we got the drift that she thought we would change our minds and not want to adopt her. It seemed she was thinking, as she had when we were there, that we would somehow be mad at her for not wanting to be adopted without her sister. We're not sure what made her think that, especially since many of our conversations focus on when we are planning to return to Ukraine, but she was obviously concerned.

Richard was following the text of our conversation on his computer while working from home. He came right in to see what she was talking about. I reassured her that we loved her and told her that I knew she had experienced disappointments in her life, but that we would not disappoint her—at least not in terms of the adoption, I quipped. "I'm sure when you are a teenager, I will do something to upset you, but we will adopt you!" I added.

She was crying a bit and the educator there comforted her. I wished it was me giving her a hug, but was grateful that someone was there to do so. She said she loved me and that she had never known such a nice family. It felt great to be appreciated. (Not sure how that will last in the teen years!)

Then she spent awhile looking up the right words to express what she wanted to say. (Sometimes on our Skype calls there are silences as we type our thoughts and put them into Google Translate.) Then it appeared. She wrote, "Can I talk to you mom?" Meaning, "Can I call you Mom?" Now I was crying and said yes. Then I translated, "I would love it if you feel comfortable calling me Mom." Then she typed, "Mom, I have to go. My friend wants to speak to her family."

We hung up and I called Richard and we basked in the beautiful moment that had just transpired, an example of love and trust deepening. I love the bond I am creating with her and I CAN'T WAIT UNTIL THEY ARE HERE!

October 1, 2011: New Middle Names
We had another great Skype call today. (Boy, are we blessed to be able to speak with them regularly!) Both girls were there and asked again about their middle names. I suggested that it may be easier to speak about it in person, but they already had it figured out. I told them that it was up to them whether they wanted to change their names at all. Currently, their middle names are their birth father's last name and their last name is their birth mother's last name, which makes their names very long, especially when you add our last name on top of it. I mentioned the idea of using the initials of the names to form a new name, but they already had names picked out.

We are being cautious in not sharing the actual names here yet, but I wanted to write that the name that the younger one chose, unknowingly and with no suggestion from me, was my maternal grandmother's name. Both boys have either their middle or Hebrew name for her. I was amazed and thrilled, as was my mother.

To top it off, our younger girl said, "Mama and Papa, I love you!" This was the first time she had called me "Mama." Our older girl seems to be getting used to calling me Mama. She sometimes calls me "T.J." and sometimes "Mama." I told them, as I tell our other kids, "I love you more than all the stars in the sky!" And I do!

CHAPTER 13

Second Trip to Ukraine

After six long months of waiting to hear when we can return to Ukraine to see our daughters, we finally learned that we can go in December 2011. This begins another round of challenges in the adoption process and opportunities to spend more time learning about our daughters and where they are from.

December 6, 2011: First Snafu

As we sat down to our first meal of the day, at 2:30 p.m., I said to Richard that it feels like we just paid admission to get on the roller coaster again. Have I mentioned I hate roller coasters? Richard is understandably anxious and frustrated. He hates other entities directing where he can go, and when. I can't blame him, although I have a different level of acceptance for things I know I cannot change.

This is a place where the government is essentially a dictatorship. They thrive on having all of the power and exerting it over people to get what they want. Our old facilitator, who we met for dinner the other night, explained that there are people who own businesses and the government will basically say to them, "You owned 100 percent. Now you have 50 percent. You don't like it? Okay, now you have 20 percent." It sounds like the Mafia to me. There is no incentive for people to improve their lives because their gains can be taken away at a moment's notice.

Our schedules are completely unpredictable and are made even worse as we continue to adjust to the time difference—seven hours ahead. Last night, I was falling asleep at dinner, at 8:00 p.m. Went to bed and slept from 10:15 p.m. to 11:45 p.m. Woke up and stayed up, wide awake, until about 2:30 a.m. Got to Skype with the boys and my parents, which was good. Eric even asked, "Mom, why are you up so late?" Nice that he understood. We slept on and off on a rock-hard bed (that they had to spend two hours fixing) and woke up at noon. Very grateful that we could sleep in.

So much for breakfast. We showered and then got news that we needed to go be ready, in case we got the referral, which is why we didn't get to eat until 2:30 p.m.

December 6, 2011: We Got the Referral!

Just a quick update to let you know that miraculously, we got the referral tonight. And by tonight, I mean nearly 7:00 p.m. (They are supposed to close at 6:00 p.m.) We got a call from our facilitator at about 4:45 p.m. saying that there had been some movement. No promises, but that we should show up at the Ministry of Social Policy (MSP) at 5:45, just in case. I asked if I should pack up our things. He was noncommittal, but we did, just in case. Good thing.

When we arrived, there were several families waiting. Some had bought train tickets already to travel to their region. After a while, one of the ladies in the office, who was connected with our appointment, left the building in a bit of a rush. I couldn't tell if she was just done for the day or if she was doing something with our documents. Apparently, it was the latter. She was driving to the other side of town where the legal offices are located. (We thought it was just up the street, but we were wrong.) She went there, got everyone's papers stamped, and drove back. We went to get a cup of coffee so as not to wait out in the cold for forty-five minutes.

When we returned, there were even more families waiting there. One by one, they went in with their facilitators and came out with their documents. We were one of the last, given that we had no plane to catch. Now it would be too late to see the girls. I was really sad about not seeing them tonight and hoped that someone would explain it to them.

We went back to the apartment and I made myself a "soup by hand" that I had brought, knowing that would be dinner. In Ukraine, we've learned that you should always eat when you can, sleep when you can, and use the bathroom when you can,

114

because you never know when the next opportunity will be.

Then we were off to Elisavetgrad, arriving in just over four hours.

We are now in our hotel and must go to sleep. It is 1:00 a.m. and we have to be up at 6:00 to shower, so we can eat at 7:00 (downstairs). Our new facilitator, who called on the phone and sounded nice, will meet us at our hotel at 7:45 a.m. Apparently, we will take a bus to CPS to be there by 8:00 a.m. They will decide whether to have the director bring the girls there or if we will go to where they live (I think it will be the former). They will skip school tomorrow and spend the day with us—finally! Yeah!

More tomorrow. Good night.

December 7, 2011: The First Day with Both of Our Daughters

After another night of not enough sleep (maybe five hours), we went down to a nice buffet breakfast at our hotel in Elisavetgrad (included in the $70 per night rate). By 7:45 a.m., we were waiting for our facilitator, who arrived soon after. Last time, we'd had a car and driver all day to take us everywhere; not this time, which was sort of okay.

The first order of business was to find a place to copy our dossier—all 100 pages of it—in case they asked for a second copy. I have the English version, but she wanted a full set, with the Russian. Nothing was open, and finally, I told her I recalled that CPS had a copier, so we went there, which is where we needed to be anyway. Finally, they copied the whole thing. They immediately knew it was for an adoption and were very nice about it.

Next, we saw the people we'd met with last time, who seemed to personally know the girls. They are in a new office now. This building, along with many others, is under construction. They were on their way out, but they told our facilitator they would be right back, and they would meet with us then.

When they returned, they reviewed the file and did seem to recognize us and know our case. They were also very nice. The director asked if we had any questions, and we said, "Nyet, spasibo." (No, thank you.) She called the director of the center where the girls live and arranged for him to come there with the girls in twenty minutes. She told us the inspector would take it from there.

We anxiously paced and waited. I kept coughing, which prompted her to ask our facilitator kindly if I was coughing because I was cold.

"No, I'm fine, thanks," I said, explaining that it was probably the dust.

I appreciated everyone's concern. I wished I wasn't coughing, but there wasn't much I could do. We'd taken more than 130 cough drops with us, hoping that would be enough to calm my throat for an undetermined length of stay after my pneumonia! (Since we didn't know when we would make our second trip, I front-loaded a lot of my school trainings in October, running myself ragged. By the end of the month, I wound up with pneumonia and had no voice for two weeks. By the time we traveled, in December, I was mostly better, but the hacking cough remained.)

It was about forty minutes before they arrived. I looked down the long hallway, envisioning the girls' arrival and us running down to meet them. Finally, I got to act on what I was picturing. Oh, what hugs and kisses and squeezes! We were all ecstatic to see each other after six months of waiting! Our joy bubbled over into squeals of delight at being reunited. Such a great moment!

We went into the inspector's office. She briefly asked our younger girl some questions about whether she wanted to be adopted by us and made sure she understood what that would mean. Our girl kept meekly nodding. I stopped trying to follow the Russian conversation (not that I could understand much, anyway, and no one was translating). I easily focused on continuing to hug and kiss my daughters, as did

Richard. He had already picked up the younger one several times and she squeezed me so tight, I thought I might burst. It was great!

Finally, it was politely suggested that we take our exuberance into the hall. The inspector's gestures required no translation, as her hands guided us out of the room. No problem.

I mentioned to our older girl that we had presents. She sincerely said, "Thank you, but this is what's important, not the presents." I have such respect for her. She is truly an amazing person, a really good person. She made other comments during the day that were so unassuming and grateful. She and her younger sister thanked us many times for everything.

After a short time, the director came out and told us we could spend the entire day with the girls! He asked us to get them winter coats, hats, scarves, gloves, and boots, because they have none. Both were wearing medium-weight jackets. The younger one had a stained hat with a hole in it; the older one was wearing the boots I'd sent for the younger one, which had to be too small. Neither had scarves or gloves. I gave the older one my scarf to wear. She immediately asked if we should give it to her sister to wear, so she wouldn't be cold. (I'm telling you, she is a great kid!) I said, "No, she has a hat; you take this until we buy you your own."

At first, I tried my hat on her and saw that it was too big; then I found a way to put it on her that worked.

We went to lunch at 10:30 a.m. across the street. Our younger girl just might eat more than Eric! She had some fruit salad, three slices of pizza (smaller size than in New York), a soda, and a big cup of Jell-O. About two hours later, while we were shopping, she started to whine and rub her belly, saying she was soooo hungry. (Just like the boys!) I gave her some crackers, which worked for a short time, but by 1:30 p.m., we were pretty much done shopping. We walked quite a distance to a restaurant the older girl knew of. Even I was tired and hungry by then. (All I'd had at 10:30 a.m. was borscht, thinking that soup would be good for my cough.)

Our younger girl ate meatball soup, a large banana drink, and two scoops of ice cream. We next ate around 5:00 p.m., when we ordered fifteen pizzas (medium size by New York standards) to be delivered to the place where the girls live (at the director's request). Our younger girl had three more slices there. When we got to the other location, she had a banana. That is not counting about ten pieces of gum and about half of a big lollipop that I brought from Dylan's Candy Shop in NYC, with a "V" on it (for her full name and one with a "P" for our older daughter). It was a busy day with a lot of walking, so I guess she was hungry. Fine with me.

Shopping was awesome, except that most of it was in a place like an outdoor flea market. I wore shiny loafers for CPS, not my UGGs, not having planned on being outdoors before going back to the hotel. I was pretty cold and coughing a lot. Tons of people smoke in Ukraine. Ugh! I will definitely bring my comfortable tall boots on the next trip, and skinny pants. That is what many people, who are not wearing miniskirts, are wearing.

We bought them everything they needed, and of course, a few other things. It's hard to resist getting these kids who have had almost nothing pretty much anything they put their eyes on. Earrings? Sure. Sunglasses? Why not? A purse? Of course! After the older girl chose a gray coat, the younger girl would only try on one gray coat. Fortunately, it fit. She completely looks up to and wants to be like her sister, who, not surprisingly, has a completely different personality than she does. Our facilitator laid out some grevna for us (hryvnia is the Ukrainian currency), and we will exchange more tomorrow.

I used a squat toilet while wearing pants for the first time today. Picture a hole in the floor with nothing to sit on. You need to have good balance and strong legs. It's hard enough in a skirt, but with pants, you have to make sure you don't mess yourself because you sure don't want to have the pants low enough to touch the gross floor! I had to hold on to the wall (eww) to get up, and of course there is no soap. I used hand sanitizer. When you gotta go . . .

We took a bus with our many packages (the girls wore their new shirts, pants, boots, jackets, scarves, hats, and gloves, so most of the bags had their old clothes in them) on a short bus ride back to our hotel.

At the hotel, we gave the girls the other presents we had brought for them, since we didn't know they would be coming and had them laid out on the table. I packed up the computers for Novyy Dom (one didn't work, so we have to figure that out) and gifts for the other children and teachers and we walked, not too far, to the newer building of the center where they live. There are two locations about ten minutes from each other. The girls live in the older building and mostly older girls live at the newer one, but it's nicer at the latter building, so we hung out there. The newer building has an off-white couch that had not yet been stained by children, with an open kitchen overlooking the living room. Paint isn't yet peeling inside or out, as the new building was probably built in the past five years.

One girl, age fifteen, had baked an apple cake, apparently for us, while we were there. It was very sweet of her and very tasty! Later, she asked if she could show me her room. I said, "Sure!" She knows a good amount of English and may want to be either a translator or makeup artist when she grows up. She loves to read and showed me her books. She is reading Dostoevsky! She showed me her "Dream Wall" on her desk. I was honored. It included pictures that depicted her wish to have her own "flat," taking vacations with her boyfriend (when she's older), playing volleyball, and traveling. She was really sweet!

Our facilitator stayed much longer than we planned. Eventually, we took a cab with the girls to the location where they live. Our facilitator dropped us off and we were bombarded by excited children trying to speak to us in Russian. Several were desperately trying to communicate in

English. "Hello. How are you?" Especially our younger girl's best friend. Another really great girl, she was trying so hard to use her English. She showed us around and asked us things. A bit frustrating, but she was determined. She pointed to a table and we said "table." She said "stu" as she pointed to a chair and we said "chair," and on it went. We did okay.

Another boy was using an ancient, tattered English book to try to speak to us. All of the children there are truly wonderful people. Each one seems to be both scarred and innocent, trying to impress us, trying to learn, and at the same time, just being kids. They all deserve families, if they want them. (Not all of them do, but more on that another time.)

The children and adults ate the pizza we had provided, along with noodles and meat from Novyy Dom where they lived. (They offered us some, but we were full.) Our girls' older brother, Nikolai came to see us. He was so thoughtful. He had asked our older girl earlier if we liked wine or chocolate and had brought us a present of chocolate. How sweet was that? I am looking at it right now: fifteen heart-shaped chocolates. We are taking his sisters away and he is buying us a present! I can't imagine the mixed feelings he must have had. On the one hand, his sisters, whom he loves, will now have a better life. On the other hand, he is staying behind, too old to be adopted, so he won't see them for quite a while. Yet, despite how conflicted he may have been, it was important to him to show his support and appreciation for what we are doing.

We had a gift for him, too: an expensive watch which Richard put on him and he seemed to appreciate. Yuri, the director, also seemed to like his watch. It was great to see him interact with his sisters. I feel so bad knowing they may not see each other again for a very long time. Our older girl did say she wants to retain her Russian, which I am happy about. That way she will still be able to talk to him and her grandmother. We bought her a locket while shopping and hope to have it engraved tomorrow and put the girls' pictures in it, so she has something to remember them with.

The older girl finally gave out the gifts and just as we were wrapping up, Eric called on Skype. How strange to Skype with Eric from where our girls live, to see our kids on the other side of the computer from where we were.

Finally, our cab arrived and we went with the girls back to the hotel. I was really tired, but Richard is now asleep at just after midnight and I am writing this, trying to capture everything about this long and awesome day! Sorry for the really long post, but a lot happens in a day in Ukraine!

Tomorrow, we will get things notarized, get on the agenda for the board of trustees for Friday, and the girls will be pulled out of school at noon so we can spend more time with them. I'll let you all know how it goes. Good night!

December 9, 2011: Board of Trustees Votes Unanimously in Favor of Our Adoption

Another exhausting, amazing day! We met at the CPS building and were immediately greeted by hugs and kisses from our girls. They were with one of the educators, and the director of where they live joined us shortly afterwards. We went to the second floor, which was more ornately decorated and official-looking. Carvings etched in the crevices between the walls and ceiling, the winding staircases and pillars, and the rich mahogany colors offset the drab furnishings of this fixture of Ukrainian government business.

We waited outside the room where we were told there would be about eighteen people. We reviewed what we were supposed to say if they asked us about how we came to know the girls: "We came to know the girls through a friend who adopted from here, Sean Darren. He told us about them and showed us pictures."

I have cousins, two brothers named Darren and Sean. I had to practice so as not to mix up the name. I hated this part, because it was preparing to lie, which I hate doing and don't do well. In truth, we had never met or spoken to this man. So far, we haven't had to lie or tell this made-up story. No one has

121

asked, but we were sternly warned. People can and do get in trouble when they try to find ways for kids to be adopted, so there are ways they want you to say it so no one gets into trouble, and they can keep using the few methods they have to get people to know about these children.

Finally, we were asked to come inside where seven people (not eighteen) sat at a long table. We were seated with the girls, the two people from where they live, and our facilitator, next to me along the wall on the side. We were relieved that it was only seven people, though we had no idea who they were. It wasn't like we could ask. These official people would lead the inquisition we were prepared for; we just had to follow along.

The woman we met with during our first visit to CPS in June, who we saw again initially this week, ran the meeting. Our facilitator translated, "We have read your file and have no questions for you, only the children."

"Okay . . . great!" is what we said. Really? is what we thought, since we had each lost many hours of sleep, dreading the questions they might ask that could keep these girls from joining our family.

She asked the girls, "Are you sure you want to be adopted into this family?"

"Yes."

"Do you know you will have two brothers?"

"Yes."

"Will you play nicely? Share toys? Not fight?"

"Yes. Yes. Yes."

We laughed. The director chimed in to say that in the six months we had had to wait, he had gotten to know us and knows we are a great family. We even want to bring our boys to see where the girls come from. (Nice to hear that was a positive, because he'd laughed and shaken his head playfully when we'd told him that yesterday. "You sure?" he asked us at the time.)

Next we heard: "All in favor of this adoption, raise your hand."

The knots in our stomachs grew, as we anxiously waited to learn the fate of our family.

Then, suddenly, all the worry and angst of the past half year evaporated as we watched the miracle of all seven hands going up. That was it. We were done!

We all hugged and Richard and I looked at each other saying, "Really? That was it? Not a single question?" When I think about how many hours' sleep I'd lost over the past six months—we hadn't even known about this step before coming last time—it's crazy! It just shows how worry is a wasted emotion.

Apparently, our court date will just be a technicality. I'd asked our facilitator about what could happen in court; could they oppose it just because they felt like it? Apparently, no one opposes adoptions, as a rule, so while the court could ask us some questions, they will ultimately approve it. It seems that once children have been made available for adoption locally and regionally, if no one offers to adopt them, they can be made available for international adoption. As I mentioned yesterday, they could either waive the ten-day waiting period, or allow us to do what we need to do during the waiting period. This is very good.

We took the kids for pizza again, at 10:00 a.m. I celebrated by eating one-quarter of a chocolate mousse and having some tea. The kids devoured two pizzas and soda. Rules? Restrictions? Not yet. I keep hearing in my head what at least one person wrote in their blog, and probably heard at the adoption conference, about not trying to parent while you're in the child's country of origin. When you are trying to adopt, you are taking children out of an environment where they know the written and unwritten rules better than you. When you are adopting older children, you don't want to set yourself up for battles or embarrassment by trying to enforce too many rules and new things. It's enough for them just to try to get used to being with new people and new routines, and preparing to leave behind everything they have ever known.

We are just trying little things, but we are definitely being more lax about sweets than we will be in New York!

While we were eating, our facilitator ran around trying to get more paperwork taken care of. When she joined us, she said we had to wait for the document from the committee to be signed by several people, showing their support for the adoption. She said there was a 95 percent chance that it would be today. If not, we would have to stick around until Monday. Really? Let's hope it goes through. We are planning to leave on Sunday.

We decided to get the girls manicures very close by, which they were very excited about. Our younger girl got bright pink polish with sparkle dusted on it. As a bonus, they blew out her hair for free. This child can ask almost anyone for almost anything, and get it, so watch out, friends! Sadly, she has had to perfect being cute and precocious. Batting her beautiful long lashes and asking for things in her sweet, lilting voice helped make her a good beggar. It got her food when she was hungry and things she needed to survive.

Before long, the manicurist had given her a nail file, three bottles of nail polish to keep, and a little flower sticker. Our clever little princess proceeded to ask the obliging manicurist about every jar, tube, cream, container, and item on her table. They were extremely nice to our little girl. It really is hard to refuse her. Trust me, we are working on that ourselves! It is easy to get caught up in her sweet appeal, especially knowing how much she hasn't had in her young life. She makes you want to give her the world, with just one look, though from the start, I've been more immune than anyone else. I see through the manipulation and want her to learn as soon as possible how to get what she needs without taking advantage of others.

Meanwhile, our older girl apparently wanted extensions and the educator said no. She tried to convince her and got sullen when she was told no. I wiped the tears from our big girl's eyes and tried to reassure her that she could get extensions when we got to America.

Eventually, she made up with the teacher and chose white nail polish with a black design. They have some amazing designs, layered into flowers, and the style here is super-pointy tips. I wish we had them in New York. Of course, nothing was sterilized or even cleaned off that I could see, though the place looked nice enough.

Our big girl got her hair cut shorter, which came out pretty well, though I still want both of them to have haircuts in New York. It will be nice to take them to a place I know, where the hairdressers are well trained and the atmosphere is clean and inviting. But here, you can't beat two manicures and one haircut for about $14 (100 grevna including the tip I didn't need to leave, but felt I had to, given what our little girl was taking home). I told our big girl that my haircuts cost $65 at home; no wait, they had recently raised it to $70 plus tip!

We finished right at twelve noon and went back to the arcade, where we stayed for three hours. Our other kids will love this place. It's similar to what we have at home, but for the first one and a half hours, they had the place to themselves. It was perfect. They went through a maze and slid down a slide into a ball pit a million times. It was so sweet to watch our big girl be a child. She probably won't be for much longer. Her slender twelve-year-old body still fits down the slides and she giggled with pleasure at being allowed to play.

We put more money on the card (several times) and they played games just like at the arcade back home. There was a game where you take a soft mallet and try to hit the mice as they pop out of holes, but not the cats (the pieces turned—it was pretty cool). They did a dance game where you step on the lighted tiles, but not to popular music. There was air hockey and mini basketball and mini bowling and catch the popcorn in a net. They had a blast! Richard and I were beside ourselves with joy, making good use of our video cameras.

Our big girl asked for water with a detour for "I play one game?" Which turned into thirty minutes or more of games. We didn't care. We were all so happy! She eventually got water, while Richard and our little girl got morozhenoye (pronounced "morozjana", meaning ice cream). I was hungry for actual food, as it was now 1:30 p.m. Our big girl helped me figure out what there was to eat. (I had a pork cutlet.) Then back to playing.

I sat watching our younger girl back in the ball pit and maze, while Richard watched our older girl. At one point, a little boy's father started talking and I couldn't tell if he was talking to his own child or reprimanding our younger girl. (I'm so used to that with our kids!) All I could think of to say was, "harasho?" (Okay?) He gave a slight smile, so I assumed all was okay.

Meanwhile, our older girl was trying to coordinate having her brother meet us at the arcade. Twenty minutes is often two hours here. She initially told us that her brother was with her younger brother. Richard and I looked at each other. What? I started to ask about this other brother. He is our younger girl's age. "Okaaaay . . ." Turns out, she meant cousin. Whew! We were prepared for surprises, but would think that the existence of another brother would have come up before now. Okay. Sure. Your actual big brother can bring your little cousin, but they should come soon, because we don't know when we will have to leave.

As it was, they showed up about five minutes before we were supposed to leave. We bought a snack for the cousin, who I would have imagined would be disappointed about not getting to play anything, but he didn't complain. Unlike our little girl, who was upset when we told her no more snacks. We ended up taking a crowded bus back to the government building (for Elisavetgrad locally; another across the street is for the rest of the very large region—think New York City vs. New York State). A babushka sitting there kindly had our younger girl sit on her lap. Total stranger. No problem.

We soon arrived at the building and met our facilitator.

After a few minutes, the papers were finally ready for us to sign. Richard and I went into the inspector's office, while the older brother watched the three children in the hall. We signed. She congratulated us and wished us luck in court. Then we went across the street with our crew for Richard and me to notarize the document. Passport? No, says our facilitator. You were here yesterday. Okay. Whatever you say.

We took a cab back with the brother and cousin to where the girls live. The children there are a bit wild and chaotic, but even as they play, none of the children are hurtful to each other; they are hospitable and all have responsibilities they do willingly. (Can you imagine an adult trying to wipe a table and the child saying, "No, I'll get it"? Not in my house with my kids. Maybe they will learn something!)

Immediately, one female child asked if we wanted chai (tea). "Da. Spicyba" ("Yes. Thanks.") Another male child quickly set out cake and cookies (Charlie's favorite, wafer cookies). They wouldn't let us clean up our own cups; really sweet!

We stayed a short time while the children begged for turns with our devices. My Russian is improving. I gave them numbers in Russian to indicate the order of their turns, which mostly worked. Finally, our younger girl got the number of a cab from her brother. When it came, she again ran out with her boots and no coat to see us to the cab. Good thing, though, because there were two, and they were not in front. Our younger girl didn't cry this time. Progress. Tomorrow, she and her friend will apparently put on special outfits and perform a dance for us.

As we rode in the cab, the vehicle conked out a few times. It finally died on the side of the road somewhere. Richard and I looked at each other. The driver fortunately spoke a little English. He told us there was a problem and another car would come in five minutes. It did, and the initial driver wouldn't take any money. Very nice.

Tomorrow we will spend a final day with our girls. In the evening, a driver will take us back for one more night in

Kiev before we fly home Sunday. We will leave at 2:10 p.m. and arrive in New York, after a stop in London at 9:00 p.m. Interesting amount of travel time with the time change.

Hopefully, we will get a court date in about two weeks and will return with Eric and Charlie. The next time I fly home will probably be with our two new daughters!

CHAPTER 14
The Price of Children

At this point, we are back at home waiting for a court date, for what was supposed to be about two weeks. We don't understand why we can't seem to get one, and are frustrated, as the holidays mark the passing of more time without our daughters.

December 22, 2011: Another Potential Problem— When Will It End?

I never thought that my own blog would help me out in moving this process along, but thanks to someone's comment, it may do just that. In case you missed it, some kind soul, who has obviously been down this road before, noticed that if we change the age in our home study, it might be a problem for USCIS. The issue is that our I-171 form, that we had so much trouble getting originally, would now be inconsistent with our home study. Further, because our older daughter would potentially be thirteen when we apply for her visa, they may not grant it because the form they approved, based on the home study, said up to age twelve. It's getting surreal at this point. I had one glass of wine tonight and I am ready to scream and cry! How many more roadblocks can they possibly come up with? Why can't I just bring my daughters home already?

Richard called USCIS when he got home from work. (Amazingly, they are open until 8:00 p.m.) The person he spoke to knew nothing about it, but tried to be helpful. We purposely left our huge folder with all our documents at the home, where the girls live, so we wouldn't have to schlep it. Not in my wildest imagination did I dream we would need it here. We searched our computers for the old files after finding our original, and finally realized that we do need this document updated. Then he checked my blog to see what steps we had to take with the I-171 to get it to where it needs to be.

Our facilitator in Michigan said that USCIS could take weeks to issue a new letter! We don't have several weeks; at least, we hope we don't! Richard sent the information with an urgent request to a representative from USCIS, to please do it quickly, and also to our congresswoman, whose office helped last time. We hope she will see our urgent plea tomorrow and make this simple change quickly. Richard just heard from our Michigan facilitator, that USCIS probably won't need an Apostilled version, (which basically means that someone in an office puts a stamp on a document saying that the document that was notarized, was done so properly) and that an e-mail may suffice. Let's hope so. I am quite concerned about everything working just right and resulting in a court date Thursday. As much as I want that to be true, I'm losing faith.

So, thanks again, anonymous comment poster, and thank you to all who stay interested enough to keep reading.

December 27, 2011: One Year after We Found Them, the Court Won't Give Us a Date

I've spent the last few days packing for the four of us to go to Ukraine. Yesterday, I alternated between calm and crazy. I went to bed after midnight, when I finished packing the little gifts for the boys to keep things interesting on our trip. I also packed one small Christmas gift for each of the girls. I woke up and couldn't get back to sleep when Richard came to bed about two a.m. It was on and off all night.

We were supposed to learn this morning whether we would leave today and hopefully have our court date on Thursday or Friday. My hope, or incorrect assumption, was that even if they said no for this week, that we would get the date today, probably for next week, after the holiday, or at worst, the week after. WRONG!

8:20 a.m.: False alarm. Call from my contractor who would be stopping by shortly to do new paint samples for the girls' room.

8:40 a.m.: The fateful call from our facilitator (earlier than the planned time of 9:00 a.m.), who told us the bad news. No court date this week. When we asked when court would be scheduled for, he told us that our local facilitator was told to register everything with the equivalent of a court clerk. I assume she meant the new document, which did arrive as planned. Later we learned that once again, the judge would not even actually see her, despite being told she had an appointment this morning.

Our main facilitator feels that the judge is young, new and inexperienced. She does not want to be accused of doing anything wrong and "selling children." (Yes, he actually said that.) She is going by the book. The problem is that unless he can find someone to intervene, our case may get put on the regular court docket, which could be weeks away! I could understand having to wait if there was a problem or if someone opposed the adoption, but everything seems to be in order, and everyone is supportive, so what's the holdup?

From the blogs we have read and from what everyone has told us, after we get approval locally, which we did, court should be in one to two weeks, and the court officials should approve our adoption. I can't understand why that is not happening for our case. No one cares that we have waited an extra six months. No one cares that two girls will miss another holiday season with their family. I find the whole thing incredibly frustrating, maddening, and absurd!

I think our local facilitator is trying, but cannot penetrate the crazy court system. She is not an attorney. The judge has probably never had an adoption case before. Why must we be the guinea pigs? It takes a lot for me to lose my patience, but this had done it. I screamed at Anita, our facilitator, while Richard watched in shock, since he's usually the one yelling while I'm almost always calm.

"Anita, I need you to sit and wait in that courthouse until the judge emerges. I don't care if you have to follow her to the bathroom!" I said. "Follow her to her house if you have to! You need to confront her and get a straight answer about a court date! I am tired of this bullshit. What kind of system is this, that doesn't give you a court date and doesn't let you speak to anyone who can tell you why?! Find her and speak to her directly. Enough of this already!"

"T.J., I can't," Anita said, in meek reply to my tirade.

"Yes, you can! You have to. I am directly instructing you that you need to stay in that courthouse until you speak to the judge directly and get a date!"

"I'm sorry. It doesn't work that way."

"Well, then, maybe we need to change the way it works, because this isn't working!"

"I'll let you know as soon as I hear anything."

"Yeah, right. Thanks a lot."

Click.

Fortunately, the kids were at school, so I had the rest of the day to calm down.

When Eric returned, I told him that we still didn't have a court date and tried to console him when he was sad that we still weren't going. I tried to get him to look at the bright side, saying that now we'd have time to get their room all set up before they arrive (which will further torture us). Now we can spend New Year's with friends (we are fortunate enough to have choices as to where we'll spend it, which is more torture, since the girls aren't here).

Not that we are in much of a celebratory mood. Now we don't have to get a tree. (I guess I can pack up the ornaments I bought.) Not sure what to do with the suitcases that are packed all over the house. They are a further reminder that we are still here.

Okay, I'm not as good at looking on the bright side today.

I told myself yesterday that if we were able to leave today, I'd run around doing what I needed to do, which wasn't too much, since I was almost completely ready to go. (Kids' haircuts were on the list.) If not, I was going to bake brownies. That was my plan.

I'm still in my PJs and it's after twelve noon. Not in much of a mood to get moving anywhere. It's going to be a day of too much TV and DS for the kids, because I have no patience to battle with or otherwise engage them.

By the way, it was one year ago tonight that Richard first found our daughters. The wait continues.

December 28, 2011: We Thought . . . (aka, What We Hoped or Were Led to Believe on This Journey)

We thought, one year ago, could this be possible? How likely was it that we would actually be able to adopt the two girls in the photo?

We thought, shortly afterwards, "Yes, maybe this could happen."

We thought, maybe we could see our younger daughter on her eighth birthday in June.

We thought we would bring the boys and see both girls together in early June.

We were elated to meet them separately in late June.

We thought we would bring them home in early August.

We thought we would bring them home in late August, at least before the new school year.

We thought we would see them in October. Maybe they could be here by Thanksgiving.

We thought we might not be here for Thanksgiving.

We were excited to see them in early December.

We told them we'd be back in two weeks.

We thought we wouldn't see them until the New Year.

We thought we would have them home for their Christmas and our older daughter's birthday.

We thought we would be leaving on four hours' notice.

133

We thought we would be in Ukraine for New Year's.
We thought we'd definitely be there for our older
daughter's birthday.
We thought we might have to wait at least six more weeks.
We think we might know something before January 10.
We don't think we'll go until at least mid-January.
They may not be home with us until February.
We just don't know what to think!

December 29, 2011: A Few Answers

Yesterday we learned why our judge was being so difficult, but we cannot disclose the particulars here. Suffice it to say that we are withdrawing our application from this judge and will re-file after the New Year with another judge. Yesterday, they told us that nothing would happen until after January 10. Today, there is some hope that it will be re-filed on January 3. I'm afraid to even speculate on a new timeline.

Our main facilitator, Andre, finally explained what was really going on.

"It seems the problem is a gift that is needed."

"A gift?" I questioned.

"Well, sometimes in these cases, there is an expectation. The judges are not very well paid . . ."

"You mean a bribe? After all this time, after jumping through every hoop for a year, now at the final step, the judge doesn't want to go by the book. She wants a bribe?"

We had heard this could happen, and we'd seen it ourselves when our driver got pulled over by a cop. After the driver handed the officer some cash, we were able to get on our way, but the judge? Wow.

"So, what do we do?" I asked Andre.

Andre intentionally never confirmed that my guess about the bribe was correct. Instead, he said, "There will just be an additional fee to cover the gift. We will take care of everything and keep you out of it. Then everything should go smoothly and you will get your court date."

Richard and I looked at each other. What choice did we have? We couldn't say "never mind" to the girls that had already become our daughters in our hearts and minds. We would have paid anything at that point, despite the moral dilemma, to finally bring our daughters home. Sadly, the judge probably knew that.

Thankfully, we could afford to do so, but there are so many families that painstakingly raise every penny in order to adopt. How many hearts get broken in this corrupt process? It was bad enough when Russia suddenly stopped allowing adoptions, despite where people were in the process, or the pain and damage to the children and their potential families. Then Ukraine abruptly changed the rules, not allowing anyone under the age of five to be adopted without significant health issues. So many families were in the middle or close to the end of their long, expensive process. Who lost the most? The children.

At long last, we got our court date. This time, the boys joined us on the long flights to Ukraine to finally meet their sisters in person.

CHAPTER 15
Final Trip to Ukraine

After addressing the latest hurdle of the judge wanting a "gift," we finally got our court date and headed to Ukraine for the third and final time, bringing our boys to meet their sisters and experience where they came from.

On January 16, 2012, our long-awaited court date, our local facilitator Anita met us with two cabs. (We took a ton of cabs in Ukraine for about 20 to 25 grevna, which was about $2.50 to $3.00 each way, with between three and seven people in each cab. Note: They were all tiny cars, which meant we often sat on each other's laps.) We arrived at the courthouse at around 8:45 a.m. for our 9:30 appointment. We waited outside in the snow for about ten minutes before being allowed to go in. We all waited in the hallway outside the judge's office for about thirty minutes before learning that the hearing would be held there due to the renovation of the courtroom.

Finally, they ushered us in. Paulina and Niki sat with the director, Yuri. Richard was near Niki, then me, Anita, a woman from Child Protective Services, the prosecutor, and three elderly female jurors (looking bored as can be), sitting next to the judge. While I was thrilled with the result, I was still angry at the judge, and found that I had a hard time looking at her. I smiled, but couldn't think of a single nice word for her in my head.

When the girls arrived at court, Paulina was holding a cow stuffed animal. My first thought was, "How sweet. The younger side of Paulina." Then I learned that she had brought it to give to the judge, which she did after she approved the adoption. A nice gesture from an innocent young girl.

I did not want to give that woman anything, including a minute more of my time. If the nonsense hadn't gone on for so long, I would have thought differently about her, but I still can't stand the thought of her. Maybe receiving a stuffed animal from a child will help her to realize who this is about in the future.

We each stood and stated our names, dates of birth, and addresses. She asked us what we asked of the court (to adopt Paulina and Niki). She asked us each to make a statement. I was a bit unprepared for such an open-ended question. Richard went first and said something to the effect of how he loves them the same way we love our other children, and he thinks we could give them a really good life in New York. I answered similarly that we had gotten to know them and we love them and they love us and we already consider ourselves to be family.

She asked Yuri for a statement and he responded by saying that we originally came six months ago to adopt them, and when Niki wasn't available at that time, we waited patiently so we could adopt both. He said he has gotten to know us well over that time, and that he couldn't think of a better family for these girls. (Really nice to hear, and he sounded genuine.) The inspector from Child Protective Services answered similarly, stating that we had waited for both girls to be available, and that they fully supported the adoption as being in the best interests of these children. (I was glad to hear that this was actually a standard, because from earlier events, I hadn't been so sure.)

The judge asked a few questions, including having us describe our house, income, and jobs. Interestingly, she asked only me if I would have time to take care of the kids along with my job, not Richard. This is a female judge asking. Clearly, she has no children!

The prosecutor asked Yuri about the health of the children. He said they both have poor eyesight, but they can't afford glasses. He talked about a minor medical issue, but kind of made it sound a bit worse than it is, dramatizing how we can cure it in New York. He basically showed that we could take care of the needs of these children, financially, physically, and emotionally. She asked us to describe our house and we told her that the boys each have their own room and that the girls will share. I offered to show a picture, but the judge didn't ask to see it.

Then she summarized the more than one hundred pages of our dossier, reading the basic concept of each page, with Anita translating. At one point, Yuri asked the court if the girls could wait with their teacher, Katya, who had come with us, and that is what they did.

Finally, the judge asked us if we had any questions, and then asked us to repeat what we were asking the court to do. Then we were told to wait outside. We waited for about ten minutes before they called us back in.

After reading a few preliminary statements, the judge said, "The court has agreed to satisfy your request." Richard and I squeezed each other's hands throughout her words.

At the end, she told me to stop crying. I did say Spicyba (thank you) to all. We walked out wiping our tears and told everyone the great news.

We're Finally the Kyri Family of Six!

Finally, we can use our daughters' new names: Welcome, Paulina Elena Kyri and Veronika (Niki) Sarah Kyri! We took a photo to remember this momentous occasion right after court, which was held in the judge's office, since the courtroom was being renovated and was unusable.

Another big thank-you to the Webber family, who were in the process of adopting Paulina's friend, Zoe, for getting up early and watching our boys, since there was truly no room for them to be in the judge's office. I am so happy the boys could be there, just outside the room, for us to tell them the great news immediately. They were ecstatic! We all hugged and kissed and did a "Kyri Family Squish"! When we took the picture, I suggested we all say "Kyri Family" instead of "Cheese."

138

In later group photos, Niki kept repeating "Kyri Family," with a big smile. It made me smile big, too, to hear her say it.

After the hugging, kissing, and squishing, we went outside where it was snowing and took a few more pictures. Then we took a couple of cabs to Camilla's, a restaurant we'd eaten at during our last trip, that Niki likes. Nikolai, the girls' eighteen-year-old brother, joined us, for a total of twelve people celebrating, plus baby Sammy, the Webber's infant son, who was born just weeks before they got their date to travel to Ukraine. He has yet to cry since I've met him!

I gave Paulina and Niki their little gifts. Paulina got some earrings and a bracelet that said "Big Sister." Niki got a pink headband and a bracelet that said "Little Sister," which she may have already lost. I also bought them little rings with a "P" and "V" for their English names. (They are different letters in Russian.)

Tomorrow, Anita will pick us up with a cab at our hotel and we will go to get new birth certificates stating that we are their mother and father, then ID cards, then hopefully passport photos. Yuri asked us to get a portrait of the family. Sure! Another tradition we will follow is buying a plant for Novyy Dom, to represent each child being adopted. Gladly!

If all goes well, we should be home in about a week and a half. We'll see. The important thing is that the girls are now ours! Finally.

January 20, 2012: To Stay or to Go, and Happy Anniversary

There are so many things that I want to write about, but by the time we get back each night and figure out sleeping arrangements and get everyone to sleep, I really want to go to bed myself!

We learned that it would take three working days to process the passports, not counting today (Friday). That means the earliest we could leave would be Tuesday evening, but it will probably be Wednesday. We were really upset (putting it mildly). Richard stormed out and started looking into flight arrangements to go home with the boys since everything was taking so long. I stayed in the room, trying to sign documents while talking to Anita and Andre (by phone) at the same time, which really wasn't working. Andre was telling me important information about the process and I was trying to properly sign my full name within a small box without making a mistake. Paulina and Niki sat there eating apples (which they love) that the passport woman had given them.

I was trying to make sense of everything. It wasn't that it was so ridiculous for it to take three working days; they had initially given us a range of two to five days. It was partially that Anita said the request for passports was sent the day before (Thursday), and now we were losing a weekend. We'd also lost a weekend with court. We lost a day after court because the birth certificate place was closed on Monday. We lost three days with the birth certificates. All of these days were adding up. The boys have been out of school and, most critically, I will run out of one of Eric's medicines on Monday. We expected to be here between seven and ten days. We've already been traveling for more than ten days, and it will probably be at least another week. We all just want to go home!

It was very stressful going back and forth about whether Richard should leave with the boys or stay. We tried different options for the medicine. Anita's mother, a neurologist, suggested three different herbs in pill form. We thought that this might be better than nothing, but when I finally called his doctor directly, he firmly said "No!" Normally, this pill cannot be split, but he said we could for these purposes. First, we were going to have my friend Susan send me some. Then Richard decided he was going to take the boys home and started analyzing flights. I didn't disagree with that decision, but I didn't want it made single-handedly, in a huff.

Finally, we decided that my neighbor could get our pills from our house and ship them DHL overnight. That is what we did, even though we knew it was a risk. DHL says the package will get to our hotel in Elisavetgrad by Thursday. We hope not to be here by Thursday. We hope to be having our visa interview in Kiev on Thursday, but who knows; it's Ukraine! Folks here swear that DHL will deliver faster than they say, but you all know how much faith I have in these people at this point, especially when it comes to how long something will take. So much more to say, but it's after midnight.

Happy eleventh wedding anniversary to us.

January 23, 2012: Odds and Ends

Amazingly, we got Eric's meds just in time. Our wonderful neighbor carefully wrapped them in a magazine, and they arrived at our hotel, hours before we checked out!

Paulina and Niki have a very interesting relationship. They are extremely close, but I suppose, like many sisters, they yell at each other. Paulina basically "tells" Niki what she wants or doesn't want. She will sometimes pull things away from Niki, making her cry (which she does easily). Then, Niki will seek out Paulina, who will hug and kiss her and make her stop crying. This will become much more interesting when we know what they are saying to each other. When I teach conflict resolution and diversity, we often talk about how much is communicated nonverbally. It is very interesting to see how true that really is. We mostly understand the concepts of what the girls are saying to each other without understanding the language.

I'll end this post with a child's view of how things are going. Charlie gave me permission to share the following e-mail that he sent to my parents:

Niki is so much like me because she likes to hide, she likes food (especially unhealthy food), and she is not really patient.

We are like friends. When she is sad, I give her a kiss. When I am sad, she gives me a kiss. Paulina REALLY likes to eat! Paulina loves the computer! Paulina sometimes makes Niki upset, but the family fixes it. They are my sisters and I love them!

This sums it up and makes everything worth it!

CHAPTER 16

Heading Home

January 27, 2012: "Tomorrow go home?"

After nearly three weeks here with all of our children, our third trip in total, we are finally going home tomorrow, Saturday, January 28, as a family of six!

I was packing up and briefly looked through the folder I have for the adoption. I found the first e-mail from Paulina that I'd translated. It's not dated, but I think it was in early April of 2011. I showed it to her and explained that the whole file, with all of its paperwork, represented what Mommy and Daddy had done to adopt them.

Her reply was, "Tomorrow go home?"

"Yes," I replied, with tears in my eyes as I thought about our journey, with all its twists and turns.

The driver is picking us up at 4:00 a.m. to take us to the airport for our 6:30 a.m. flight to Munich, which arrives 8:05 a.m. local time. Then we board another Lufthansa flight at 11:45 a.m. to arrive at JFK at 3:00 pm. We have been told three times that we must carry the paperwork from the embassy with us, along with, most importantly, the court decision, to give to the immigration officers.

I'd thought that if they had a passport and visa, we were done. Apparently, we are not done until the United States stamps their passports, which will make them American citizens. That is why our "Gotcha Day" will be the day we arrive in New York and the girls' passports are stamped. The immigration officers will keep the documents that are in a sealed envelope with a special stamp (which everything has). Once we are home, we can, and should, immediately apply for US passports for them. Social security cards should come automatically, since I checked that box on one of the five or so forms (completed in duplicate) that I filled out at the embassy.

By the way, the "interview" didn't involve any questions. It was just us signing all those documents in front of the officer, who notarizes them. We stood the whole time on the other side of a glass window, like a teller in a bank. Other than curiosity, the kids weren't part of it. They were off playing in the little play area. Unfortunately, they had the world's loudest toy, like a lawn mower, that Niki insisted on wheeling back and forth to where I was standing. I swear, I was about to lose my mind. I couldn't hear the officer and I couldn't think straight to even sign my name. The guy laughed with his colleagues and promised that that toy would be removed by tomorrow. Thanks. Doesn't help me, though I hope it helps our friends and other future families.

We met two other families who were finishing their adoptions today. One person will be on both our flights and was adopting her second or third baby with Down syndrome. I have read her blog. The boy is sweet; he's about three and a half, but looks around eighteen months. He wouldn't walk in the orphanage, but I saw him walking while holding hands with his mom, a big smile on his face. Paulina got to hold him. Perhaps I will tomorrow. It was a bit sad for me, as I thought about Collier, my third child who had Down syndrome, and didn't get to join our family. The other family was adopting three older siblings, now that their three kids are all in college, or beyond.

This morning, Richard went to the little store, twice, to get stuff for a slightly better breakfast. Then, as we were getting moving, the lights went out. Apparently, it wasn't just us; the whole building lost electricity. No electricity meant no shower, because there is no window and it was pitch black. Thank goodness it was during the day so we could function. We used the flashlight I'd brought along, until it died. Anyone coming here should definitely bring at least one or two small flashlights, especially so you can see in the very dark hallways to put your key in the lock.

We took the family to the Dream Mall, near our apartment, where we endured more credit card frustration.

While each place says they take credit cards, some saying they will accept them without a pin code, most don't, which leads to a lot of wasted time and annoyance. We bought a few things, then went to our final restaurant in Ukraine. Andre joined us for a while and we said good-bye.

I have to be up in about three hours and haven't bathed today, so I will end this here.

More from home!

January 30, 2012: Our Trip Home
As you can imagine, we have been quite busy since our return. The following is what I wrote on the long plane ride home. I will add another post soon about what has gone on since coming home.

We are on the second leg of our flight now, from Munich, Germany, to JFK. It is a really long flight, over eight hours, plus the seven-hour time difference from Ukraine. Paulina and Niki have seats behind Richard and I and the boys. It makes it a bit challenging to be helpful, but they have individual screens, so fortunately, everyone is quiet and occupied. Charlie, Richard, and I each slept a little, but certainly not enough to make up for the lack of sleep last night. I think that will take a while.

While we were on the first flight, straight across the back row, there was a woman sitting in front of us who helped translate some things for Niki. She smiled at the kids and was helpful. When the plane landed in Germany, I wasn't in a rush because I figured we would get off last, being in the back row.

Suddenly, they opened a door in the back and Richard told the girls to go to the bus that was waiting. That put me in a panic, to have them waiting on a bus in a strange country without us. I was in the window seat without my coat or our bags, which were overhead. The woman said, "I can look after them," and I quickly agreed and thanked her. Richard pulled down everything and I sent him after the girls and boys while

I gathered everything.

Two people were filing out ahead of me when they had some of the people come back up, because apparently, the stairs were broken. Richard later told me he had to jump down a few feet to the ground because the stairs didn't reach. Apparently, the woman behind him didn't feel comfortable with that and they realized it was a problem and closed it. For me, that meant I was one of the last off the plane, because I had to go out the front.

When we got inside, we waited in line for someone to check our passports and boarding passes. Paulina handed me a note that the woman apparently wrote and gave to her to give to me. This is what it said:

"Sorry for staring at you all the time. I can't take my eyes off your beautiful family. God bless people like you for what you are doing to these little girls, for giving them the best and priceless gift in this world - caring parents and family. Looking at little Niki makes me smile and cry all the flight. How you are kissing her and she is saying, "Dad" "Mom." It is like when the child is born into this world, his or her first words are Mama and Papa, Niki and Paulina is kind of born for a new happy life, full of love and care, and her first words in this new life and language are the same. I wish you all the luck, joy, patience and happiness. It is so great that you haven't separated sisters. I wish there were more people like you because you make this world a better place. Sorry again for inconveniences. Should there be anything you would probably need help with back in Ukraine, I would be more than happy to help with anything."

Wow! You never know the impact you may have on someone else! I didn't even really talk to her other than saying they were sisters and Spicyba for helping. Fortunately, she gave me her e-mail address. I will definitely contact her. When I looked around at the airport for her, she was already gone. Maybe she'd gotten through the line quickly while I took Niki to the bathroom. It's also interesting to know that she is apparently from Ukraine, because the general philosophy there is against adoption. There are good and not-so-good people everywhere.

We have been fortunate to connect with other families who are adopting, as I have mentioned before. I just spent some time talking to Sunny, who is here with her two older boys, adopting Conor, age three, whom she found on Reece's Rainbow, for children with special needs. Check out www.reecesrainbow.org if you are interested in adopting or are willing to help another family with some of the costs. Even small amounts can cover a meal or a bus or a phone card. There are grants that you could be part of, to help cover the costs for some of the children and the families trying to scrape together enough money to give these children a future.

When I told her about the drama of our process, she was surprised, because apparently, her process was much easier. She only spent a total of about a month in country over two trips.

What she is doing is amazing. Conor is the second child in her family who has Down syndrome and was adopted from Ukraine. He will join his new sister later tonight, and has been having a great time with his older brothers. They have another flight to Upstate New York after landing in JFK. Apparently, they lost her stroller, which she told me had been donated by a local store, who knew what she was doing. Hopefully, it will show up at JFK.

It should be "only" about three more hours until we touch down in New York. Sunny said that customs should be about a half-hour, though it could be more for us, since we have adopted two girls! (I like the change in verb tense from "are adopting.") As we went through immigration in Ukraine, we held up the entire line while the officer read through every word of the court decision for both girls, checking it against the passports. I don't understand; if you see the kids standing in front of you and their faces match the pictures on their passports and visas and the court decision, what does the rest of it matter to you? Read the conclusion. It tells you they are ours and the passports confirm it. By the time we got through the line, they were boarding the plane.

There were two Indian gentlemen, heading to Toronto, behind us both when we checked in for the flight and for immigration. We all chatted a bit and they talked to the kids. Everyone else got off our line, one by one, for the other line. By the time we were done, they were the only ones left. She literally closed the gate behind them. We were relieved that she let them come through first.

We are really excited to have some of you meet us at the airport! It can't be soon enough. Thank you all so much for you interest and support in seeing us through this incredible journey. Stay tuned for the next phase—in America!

CHAPTER 17
Homecoming

I continued to update the blog sporadically, now that we were home. I found it challenging to find the time, and I wasn't sure how much I should share about the struggles and triumphs we faced in the early months at home, now that these formerly nameless children were part of our family. I wanted to protect their anonymity, yet I felt it was important for people who had been following our journey to have a sense of what it was like now that our "mission to adopt" had been accomplished. Here are a few glimpses of what occurred as we tried to blend our family. We worked hard to help our daughters, who had left everything and everyone they had ever known behind, to adjust to the life that lay before them.

January 31, 2012: First Days Home
It seems like I haven't updated this blog for a while. We have been pretty busy since arriving home. I will fill you in on what has been going on.

There have been many firsts. For Niki, seeing anything beyond Elisavetgrad was a first. Being in the elevator in our hotel and riding an escalator at the mall in Kiev were firsts. It was her first plane ride and possibly her first time wearing a seat belt, which she now does automatically in my car. It may have been the first time either of them were in a mall. We went to the one in Kiev, where we had endless frustration with our credit cards again. Today I took them to the Westchester Mall, which was much easier! More on that later. It was certainly their first all-out shopping spree. We had taken Paulina shopping in Elisavetgrad and bought her several things back in June, but that was nothing like what happened when we got here.

I have to mention the amazing homecoming that we received and give a huge thank-you to everyone involved. At the airport, we had my parents (who brought flowers), my aunt Judith and Todd, with bonus baby cousin Ariella, plus friends Lauren and Dustin with their kids, Tyler and Noah, plus neighbors Louisa and Russell with their kids, Shelby and Erin. Louisa was brilliant enough to arrange a minivan to drive the six of us home.

When the car pulled in our driveway, I had tears in my eyes. There were more than half a dozen handmade signs and balloons welcoming our family home, from different neighbors and their children. It was wonderful!

On the way home, at about five p.m., Richard and I had discussed what to do about dinner. We knew that we had no milk or food in our house. He had wanted their first meal out to be pizza at Frank Pepe's (if you are anywhere near one, you really should try it). None of us were in the mood to go out, but I couldn't function enough to figure out what to order.

No worries. My wonderful next-door neighbor, Catherine, who adopted her children, had that covered. We came home to a giant bowl of bagels and bread, and my fridge was filled with dinner and groceries. She had even bought a Carvel cake that said "Welcome Kyri 6"! (We are still enjoying that.) Louisa dropped off a tray of cupcakes the next day. I cannot tell you how blessed I feel to have the love and support of so many great people; thank you, one and all!

When the girls walked in, Niki went straight for the piano, which she has played a lot since her arrival. I had already e-mailed our piano teacher to let him know that he has at least one, if not two, new students. Paulina sat down to play several times and even brought some Russian sheet music with her. They went through the house and seemed to like it, including their room. Paulina was completely unpacked in less than an hour, given that they only had one small suitcase between them, having left most of their things behind for the other orphans. Their room was fully decorated shortly after that.

After sort of sleeping—except for Paulina's boyfriend Skyping at two a.m. our time and some crank call at five a.m.—we woke up relatively early. The girls had pierogi (vareniki—little dumplings filled with sweet cheese) for brunch and enjoyed it. A bit later, we went to Frank Pepe's, which the girls liked.

They desperately needed socks and underwear. They had two of each that they had brought with them, instinctively washing them out after wearing them. (Oh yeah, the clothes dryer was new too. Niki didn't want Richard to put her things in the dryer. I found her trying to use a blow dryer on her shirts.) Finally, I showed her and convinced her that it was okay to put clothing in the dryer.

I am falling asleep, so I will catch everyone up on our shopping next time.

CHAPTER 18
Kyri Family of Six Finds
Their Flow

February 4, 2012: Getting back to a "New Normal."
We've been home nearly a week and I'm finding that I can't stay
up to post like I did in Ukraine. Maybe it's because I have to get
up early to get the boys ready for school. Maybe it's because, at
home, I'm in my comfy rocking chair that I used when I nursed
the boys and it still puts me to sleep!

We are returning to a "New Normal" . . . well almost. The
girls are not in school yet. We've been busy shopping and going
to appointments. Right now, it's Saturday morning and Niki
is in our bed. I am ready to go back to martial arts, as will the
boys. After martial arts, we will drive to my parents' apartment
so that everyone can swim at the indoor pool at the clubhouse.
The girls asked me about a pool on the ride home from the airport and have asked a few times since. There is some benefit to
the stores being ready for spring and summer, as I was able to
get each of them a bathing suit.

Paulina does not yet understand sizes. She fights me to
try on teeny-tiny clothes. She insisted that the size 4 bikini
would fit her. I tried to explain that it was a toddler size 4 and
wouldn't even fit Niki, but she was insistent. Finally, I told
her we should take in three different sizes and see what fit.
I told her she could try on whatever one she wanted first. She
actually got the 4 on, and thankfully acknowledged that it was
too small. She settled on the 7/8, though I think the 10/12
would have been better. She seems to like things small. She
has bought clothes in every size from a 7/8 to a 14. Generally, I
think she is best in a 10, but these are little battles. I only said
no to one thing that was too short. She does have a really good
sense of style. I can definitely see borrowing some of her clothes
in a few years. (No, not the teeny-bopper styles!)

Let me backtrack now to how we spent our week.

After visits from some neighbors on our first night home, last Saturday, we were up relatively early on Sunday. After eating some pierogis at home, we went to Frank Pepe's for their first "New York pizza experience," which they liked. Next, we went to Children's Place to get them some basics and a white dress with silver flowers, white patent-leather shoes, and a white purse for Niki. They have Easter stuff out, so how could I say no? She looked adorable and I've dreamed about buying girl clothes for years.

Monday was hard for the boys to go to school, particularly Eric. He made an impassioned plea to stay home with his sisters, saying, "I only got to spend one day in New York with them and I don't want to be apart from them for a nanosecond!" Richard and I discussed it and decided that he needed to go back. We made a deal that they had to go to school, but I would give them a "HW pass" so that when they came home, they could spend time with their sisters. That worked, more or less. Actually, Eric did very little homework this whole week because he kept falling asleep at eight p.m. The rest of us did pretty well recovering from jet lag.

Monday, Richard and I took the girls to Target, for their first big shopping trip. Niki got a bunch of things, but Paulina was not impressed. Target does not seem to fit her fashion sense. She did get a few things, including sunglasses, which already broke when she fell on top of them. Have I mentioned yet that Paulina is addicted to earrings? Really, she is! I have probably bought her over a hundred pairs since I've known her, given they come in multi-packs.

Tuesday, I took the girls to the Westchester Mall. American Eagle first caught Paulina's eye, and she bought a few shirts. Then we practically bought out Justice. Usually, if I go to a store I like, I will try on an armful of stuff and come out with maybe three things. Not so my girls. My arms were breaking with the number of things they picked, so we put them in a room and kept going. We bought more than three-quarters of what they tried on. Thank goodness they had 40 percent off! I also opened a charge card for another 15 percent off. That was certainly the day to do it. They got a lot of nice clothes, including matching black-sequined dresses. Perhaps they will wear them to the welcome home party on February 12.

We also went to Stride Rite and got Niki a pair of boots (I had to convince her to get the size 2, since she wanted the size 1, which barely fit). I also had to convince her she needed sneakers. This girl really does, although she also thinks it's fine to wear her white patent-leather shoes to play on the swingset (which both girls love). She was sold when she realized they have a disc on the bottom that she can spin on. Then she saw the black patent-leather shoes, and had to have them. Thank goodness they had her size, because she pouted when the one that was out on display didn't fit her. In Ukraine, it was generally, "What you see is what you get," so if what was out didn't fit, you couldn't get it. It was a little adjustment for both girls to realize they could ask for their size and they would get it from the back. She agreed to get the size 2 boot, as long as she could wear the black patent-leather shoes out of the store. Deal!

Wednesday we got manicures and pedicures. Paulina was only happy when they found black polish for her fingers and toes. Niki got pink sparkles on her fingers and silver crackle for her toes.

Thursday, we went for eye exams with my friend Susan's friend Roman. He is actually from Ukraine. He came to the United States when he was ten, and conducted the whole exam in Russian! Worked great, and they don't need glasses. He works in Walmart, so we even got the girls backpacks while we waited for their eyes to dilate. Afterwards, we went back to Susan's house for pizza (again!), and met her boys. They were so sweet, giving the girls books and stuffed animals.

Yesterday, we went to the kids' school, where Niki will go. I'll write about that next time. I'm off to martial arts!

February 14, 2012: Catching Up on the Past Week

We took the girls to the boys' school, which Niki was very excited about, since it will be her school as well. We received such a warm welcome, visiting Eric's class. The teacher had each of the students write a welcome letter to the girls that talked about some aspect of New York or the United States, and they drew pictures on the back. One of his teachers baked cupcakes in their honor. We stayed about forty minutes, answering questions and showing what grevna (Ukrainian money) looks like.

Niki loved being center stage with me, though she didn't have much English to answer questions, so much of it came from me. The students wanted to know the weather, what her school was like, and what kind of food they ate in Ukraine. They were wide-eyed when we told them that there were TVs playing music videos in most of the stores and restaurants.

We spent about two minutes in Charlie's class saying hello and having him introduce the girls. Then we went to meet Niki's teacher. She will be in a third-grade transition class with two teachers, one of whom speaks a little Russian from when she spent a year in Russia. We confirmed the placement with the principal, who was very supportive, and then we were on our way.

Saturday, February 4, we went swimming at the indoor pool at my parents' apartment complex. Paulina is quite the fish. Niki has no fear and loves to jump in, but can't really swim well; she would scream after jumping in, and then do it again. We (mostly Richard) had to keep a close eye on her. Swimming lessons are definitely in her future.

Sunday, February 5, we bought Eric and Paulina new computers and Richard got the iPhone 4S and gave his old phone to Paulina. Expensive day!

Paulina was quite unhappy about us setting parental controls. She stomped around the store, sulking, whining, and protesting with her head down. It seems she had very few rules in Ukraine, and there was certainly no adult oversight for technology. How dare we think we can tell her what sites she can be on, and when! She's been fine making decisions for herself for nearly thirteen years. (A week later, she's either gotten used to it, or she's found a way to get around the controls; we're not sure.)

We raced home for our small Super Bowl party, which was really great. The girls had a great time with their new friends. Suddenly, one of the kids told me that Niki was sad. That seems to happen with Niki. She goes from happy to sad and back again like a light switch. When I spoke to her, she said she was missing her brother. Understandable. I'm not sure if something triggered it, but I can imagine just getting sad sometimes, thinking about who and what was left behind. She later rejoined her friends and seemed to enjoy the rest of the evening. Go, Giants!

The rest of the week was haircuts, dentist, haircuts, dentist. No, that is not a typo. First, I took the girls to get haircuts. Niki agreed, somewhat reluctantly. Paulina outright refused. After trying to convince her, I finally agreed to take her to a more grown-up place—mine, at twice the price. She flip-flopped about whether or not she wanted a haircut. She agreed when I made the appointment and then embarrassed me by throwing a fit in the salon. She whined and protested that she didn't want her hair cut. I don't know if the size of the place and the sounds were overwhelming, or if she didn't feel like she could communicate what she wanted, or if it was just too many new people whom she perceived were telling her what to do.

Thankfully, the people there were very nice, though they don't work with kids that often. They tried reverse psychology, which worked, telling me to forget it, because she clearly doesn't deserve a haircut. It was the most stressful haircut I've had since I was a kid, and mind you, they only took off about a quarter-inch! This was not what I envisioned it would be like when I was in Ukraine and dreaming about being in my hometown, getting their hair cut nicely! Just one more difference between fantasy and reality.

The initial dentist visit went okay, despite their reluctance. They both needed dental work, so I made another appointment later in the week. Niki was great with the numbing gel and the first part of the Novocain, until she looked down, saw the needle, and got hysterical. She screamed and kicked and cried and refused to open her mouth. It was a good thing for Paulina that I was spending all my time comforting Niki. Without me, she was fine having sealant put on seven of her teeth. We were unable to do any work on Niki and will have to decide how to proceed.

The pediatrician, on a different day, was the opposite. Niki was almost excited. She played with the scale and anything else she could find. Paulina refused to do everything she was asked to do. We gave her the choice of being alone, or with just me, or with just Niki. No! I tried different approaches to see what was wrong.

"Are you scared? Do you understand what the doctor is saying?"

She said nothing.

I threatened to take her phone and explained that she had to have a physical exam in order to go to school. Finally, we convinced her to participate, but she was still really upset. We got through it, the doctor deciding to make this a friendly visit with no shots, but Paulina will need the Hep B and Niki will probably need a bunch, since her history is so lacking. I do not want to think about how it will be when they have to go for blood tests to check their immunity.

The doctor, who lives in our neighborhood, actually asked me if we could send them back to Ukraine! He wasn't joking. In all his years of practice, I don't think he had seen a child be so rude. I was appalled that anyone would say that to me, especially a professional. No, I replied, I cannot send them back. I worked hard to have them become part of my family, and now they are. You don't give back family.

We did have a bit more shopping at the Westchester, to brighten the week.

In the midst of it, I started feeling like I was getting pneumonia again, and it scared me. I immediately made an appointment with my doctor for Thursday morning. Fortunately, Richard stayed with the girls. I haven't been without them much since we got home.

The doctor confirmed my suspicion. The chest X-ray (my fifth since October) showed something and he put me on Avelox, which is helping. (Note: If you take Avelox, take it with food or it may knock you out!)

Friday, we visited Paulina's school to register her. The kids were nice, coming up to Paulina to introduce themselves. She had to be seen by the nurse, which she again resisted. (See a pattern here? Don't know what's going on yet. I know that medical care in Ukraine is limited and not very child-friendly. I wondered if she had been traumatized by treatment there?)

Saturday, February 11, Niki had her first mini piano lesson and seemed to do well. She followed what the teacher told her. I think she will continue. I felt awful that morning, I think because I took the Avelox without eating first. As the day wore on, I felt better, cleaned the house for our party, and actually went to the annual neighborhood dinner.

Sunday, February 12, was the girls' welcome home party. I was so amazed that we had about one hundred people in our house! Anyone we knew who could come, came. Family from New York and New Jersey. Friends from near and far. People who have followed our journey on my blog. A few people came whom I hadn't seen since high school or college, just to celebrate the momentous occasion of us bringing our daughters home!

Fortunately, I catered it and had help. Thank you, everyone, for being interested and supportive, and for the generous gifts. (Gift cards mean more shopping!) We even raised a little money to send to Novyy Dom. I put up a sign with pictures of several of their friends, Oksana, Symona, Zoya, and Olena, asking if anyone could help them find a "Forever Family." They really are great kids who deserve a chance at a good life.

(Eventually, sisters Symona and Zoya and their older brother were separated and adopted by different families in Ukraine. It appears that as of 2020, the brother is in jail and Symona is living on the street. We think Zoya is still with her adoptive family in Ukraine. Oksana was adopted by an Italian family. We worked to arrange several options for Olena to be adopted in the United States, but due to the greediness of Yuri, the director of Novyy Dom, who wanted the flat that Olena's grandmother left her, he forbade it. In an unspeakable tragedy, Olena turned to drugs and prostitution when she was sixteen. She got pregnant, had a daughter, and was then murdered by her pimp. This is a horrific reality for orphans in Ukraine. My heart breaks anew, every time I think about it. Our daughters continue to have opportunities most other orphans do not.)

The night ended with me reminding the girls that they needed to be ready early the next day, because we had an appointment with the international adoption doctor, Olek Rachman, about an hour away.

When older children are adopted internationally, you try to piece together their history, including academic level and emotional functioning, so you know how to best support them medically, psychologically, and in school. We were fortunate to live close to Dr. Rachman, who is world-renowned. He speaks and has materials in Russian, so unlike the schools and medical professionals, he can realistically determine where and how they are. As an experienced person in the adoption world, he can accurately determine what issues are due to abuse, learning difficulties, fetal alcohol syndrome, or other situations, and can advise both the family and the school district as to appropriate placement and accommodations.

Paulina again got very upset, and protested. Not the way I wanted to end such a great day. I tried comforting her and explaining the kind of doctor he was, and that it wouldn't be shots; it would be in Russian, and was designed to help us figure out what they needed in school and otherwise. She didn't want to go, and thought it would take too long.

Fortunately, they did get ready in the morning, again reluctantly.

Niki was seen today and we'll come back with Paulina for her full day appointment. While Richard stayed there with her, I took Paulina to the Palisades Center, fifteen minutes away. We went to DSW for shoes. She found nothing, other than more heels that I wouldn't buy. (I got two pair of shoes.)

We left and went back to get Richard and Niki for lunch. We went to the Airmont Diner, figuring they would have a big selection. All Niki wanted was pizza, and all they had was pita pizza. More, "I'm not hungry." Really? Finally, we convinced her to get a hot dog, which she ate. It is so hard to explain American food options to the girls. As a result, when we are out, they usually go with something basic they may be familiar with. We constantly have to tell them to eat protein, as we do with Charlie.

We went back and Richard and I met with Dr. Rachman for two hours, while the girls banged around upstairs with toys of every kind. At least the doctor got to see them interact a bit before and after speaking to us. Good news. Niki is fine. She is a healthy child and he agrees with placing her in 3rd grade. Though she performs equivalent to middle of 2nd grade, which is where she was in Ukraine.

He did comment that second grade is vital for learning to read; it is the year they switch from learning to read to reading to learn. He said to take advantage of ESL now, but to not get hooked on it. He made an interesting point: ESL is designed for immigrant families, where English is not usually spoken in the home. Adopted families are different because the kids are always on, being forced to learn English to survive. By fourth grade, it is assumed that kids can read well enough to learn, and that is when we will likely need to switch them from ESL to remedial reading.

Niki will be lost, no matter where we put her, so chronologically makes sense. Dr. Rachman thinks we should not get a tutor until the summer, over which time she should do about two hours of schoolwork a day. He is against homeschooling, which I couldn't do anyway.

He explained that our job is to establish emotional stability. Coming from a chaotic environment with so much distrust and abandonment, we need to find ways for the girls to trust us, so their emotional needs can now be met. He strongly advised us not to be their tutor. He said we should leave academic learning to the school.

I took the girls back to the Palisades Center until it closed. My girls love shopping as much as me! We only went to Macy's and Forever 21, and had dinner at the food court. I told them they could each pick one ride. Niki chose the carousel, then cried when she couldn't go with Paulina on the Ferris wheel. I didn't give in, and told her that if she didn't stop crying, she wouldn't go on either next time. Didn't help.

Finally, on our way out at 8:55p.m., we passed a card store that they had asked to go to earlier to buy Valentine's Day cards. I said okay. Boy, what a racket. We spent a fortune in there, but it was so cute, because I was reading them the cards they picked and they made sure I couldn't see what they picked out for me. They are great kids and I love them, tantrums and all!

February 19, 2012: Bears, Pierced Ears, and Sushi

Today we met my sister and her family at Build-A-Bear. It was the perfect thing to do with eight kids ages five to thirteen. It was nice for the cousins to spend some time together and have something to remember it with. Each one carefully picked out their own animal to stuff and got to make a wish for their new friend and put a heart inside with the stuffing before it got sewn up. Our family ended up spending seven hours at the mall, beyond closing time.

We took Niki to Claire's to get her ears pierced, since she kept saying she wanted it done. She sat on Paulina's lap and cried but did get it done, and now has cubic zirconia studs. Very cute.

Eventually, we went to East, aka the "Carousel Sushi Place." I was trying to show them other things they could order on the menu. Fortunately, and much to my surprise, they were enamored with taking things off the conveyor belt to try. I was so proud of them for trying many new foods. Some they liked and some they didn't, but I am so relieved that we can go as a family for sushi! Amazingly, Niki likes mackerel and Paulina likes flying fish roe. Niki even said, "Mmm . . . sushi good!" I am so psyched!

Paulina noticed that the family behind us was speaking Russian. They were apparently from St. Petersburg, though they have lived in New Jersey for a long time. We also heard a Russian song as we left the mall. So many unfamiliar and familiar things.

In other news, we did take them for blood tests. Paulina was great. Niki screamed. Thank goodness Richard was there. They both need Hep B and MMRs in three doses. We will get the first this week and they will both start school after the break. The next dose is in two months, then the last in six months. I will need Richard for that as well!

Paulina's visit to Dr. Rachman also went well. She is also a healthy child, thank goodness. She will be behind as well, but he agrees with putting her in the seventh grade. The middle school seems nervous to have her there because they have never had a student with her level of English, so they are not sure they can provide what she needs. They tried to have her go to a different school in Greenburgh that has a "newcomer" program, but the population is different, and all eleven kids in the program are immigrants. I tried to ask her if she wanted to at least see it (through Google Translate), but she firmly said no before I'd even finished typing. She wants to be with kids in her community and has already begun making friends. To me, the two things she needs to do from now until June are learn English and make friends. The best place to do that is in her community, building on friendships she's already made and relying on those friends to show her the ropes.

Finally, I want to congratulate my friend Joanie and the entire Webber family and welcome them home. This is the family who adopted Paulina's friend, Zoe and her brother Kieran, who are now in Pennsylvania. Paulina is anxious to see them and wants to go to Pennsylvania. She also wants to check out Las Vegas, as soon as possible. It is hard for her to understand that they don't live next door, and paying for six plane tickets is not happening right at the moment. She has no sense of time or geography or money. There is "I want it, so I should have it, since I have been deprived of everything." Such a change from the grateful Paulina we saw in Ukraine. Eventually, we'll go, or maybe I'll take one or both girls. For now, we are adjusting to life. The real routine will start next week when they go to school.

February 22, 2012: Laundry

I was in the kitchen when something told me I should check the laundry room. I went down and found Paulina and Niki there, arguing in Russian. I also saw that the floor was soaking wet, there was about a gallon of water sitting in the now-empty washing machine, sopping wet clothes in the dryer, and the clean laundry that was finishing in the dryer now spread out on the floor.

The girls had run upstairs while I was taking in the situation. I called them down and tried to be composed. I told myself that they were trying to help and I should try to calmly explain how laundry is—and is not—done.

When they returned, I told them that I understood they were trying to help. I unsuccessfully fought back tears as I told them that clean clothes do not go on the floor. I tried to explain that you can't stop the washing machine in the middle of a cycle and put really wet clothes in the dryer. They may not have had dryers in Ukraine, but I am sure they did not take sopping-wet clothes out of the wash to hang up. I said that if they wanted to help with the laundry, I would show them how.

About that time, Richard came down. He tried to help me figure out what to do. He handed me items of clothing, one at a time, and I wrung them out in the sink before he deposited them back into the washing machine, full of water. We took a towel and dried the inside and outside of the dryer and the floor. He went upstairs to talk to the girls while I finished cleaning up. Apparently, Niki had done it and Paulina had tried to help. They came back down and apologized, and through tears, I told them that I was very upset, but that I still loved them.

I couldn't help but think of how late I would have to be up to finish three loads of laundry before we left for our overnight trip to Manhattan the next morning. I had been halfway done with the second load and now I had to start all over again plus clean up this huge mess. Being rational and saying "It's only laundry, and they were just trying to help" wasn't working for me.

I felt frustrated, tired, and defeated, yet somehow I knew I had to get it done, so I started the sopping-wet load again from the beginning. When that finished around ten p.m., I ran the clean clothes from the floor on a speed cycle, but still needed to wait for the original load to dry. Finally, I did the wet towels and was able to transfer them to the dryer and pack suitcases from the clean clothes about midnight.

It all worked out, but it was a very stressful evening. It reminded me of the song from *Free to Be . . . You and Me* that says, "Sometimes the help is the kind of help, that helping's all about, and sometimes the help is the kind of help, we all can do without."

February 25, 2012: We'll Take Manhattan!

We had decided to take the family to Manhattan overnight, and we'd booked adjoining rooms at the Marriott Marquis in Times Square. Everyone was very excited to go!

Lunch at Planet Hollywood, a quick stop in a souvenir shop for an "I Love NY" shirt for Paulina, and then on to the M&M's store, where the kids were excited to each mix their own bag of assorted M&M's. When we went to the register, the total was $81! I gasped and said, "Eighty-one dollars for M&M's!" Fortunately, the cashier allowed us to spill some back into the containers, bringing the total down to a mere $31. Oy!

Tomorrow, we may go to the Empire State Building, which Paulina truly thought was the "Vampire State Building." (Might be a nice Halloween theme for them.) Maybe we'll make it to the Ukrainian restaurant for lunch. I want to be home early, since everyone got their first round of shots and will be starting school Monday. Yeah!

CHAPTER 19
Blending Our Family

May 19, 2012: I Love You
I have started to write many posts, and to be honest, I have written some that I haven't published because I'm trying to figure out what is appropriate to share. Today I went to two different conferences (one for conflict resolution and one about parenting adopted teens) where I met people with whom I spoke about our adoption, so I thought it would be a good time to share.

The girls have been here almost four months now. It has certainly, as expected, been an adjustment for everyone. They are getting used to school and their English is coming along. At home, there are days where I feel like Chucky with my head spinning from four different kids screaming "Mommy!" incessantly. We have had our ups and downs, and I have no doubt that it will continue like this for quite a while.

When we were going through the crazy adoption process, I told people the most stressful thing was that nothing was in our control. We were pawns in a process that changed every five minutes, sometimes literally. I believe that despite our current challenges, at least here, I have resources. I can call people. I can read things. I can get in my car and go where I need to, whether that is to a doctor or just out for a break, to escape for a while. Having the girls here, as challenging as it can be sometimes, is way better than the process we went through to bring them here. And it's totally worth it!

It's worth it when we are out to dinner and Niki puts her arm around Eric and says, "I love my brothers!"

It's worth it when Paulina gives Eric and Charlie a kiss.

It's worth it when I "eat" Niki's belly.

It's worth it when I get to tickle Paulina and make her smile.

It's worth it when they make me look deep into myself as I strive to become a better parent, and person.

It's worth it when Charlie and Niki play kickball together.

It's worth it when Eric wants to go with Paulina to see the Avengers movie because he thinks she'll like it.

It's worth it when I get homemade cards and store-bought cards and gifts on Mother's Day and when I see effort despite it being a difficult day.

It's worth it when Niki buys my mom a bracelet for Mother's Day.

It's worth it when I see Paulina struggle to try to let me in when she desperately wants to do so, and desperately doesn't.

It's worth it when Charlie gives Niki a kiss and when Niki comforts Charlie.

It's so worth it when it's been a tough morning and Niki blows me a kiss from the school bus window and says, "I love you, Mom!"

Like all siblings, they fight in all combinations, but they truly seem to love each other. We are growing together as we figure this out. No one said it would be easy, and it's not. Having Niki sit on my lap and pretend to be asleep while I sit rocking her and kissing her in my rocking chair makes me smile. How can it not? This is what we worked so hard for. We love them, all of them, and always will, no matter what. The boys understand this because we have had years to re-inforce that with them, though they still check sometimes. The girls are learning this, and so much more.

Whenever we tell Paulina that we love her, she always doubts us and says, "No." We understand that and repeat that we do. The other day, when we were arguing, Eric observed, "She just doesn't understand love yet." True. Hopefully, in time.

June 28, 2012: Five Months Home

I realized this evening that today marks five months that the girls have been in New York. Seems like a good time for a brief update.

A lot has happened recently. We got an au pair, Anastasia, from Ukraine, to help us with our crew. She cooks and helps get the kids ready for school, and we got her driving lessons to improve her driving so she can take the kids where they need to be. I know some people have bigger families and survive without help. All I can say is I am grateful that we can have help. Just being able to take only one child to an activity or appointment is amazing!

All four kids finished school in June. The girls did pretty well, considering they were only in school for barely four months. Niki will repeat third grade, which is a bit hard for her, but in consultation with the school team, Richard and I agreed that she will catch up that much quicker to prepare for fourth grade, which is a tough year. She will still have ESL and will probably have one of the same teachers.

Paulina took her four finals, in English. We agreed that she should have practice taking two-hour exams, though her grades are irrelevant. She needs to improve her work habits. She refused to study at all. Social studies is the hardest for her, because she has no foundation to base her learning on, particularly in this subject. This is the first time she is learning the American version of history, and trying to do so in English.

Eric and Charlie did pretty well. A few high and a few low grades.

The boys are attending a local Jewish day camp and seem to be enjoying it. Niki is at an international school that has an academic component. This week she is only swimming. Next week, she will add the academics and sports. Paulina is very reluctantly attending summer school.

Oh, we also got a dog, Carmela, and Paulina got a hamster, Brownie. My friend Susan observed that we have doubled our family in less than six months.

We had been thinking about getting a dog since before the girls came and had practiced taking care of one for another family. Richard wanted a Cavalier and ironically, when I reconnected with Annie from high school, we learned that she bred them for a living. We got to dog-sit one of her dogs, Luna, while she was pregnant and when it was time, we got the only girl of the liter, Carmela. Everyone was thrilled!

After five months, Paulina is finally learning about give and take and earning things. She had to take care of our cat for two weeks. When she showed she could be responsible and take care of something, we got her the hamster she really wanted. She is the only one to take care of Brownie, the one thing that is hers, though I told her before we got the hamster that if she didn't take good care of it, we still had the right to remove it from her room.

She is also finally catching on to the responsibility chart that we created for Niki. Niki earns stickers for various desired behaviors, and when she gets to fifty, she will get a bike. Paulina is now doing the same, and she can get a camera when she earns fifty stickers. We've been trying to "catch her being good" and give her some stickers despite her nonchalant response. Now that she is taking a photography class, she is motivated to do extra things (there is a bonus column) to try and earn stickers faster.

All four children still have crazy mood swings. You never know what will set them off. It looks different for every kid, and each one requires a different and malleable approach. Eric will roll around on the floor, protesting when things don't go his way. Paulina will ignore, leave, or argue when she is frustrated. Sometimes she "runs away" to our car in the driveway. Niki can be violent, thrashing, flailing, spitting, and kicking when something is more than she can handle. Charlie will cry or sneak off to his room when he's upset or the chaos around him becomes unbearable. Fortunately, they will all apologize later and seem to understand what they did.

Although the days are long and hard, they sometimes contain sweet and wonderful moments. It may be a cliché, but they are why I get up each morning. To see their faces and know they are mine, to see what the day holds for each and every one of us, good, bad, and everything in between—that is my purpose in life!

August 14, 2012: Welcome to Holland, and Behavior Charts

As we finish the last few weeks of summer, I am finally noticing some progress. I don't know if it's the fact that Paulina doesn't have the pressure of school right now, or that we are spending more time together, or that Anastasia, our au pair, was gone for two weeks (to Ukraine, because her grandfather passed away), so she wasn't able to escape into her native language. Maybe it's the book I am reading, *I'd Listen to My Parents If They'd Just Shut Up!* (great book!), but Paulina and I are no longer fighting constantly. The last few weeks have been better. I get some free hugs and kisses and even some thank-you's. Not to say life is 100 percent rosy, but there are breaks and smiles and moments that come closer to how I imagined things would be.

I have to be honest—I've been somewhat grieving the fact that life hasn't been what I envisioned. I pictured cooking with the girls and getting our nails done and enjoying doing lots of girly things together. While those things do happen, it hasn't been without lots of fights and whining. We fight over hair and nails and food and pretty much anything where there is a difference of opinion. They don't feel the need to respect me as a person with authority, since no one has consistently held that role in their lives before. The attachment issues feel out of my control, and all of my love isn't enough to "fix" it.

I refer frequently to the concept created by Emily Perl Kingsley, whose son has autism. I've heard her speak, since my son is also on the spectrum, and I try to keep her mantra of "Welcome to Holland" in my head. She likens being pregnant to planning a trip to Italy. You get excited about the sites you will see and buy a guidebook. When you land, the flight attendant says, "Welcome to Holland!" You say, "But wait, I was going to Italy." Italy is not to be, and you must stay in Holland. Holland is not a terrible place, but it is very different from Italy. You need a new guidebook. You need to adjust your expectations of what you will see. You also need to be prepared to hear from all your friends, with seemingly perfect kids, how wonderful Italy is.

Expectations are shattered with many children—those with disabilities and those who are adopted and even those who just don't fit the mold we thought they would. We love them all the same. We get frustrated by them. We hopefully turn to others for guidance and celebrate milestones that may be different from others. In my line of work, teaching conflict resolution and related subjects, we often teach that "different" is fine. Though it is sometimes hard to avoid comparing yourself or your children to others, we truly must celebrate the uniqueness of every child. (Which can be hard when they are driving us crazy!)

"My child got an award! Look at how well my child is doing!" We see everyone's accomplishments plastered all over Facebook, which makes many of us feel that we and our children are "less than." Part of us knows that's not reality—the tidbits our friends and family post are never the whole picture—but it doesn't make it hurt any less in the moment. We can join groups with children similar to ours and celebrate the different levels of our children's milestones. Niki read a book! Paulina sat with us for dinner! Eric didn't get in trouble at school! We revel in our own children's accomplishments and often see them as a mirror of our parenting.

It's often hard to remember that children are their own people, and while we can impact them for better or worse, their successes and failures are not always correlated to our parenting abilities. Just ask a parent of a child with autism who is throwing a fit in a store. The fact that the child made it out of the car and into the store may be a huge accomplishment for the day, but that gets obscured by our embarrassment when other parents, who don't understand, judge or offer advice.

I also try to remember something else I teach, from educational specialist, Rick Lavoie. (He created a great film called, "How Difficult Can This Be: F.A.T. City", which stands for Frustration, Anxiety and Tension. It gives people an amazing sense of what if actually feels like to have an invisible disability. Check it out!) He says, "Behavior is communication." We may not always understand what our children are trying to communicate when they behave in ways that make us look at them like they have three heads, but there is definitely something going on in their brains, be it chemical imbalances or emotional baggage or just being tired or hungry. Which brings me back to the progress I'm seeing.

Niki finally earned her fifty stickers for certain behaviors and therefore earned a new pink bicycle. Paulina had earned a camera earlier this summer, and after seeing Niki's bike, which she originally thumbed her nose at, asked if she could earn a bike for fifty stickers too. When I agreed, she made herself a new chart. Buying into a reward system is a milestone worth celebrating with Paulina.

I created a five-point system for Paulina, who needs more immediate gratification. When I take away her phone or computer for bad behavior, she has to earn five points to get it back. She earns points by being nice and helpful and loses points for being rude and nasty. She curses; she loses five points. She helps set the table; she earns points. So far, knock on wood, it is working well. I took her computer the other day for her rude behavior. She had earned two of the five points and really wanted to Skype with her friend. She came to me and asked what she could do to earn it back. I had her do dishes and fold and switch the laundry. Less for me to do, and she earned back her computer. Win-win!

As with all systems I have used over the years, they don't last forever. We do need to change it up from time to time, but for now, it's going pretty well. Niki wants to work toward something else and the kids do too. Great! School starts soon. Plenty of stickers to earn!

August 15, 2012: Problem-Solving Progress
Since the girls arrived, we have had great difficulty helping them manage conflicts between them. Paulina is very protective of Niki and physically stands in our way if we try to discipline her verbally or take something away. They often yell, scream, or curse at each other in Russian, and sometimes physically lash out at each other when they are angry. We continually remind them that no one is allowed to hurt anyone here.

Finally, I think we had a breakthrough the other day.

Paulina had borrowed Eric's bike and helmet, with permission (also a good thing, that she is asking first), and the girls were thrilled when I allowed them to ride together on our block, on the sidewalk, without me. When they returned, Paulina was frustrated, but rather calmly explained why she was mad at Niki, while Niki seethed, but didn't yell, cry, or try to hurt anyone.

Apparently, an issue arose about following through on a deal they'd made with each other. What was so amazing was that they came to me for help, allowed me to "do a version of my mediation thing." Adapting the parameters of mediation, I asked them to agree to some ground rules, like one person speaking at a time, and trying their best to solve the conflict. I listened to each one and paraphrased what they said. With encouragement, they actually stayed with it until they reached an agreement. Paulina was able to explain, very maturely, what was really important to her in the situation. Niki, on some level, was able to see the consequences of what would happen if the situation occurred again. It was the best problem-solving I have seen with them yet!

Tonight, I was in my home office working, when Paulina asked if we could go out for dinner. I told her if she could get agreement from all the kids, without demands, bribes, or threats, then we could. She eventually came back and announced that Anastasia had written "Pizza" and "Sushi" on two pieces of paper and sushi won, so everyone agreed.

I thought, Wow, that worked well. We should do it that way more often.

But then, while I was on a call, Eric threw himself on the floor, whimpering in protest.

When I finished my call, I spoke to him and he told me that he felt it was done unfairly. I tried many angles to talk to him and the others. At one point, I said, "Forget it, we'll eat at home," to which I received a chorus of "Nooo!" Everyone was upset. I figured, "You win some, you lose some."

But sometimes, you just have to keep trying. Everyone agreed to me doing a coin toss. I explained the procedure. Sushi won. Eric was still not happy, but I came up with what I thought was a creative solution. I made pizza for Eric at home and he sat with us at the sushi place. If everyone behaved, which they sort of did, we would go to Nuts About Yogurt, which was what everyone really wanted more than dinner. Everyone loved that solution. Eric said, "Thank you." Niki gave me a kiss. Another lose-lose turned into a win-win. What is that quote from George M. Moore Jr.? "A winner is just a loser who tried one more time."

Finally, the icing on the cake today: While Eric ate his pizza, Paulina asked what necklace I was wearing. She showed me that she was wearing the "Daughter" half of the necklace that she had me buy for us a while back. I asked her if she would like me to put on the "Mother" half. She excitedly said "Yes."

Mothers and daughters. As it should be.

CHAPTER 20
Israel

Things were starting to settle down a bit when I was given the opportunity to join other nonreligious moms on my first trip to Israel with an organization called J-Inspire, now called Momentum. This ten-day trip in December of 2012 was one of the most memorable experiences I've ever had. It was remarkable to be in a place I had never been, that immediately felt like home. I didn't need to explain to anyone about how I did or did not practice my religion. I was immediately accepted for who I am. The trip was sponsored by people who are far more religious than I. These religious men and women broke down prejudices I didn't know I had. Most women dressed modestly and wore sheitels, which are wigs to cover their natural hair. I thought they would be stuffy and not fun. Boy, was I wrong!

One of our group leaders, Esti, turned out to be the biggest partyer I've ever known! She got up on the bar and danced and sang at one of our events at a place called Decks. She was larger than life, wearing full makeup, encouraging everyone to share in her boisterous, theatrical manner.

The bus I was on contained a mix of women from Miami, Florida, and Long Island, New York. We called ourselves MiLi, and are still in touch to this day. When we first arrived in Israel, we waited on our buses for other flights to arrive. We were about one hundred women from all over the world. One of the other cities represented on this trip was Atlanta. The only person I've ever known from Atlanta is someone I went to law school with; as I looked out the window, I couldn't believe my eyes. There, on the sidewalk, waiting to board a different bus on my trip, was my friend Shayna!

I ran off my bus and called to her, and soon we were locked in an instant embrace. What were the odds of finding someone I used to know in New Hampshire, who currently lived in Atlanta, here on the same trip in Israel? Yet here we were. Beshert, as they say in Yiddish, meaning "meant to be."

As we walked through Jerusalem, one of the moms asked me what I did for a living. When I said I was a conflict resolution specialist, she replied, "So you must not have any conflict in your life." I cracked up and said, "If only!" I shared the challenges I faced in my family with my newly adopted daughters, and the constant battles with my husband. I told her that I use my professional skills more at home than I ever will at work!

We did many exciting things on the trip, including swimming in the Dead Sea, riding a camel, going to the Kotel (Western Wall) and putting notes of prayers in the wall, along with thousands of others. We also did tons of shopping, so I had plenty to bring back to remind me of the trip. We saw different temples and visited a mikvah, which is a ritual bath for women. We met with soldiers and learned about the Israeli army. Despite the fact that fighting had heated up right before our trip, which caused some people to cancel, I marveled at how safe I felt, even with armed military personnel around.

There were many lectures from religious men and women, which I thought would have been boring, but really weren't. One of the rabbis was so funny, I thought he should give up being a rabbi to be a comedian. Then there was my favorite lecturer, Lori Palatnik. We heard from her on many different subjects. When she spoke, I felt as though she were speaking just to me. Everything she said was so relatable. One of the things she said became sort of a mantra in my life: "G-d tests you most at what you are best at." As I struggled in my marriage and family, I thought of those words often. Here I was, a conflict resolution professional, yet I was surrounded with conflict. I felt I was constantly being tested, and would sometimes think, "Did I pass yet?"

J-Inspire had started running these trips a few times a year. I was one of the first people to start a daily blog about our experience. After me, they selected someone to do it for each trip. Below are some excerpts from my blog.

A few of us did a bit of shopping before heading back to the hotel. Some of us stopped at the Arab market to see their wares. I have to say, I felt a palpable difference in values there, and I don't mean money. One merchant was quite rude to us when we didn't make a purchase. He was angry at what he perceived to be us wasting his time taking scarves off the wall for us to see. He called us some names and told me, "Move away from me. Move! Move!" I was a bit stunned. At another shop, I looked at a scarf and apologized, saying I didn't want to refold it incorrectly. He said he would do it and when I went to look at another one, told me not to open it. It occurred to me that none of the store owners in any of the Jewish areas would ever treat a customer that way.

I went back to the original shop owner who was rude. Being a mediator, I don't like to leave things in conflict. I explained that we meant him no harm and that in America, shop owners will usually eagerly show their wares, whether or not customers make a purchase. He said, "That may be in America, but this is Israel." I conceded that point and said that that is what we know. I apologized for any offense caused and told him that it was not our intention to be rude. He was upset that the other person changed her mind and didn't make a purchase and didn't apologize. He called me "friend" and apologized for being rude to me, saying that I was a nice lady.

This was such a clear example of a cultural difference that led to a misunderstanding. In my workshops, I often speak of the difference between perception and intention. People say and do things, most often, with good intentions, but based on what the receiver brings with them, they may perceive it in a negative way. It is only through education about each other that we can learn to understand and accept each other. I was really glad that I went back to try to clarify. I'm still not sure I like that shop owner, or his values, but I understand why he was upset and I feel better leaving there with no hard feelings. Lori said, "The greatest act of creativity is to bring G-d's presence into the world. If you don't take the elevator and then shut the lights, it doesn't erase the mitzvot of not taking the elevator." I appreciated knowing that. I felt Lori was talking to me when she spoke about feeling like a hypocrite, lighting Shabbat candles and then eating something not Kosher and going to a movie. It's good to know that whatever you do is accepted.

One of the speakers mentioned something about the fact that, when you are in America, you practice the religion of Judaism. Here in Israel, it seems to me, people embody their Jewish identity. You don't have to explain to anyone what it means to be Jewish. No one here thinks you have horns. No one here wonders why some people dress modestly. Here, there are Jews who practice their religion to many varying degrees, but all have pride in their heritage and understand the history that brought them to this place. I think it is hard to recapture that when you are not on this soil.

We went straight from dinner to a Chanukah party at Esti's fabulous apartment. We lit menorahs, had yummy treats, and were soon joined by the Miami part of MiLi. Lori and Ariella joined us as well, and we went around the room saying what we are thankful for or will take back with us from Israel. I made the following list and Lori videotaped what some of us said and sent it to the wonderful funders of this experience. I'm glad they will get to hear how beneficial it was for us.

- Patrick, our amazing tour guide: Leave stereotypes behind
- Keep Shabbat; turn off everything
- Eric: Trying to impart these values, particularly with him
- Values of the Jewish people, particularly on education and being peaceful compared to other religions
- Army—how the soldiers gain maturity
- Peaceful—being in a war-torn place among a peaceful people

178

- Men's trip—the dire need to have a men's trip and the hope that having one soon could help save my marriage
- I don't know how to bring it home when the values are not shared in my family
- Bringing Judaism into my home with things I bought. If I go to Mexico and I bring things home, they remind me of where I've been. When I bring things home from Israel, I am bringing more Judaism into my home.

Our last day began with the lecture I was waiting for from Lori Palatnik, "Bringing It All Home." Even before the trip began, I wondered how to take my beliefs home and help my family to see the beauty in our religion, especially my newly adopted girls who are not Jewish. I can't wait to listen to "Sharing Your New Excitement about Judaism without Blowing It," which fortunately is a CD included in our packet. Lori also mentioned additional lectures and resources at www.aishaudio.com and www.goisrael.org; the latter sponsors trips to Israel for teens and is highly subsidized.

Lori's lecture talked about "Bridging the Gap."

Bridging the Gap
1. Cool it—don't be overzealous.
2. See it from their side.
3. Be positive, never critical.
4. Don't expect them to be like you.
5. Don't judge them; respect their journey and know it will be different from yours.
6. Love them.
7. Don't make them feel whatever they do will never be enough; validate every step they take.
8. Understand what motivates them.
9. Make Judaism great for them; make Shabbat amazing for them, food they love, friends.
10. Introduce them to learning—books, tapes, etc.
11. Let them hear it from someone else.

12. Be a living example; be low-key, but consistent.
13. Get the right rabbi.
14. Remember: This isn't about them at all, it's about YOU.
15. Be patient.

She said to remember that your parents didn't raise you wrong—they inspired Jewish values—and for you to teach them and make your own decisions.

I prayed that they would create a men's trip. They finally did, and eventually changed the name of the organization to Momentum, which has the word "Mom" and the word "Men" in it. I begged Richard to go, hoping he would be as moved as I was by the trip, and that it might improve our marriage. Sadly, he refused to go, and things between us continued to deteriorate.

CHAPTER 21

Happy Fourteenth Birthday, Paulina

January 6, 2013: Bashed Birthday

Today was Paulina's fourteenth birthday—her first, celebrated with us here in America. She had been contemplating what to do for months. Finally, we decided to invite several of her friends over. Her best friend, Zoe, from Novyy Dom, drove up with her family from Pennsylvania. My friend Annie and her kids came from a different part of Pennsylvania with the child they are hosting from Ukraine, who they hope to potentially adopt, and my parents came from New Jersey.

We decided last week that we would make it a karaoke party. I spent hours checking out the DJs and making arrangements. We went to Party City twice to get exactly what she wanted. The theme was black and white. After debating and drawing pictures and looking online, she decided exactly what type of ice-cream cake she wanted, which I ordered.

She was very particular about the food she wanted. Sushi and Italian food. She insisted on chicken Caesar salad and also grilled chicken. She would not hear of getting the grilled chicken on the side! I also got penne vodka.

After being out late last night for my friend Shannon's birthday, I woke up early to take the kids to Hebrew School and get snacks and drinks for the party. I even got bagels for the Webber family and ours for breakfast. Richard went to pick up the balloons around three p.m.

People started arriving, and Paulina looked very pretty in her purple dress. It pretty much went downhill from there. Paulina, without our knowledge, had had some vodka and gotten drunk before people had even arrived. I took one look at her and knew she was either drunk or high. Fortunately, it was the former, since at least she hadn't found a way to buy drugs. Richard couldn't believe it. I saw her glassy, dilated eyes and watched her sway. Then she hugged me twice and I knew something was wrong. She started complaining that her stomach hurt and she wanted some Pepto-Bismol. I didn't think it was an ordinary stomachache. She was slurring her words.

We went upstairs with her and she ultimately admitted that she had been drinking. At first, we thought it was wine, which several adults were drinking. Later, she confessed that it was vodka. She was crying and screaming the same things over and over. She said she liked to drink and does it all the time. (I think she has done some drinking before, but I believe it was only once here.) She said her mother used to let her drink, and she misses her mother. She said she hates us because we won't let her drink. She tried to threaten us, saying, "You see, I can drink—even if you say no, I still will. I'll drink every day." I told her that I knew that if she really wanted to do something, she would, and we would not be able to stop her.

Through her tears, she declared, "I feel better when I drink." Looking at her, I couldn't help but think, Really? You don't look like you feel better. Richard actually verbalized the connection with her mother's drinking, telling her that her mother didn't solve anything by drinking. I cautiously added that if her mother didn't drink, she would still be with her.

Paulina also seemed concerned when she repeatedly stated, "I don't love you." We told her that was fine. She didn't have to love us, and we were not trying to take the place of her mother. We told her that we loved her and that over time, she might grow to love us, or not. (We know she already does, somewhere in there, but I also know her feelings will grow over time. There's no rush.) I also commended her on telling the truth. Richard and I agreed not to punish her. She still doesn't believe that we won't. I think she realizes how wrong drinking was. The way she thinks and feels will likely be punishment enough.

The counselor the kids are seeing, Lindsay Jacobs, warned us that birthdays are tough and kids often think about their mothers and wonder if they are thinking about them. We knew Paulina's birthday was stressful for her. We went back and forth about whether to do a party, and how big it should be. Ultimately, she not only decided her guest list, but she also refused to share it with me until the day before the party. I prayed that her friends would come, since none of them had RSVP'd, and fortunately, most of them did.

They all had a good time with the karaoke and the food. We told everyone Paulina wasn't feeling well. Throughout most of the party, we were with her in her room. She tried to leave her room, but could barely stand up. We gave her a bagel, some crackers, and a small can of Coke, which she spilled all over herself. She could barely hold the cracker. It made me sad, watching her, a mess, alone in her room, while her first birthday party was proceeding without her.

At one point I felt like telling everyone to leave, but they were having a good time. The DJ was playing (Niki was queen of the mic), and we had a ton of food coming. (I was also sad because I like karaoke, and was looking forward to having the time to try it in my own house. I got about one minute to look at the list and sang for about a minute with Niki and Charlie.)

Eventually, I went downstairs to try to be social. Then I learned that Paulina was throwing up. Not shocking. Better, actually. I went up to assist Richard. This would have been a good party to have my housekeeper Gabriella helping, but I didn't ask her, so I helped with everything as best I could.

The dips, some appetizers, and the fruit bowl never made it out, and the bread never made it into a basket, but I don't think anyone minded. The sushi went over well, with several people trying it for the first time. Her friends didn't like it much, but our friend, Stan Webber, did.

After a long while, Paulina showered and came downstairs. She ultimately changed her clothes four times. Her appearance didn't last long, as she threw up again (fortunately, in the garbage, and not many people saw). She went up and down a few more times and finally seemed to be feeling a bit better. I asked her if she wanted us to get her cake and sing Happy Birthday, or if she preferred to wait and just do something quieter tomorrow with us. She wanted the cake, so Richard ran out at 6:45 p.m. to get it.

Annie and my mom helped me clean off the table. When Richard returned, I lit the candles and we started singing as Richard walked from the kitchen to the dining room with the cake—only to find no Paulina. I went upstairs and found her on the floor of her room. She pulled it together and came down long enough for us to sing and take a couple of pictures, before running from the group photo to throw up again.

Eric, Charlie, and her friend Rosalie were concerned for her. Eric and Charlie felt really badly that she was missing her own party. They didn't know what was happening. Amazingly, neither did my parents. I'm not sure if her friends suspected anything. Charlie was particularly worried about how we could make it up to her. I'm not sure what we'll do. It was not a particularly happy birthday.

CHAPTER 22

Italy

This section contains journal entries from our anniversary trip to Italy and the children's response when we returned home.

February 2013

I surprised Richard by planning a trip to Florence, Italy, for just the two of us, to celebrate our twelfth anniversary. For many months, I have been trying to get him to understand that our relationship won't fix itself. Therapy is minimally helpful. We have to go back to finding what we loved about each other.

Especially with the chaos of our family and our constant fighting, we need to regularly take breaks and connect with each other. He has said, several times, that he doesn't want to go out because there are so many issues between us. We disagree about how to try to solve them. I think being alone together more often will help. He doesn't.

We've been at this a long time. Married for twelve years, together more than twenty. We've seen countless therapists, tried numerous exercises, and nothing seems to change the dynamic between us. In fact, I think it may be worse than ever. We are so busy with work, life, and kids (not to mention our new puppy, Carmela) that we don't take much time to just be together, the two of us. The girls also triangulate us, which is making things worse.

The beginning of the trip started our surprisingly well. After initially getting over his concerns about us being together, Richard was affectionate, loving, and interested. We went to a nice dinner and brought back some pecorino cheese to have with the champagne the hotel sent us for our anniversary. We ordered chocolate fondue with fruit. We tried to have a nice evening, but we fought instead.

That night, his mood changed, initially, because I mentioned that there was pee on the floor. I hadn't said anything the day before, but really, do I have to clean up a grown man's pee so I don't step or sit in it? Of course, he was mad at me for bringing it up. (How silly of me!)

As he tried to regain his mood, he apparently debated about whether to not to ask me about my sexual fantasies. I truly have no problem with the question, except that for me it is a loaded question. As I tried to explain, my fantasies are very simple and should be attainable, but they are not. I simply want someone who treats me with respect. He claimed he didn't understand, and that what I described was not a sexual fantasy. I tried to further relate it to Fifty Shades of Grey, which I read and he has started to read. While there are certainly aspects of him treating her horribly, there are many examples of how he shows he cares for her. I tried relating it to romance movies, explaining the courtship involved. He just couldn't understand that my sexual fantasy involves someone realizing that if they pee on the floor, they should clean it up, if for no other reason than it would please me. It would be considering me and my feelings, needs, and wants.

He tried to talk to me about it, but just grew angrier, with me now in tears. He kept insisting I wasn't answering his question. He couldn't understand what I was trying to say. It amazes me how he can place so much blame on me and be so blameless himself. He has a way of saying things that make me feel blamed. He says or implies that all of the issues in our marriage and sex life are and have always been my fault. He likes to say he lives in a sexless marriage, but we had sex about five times this trip. For the past several years, he has been the one turning me down.

We tried talking about it while taking a bath. He went on for so long that I actually counted over one hundred tiles on the bathroom wall. He wonders why I don't say anything and doesn't understand that he barely takes a breath. If I do try to speak, he either cuts me off, yells, or both. When I finally yelled at him—that he is living in the past, and that he is the one who needs fixing—he abruptly got up from our bath and the fight started anew. When I added water to the bath for myself, he returned to the bathroom, trying to speak to me, but he just doesn't know how to have a two-way conversation, much less without anger. He smacked his fist into his hand several times. As I'd practiced, I didn't flinch. He doesn't know what to do with his anger. He just unleashes it on whomever, most often me, whenever he can't take it anymore.

I teeter back and forth, relating our life to the book *Why Does He Do That?* It's about men who are abusive, not necessarily physically, but emotionally. I have so much of the book highlighted due to its relevance. I do think he is abusive. Interestingly, his mom, Elaine, used those same words just last week when I saw her. She told me for the second time that she doesn't want to reconcile with him. She said he is abusive and she just wants to cut ties with him. As crazy as she can be, there is logic to that idea. I wish I could do that so simply.

On the other hand, as I said to my current therapist, isn't something wrong when one person only sees problems with the other person and doesn't acknowledge their own role? At one point, another therapist (who was seeing both of us a few years ago) told me, "You seem to have tried everything to change. Now it's up to him."

Again, I don't claim to be perfect. He would like it if we had sex more often. He would like it if I didn't yell or criticize or complain. It would be better that way, but none of that would change the way he treats me. As the author of *Why Does He Do That?* says, anger management is not the problem, or the solution. He needs to recognize and deal with the root of the abuse in order for anything to change. It seems that very few men are successful in that endeavor. I don't think he will be either.

I admit that at the beginning of our lives together, sex was a significant issue. We tried a million therapies, and despite the fact that I often still find it painful, I still want to do it. I would also love more intimacy and romance, but that is not a specialty of his. I suppose that is what I wish for. That is my fantasy. Just romance. No sarcasm. No put-downs. Not having him control everything. No yelling. Instead, having him cater to my wants, needs, and desires. I don't think it's that complicated. I do think it would be possible to find someone who is my soul mate, who would want to please me and would understand what upsets me.

Sadly, I don't think I will find this with him, but I am stuck. We have four very fragile, needy kids. I have considered separating. On this trip, I decided that I wouldn't bring it up until I finish reading another book I started, about saving your marriage. I spend so much time trying to figure out how to improve myself as a person, wife, and mother.

I am also currently reading *Scream-Free Parenting*. I am encouraged by the author's stories, where he admits to losing it and screaming, recognizing that he is supposed to be an expert on this stuff.

The same goes for me. I think I am good at what I do; my clients have often told me so. I think it is the ultimate test that I have been given, to figure out how to use my conflict resolution skills with my husband and children. I have spoken about what makes that difficult. It is hard to be neutral when you have a stake in the outcome. However, I am encouraged when my therapist agrees with my line of thinking about how life would be if I didn't have and constantly use these skills.

None of us will ever be perfect. (I have the book *Good-Enough Mother*, too. I do a lot of reading!) I just want to use the knowledge I have gained for the benefit of myself, my family, and the people I interact with. I hope that even reading my adoption blog may be helpful to some people.

There are similarities and differences between us and the movie, *Hope Springs*, which we saw on the plane to

Italy. We have our youth, and kids that are still young enough to drive us crazy, constantly. We also sleep in the same bed, most nights. There used to be cuddling and touching. We do have sex, about once a month, sometimes more, sometimes less.

I share the character Kate's need to fix things. We both share her desperation. I could see myself giving up, after trying so hard, for so long. I could pack up and move on. But my kids are what keeps me here. I truly put them ahead of my own happiness.

Lately, Richard is so depressed; he passes me by with barely a glance. We all suffer from his depression. Sometimes he will acknowledge it, but he won't do much about it. It's almost as if he likes being that way. He has many similarities to his mother. Living in the past and being depressed and refusing to do anything about it, and blaming everyone around him every time he feels wronged, and never letting it go. No one can do right. There is always suspicion and remembering what they did wrong in the past.

In *Scream-Free Parenting*, the author asks you to imagine a time when your youngest child is twenty-five. He asks a series of questions about where you hope each of your children will be. I calculated that I will be sixty in seventeen years, when Charlie turns twenty-five. The author asks questions about me, and where I will be. The first is whether I am married. My thought is yes. To someone else. Then I think, at what point would that have happened? I have the right to be happy. So do my children. I am fully aware of how awful it would be for everyone if we got divorced, so I continue to stay. Then I also think, how will my children grow up if our relationship is the only model they see?

I am stuck. I am trying everything I know how to try. I don't believe anything will work until Richard gets on real medication and starts dealing with the issues that have been unresolved in his life for much too long. Until then, everyone suffers.

Absence Makes the Heart Grow Fonder

This old adage was proven tonight when Richard and I returned from our five days in Italy. Some people were thrilled that we were getting away to celebrate our twelfth anniversary. Others thought we were crazy to leave our four kids and go that far. Thank you again to our au pair, Anastasia, for being brave enough and willing to give us that unique opportunity.

As great as it was to be away, I was really amazed at our welcome when we returned. The kids were out to dinner with Anastasia when we returned home, so the first hello was to our puppy, Carmela. She was quite happy to see us.

Within a few minutes, everyone came home, and you could hear their anticipation when they realized we were here. No one was sure who to hug first. Niki threw her arms around us and gave us a big squeeze. Next came Eric, then Charlie. We even snuck in a hug from Paulina.

Next it was time for presents. Score! Paulina put on the "P" earrings right away and loved the camera necklace. Niki waited patiently for me to find her jewelry. She immediately put on the bracelet and said, "I'm going to sleep with it because Daddy picked it out for me." It was so sweet!

Anastasia loved the jacket we got her. Apparently, Pernod is her favorite store in Ukraine and it fit perfectly! I'm not sure what Eric thought of the T-shirt, toy, and candy. Charlie loved the toy that lights up when it hits something. We also got him a little magnetic car and a tiny pack of noodles that has a magnet in it. (Not to eat.) He loved it all.

Everyone took turns talking to us and telling us some good and some not-so-good things about when we were gone. I ate Charlie and Niki's bellies, as I do virtually every night. Niki also asked for a million hugs.

Anastasia filled me in on how helpful Paulina was and about some issues with Eric yesterday. Other than yesterday and a fit from Niki about her tutoring program, which Paulina helped with, it seems they did very well. I am so relieved! They even had issues with no Internet or phones, and still, everyone survived.

The best was after all the younger ones were in bed. Paulina came into our room and was talking to me. She told me about how she is now doing her homework before watching movies and that she did really well on tests in several subjects. She showed me some work that she did in class and told me she will show me her English test, which she got 100 on. There was even mention of an eighth-grade dance.

Suddenly, she threw her arms around me, pushing me back on my bed and telling me she really missed me. Boy, I didn't see that coming! She then jumped on the bed and hugged Richard. I joined them in the hug and she repeated how she'd missed us. We told her how we'd missed her and how much we love her. A few minutes later, I knocked on her door and, when she answered, I told her that having her hug me and tell me she missed me was the nicest moment of the entire year!

Tonight is definitely proof to me that there are many benefits of going away. You really do need to take care of yourselves and your marriage in order to be able to take care of your kids. They do better when they have a break from you, too. Here's to more vacations. Arrivederci!

CHAPTER 23
Mommy and Me Trips

Summer 2013

This summer, I was fortunate enough to be able to take each of the kids on a separate, mini, one-on-one getaway. Charlie and I went to Florida to see an old friend of his. Eric chose Atlanta, where we went to the Coca-Cola factory and the aquarium. Niki, Paulina, and I went to Pennsylvania to see their old friends, Zoe and Kieran, from Ukraine. At the end of the summer, I really wanted to spend time with just Paulina to see if we could strengthen our relationship. She agreed, and said she wanted to go to Washington, DC, so we drove down there together.

Here is what I wrote about our time together:

I am sitting in a hotel room in Washington, DC, with Paulina. It is just the two of us, here for a few days. She has been in the United States now for one and a half years as our daughter. She wanted to return to DC since she visited here at the age of nine on a Ukrainian hosting program.

Prior to coming to DC this week, she was away from us for the longest time since arriving. She spent two weeks with her friend, Zoe, who was adopted from the same group home in Ukraine, by the Webber family who live in Pennsylvania. Despite the distance, we have seen each other several times. They invited Paulina to accompany them on a family vacation, which she loved!

I was a bit concerned, being away alone with her, since we still fight a lot, yet I thought it would be a good bonding opportunity. Without the other three kids and Richard around, things went very smoothly.

She was polite and respectful (other than blowing bubbles in her juice at dinner tonight in the nice Russian restaurant). She did what she was asked to do and I let her be in charge of the schedule. It was great not having to hear all the others whine and to not have time pressures, so I could enable her to do what she wanted to, when she wanted to.

The typical tourist sites held no interest for her. We went to Eastern Market and bought jewelry and fresh fruits and veggies, which we ate throughout our stay, thanks to a refrigerator. We went to Madame Tussauds and the International Spy Museum, which had a really nice gift shop.

At Paulina's request, we had sushi two nights in a row, since she missed it while she was away. The first night was in Chinatown. It was a fraction of the size of New York's Chinatown, but the sushi was decent. We also found one little store that sold Asian items. We each bought a dress.

We also went to H&M and Forever 21 yesterday. To-day, we went to Payless, Macy's, where we found nothing for ourselves, and back to Chinatown, where there really weren't any other stores.

Tonight, after a filling dinner in the Russian House, we started a short walk and found that, here in DC, some nail salons are open until 11:00 p.m. and serve free champagne for the adults. I let her get a gel manicure and I got a pedicure. We took a cab back to the hotel, quickly changed, and went to the pool.

Tomorrow, we head home, maybe a little closer than we were before.

CHAPTER 24

Ups and Downs with My Daughters

September 16, 2013: Building Trust

So much has happened since my last post, and although I have been writing, I have not posted because I haven't yet figured out the balance between writing about our ups and downs and protecting my children's privacy. I just wrote the following about the process of building trust, particularly with Paulina, who is now fourteen and just started high school.

It's amazing to me that Paulina can be intensely rude to me one moment, saying, "I wish you will die in a car accident." And later transform to hugging me. (Still a rarity.) If I ask her mundane things, like, "How was your day?" I am met with either silence, her yelling at me, or, on a good day, "Uh-huh."

Yet, for the important stuff, she speaks to me. She tells me about the kids she likes and doesn't like. She asks my advice as to how to respond, and even works together with me to help craft messages on her behalf to friends and boys. Sometimes, she invites me in—to watch a video or see something she has. Most times, she screams at me to get out and slams the door.

When it comes to clothes shopping, we have gone from arguing over sizes she didn't understand, to asking me what size she should look for in what store. She even asks my opinion about most clothes she tries on. On shopping trips, she accepts the routine of try anything you want, pick what you like, and then we'll total it up and choose what we like best. Of course, other days, she wants nothing to do with me. She wanted Dad to take her shopping for a bathing suit, which is fine, but she'll say, "I don't want to go with you!", which is painful to hear.

How hard it is to live with the unpredictability and unjustified viciousness! Yet, I see the good head on her shoulders. I think she believes it when she says she doesn't want a boyfriend until about age sixteen, or when she is in a good place with her studies and Huntington Learning Center and such. (We'll see! She wants a job, but is finally putting her emphasis on school. She just started taking Spanish a week ago. After studying hard, she got a 95 on a quiz about numbers 1 through 100. It took me much more than a week to get that far!)

While I know even greater challenges lie ahead, I take comfort in knowing we were able to help her out of a situation that would not likely have a good end, and put her on a path where she can shine. And I'm sure she will!

We have been working with an adoption therapist, Lindsay Jacobs, to try to help integrate our family. In April, I wrote her the following e-mail to try to summarize what had been going on.

April 30, 2013
Dear Lindsay,

I wanted to write to you to let you know that Paulina has been barely speaking to us for the majority of the last several weeks. She is increasingly rude, angry, irritable, and oppositional, and really quite mean to everyone around her. Of course, she is worst to me.

For example, if we ask her how her day was or if she would like a glass of water, she screams, "Did I ask you?!" She yells at us to get out of her room, to not speak to her, and she won't do anything sociable, like join us in going out to dinner. She has said, "I'd be fine if you weren't here!" I have tried many ways to engage her and have remained calm most of the times she is rude. Today, not for the first time, I said, "Have a good night,"

195

before Richard and I went out for a meeting. Her response was, "I hope you die in a car accident."

She spends many hours in her room, mostly watching anime. She slams doors and is uncooperative for most things. Fortunately, she has been going to school and Huntington Learning Center. She often goes to bed early, like six or seven p.m., unless she is up late watching anime. On the weekends, she is happy to sleep until one p.m. or even later. (Waking up at four p.m. is her record, I think.)

This also affects her eating habits. She doesn't eat for many hours. She complains that she is fat, often. Then she will eat excessive amounts of food. Part of this is adopted child behavior, but it is not a healthy way to live. She does also like healthy foods, but balance is a challenge.

We are not certain what caused her apparent downward spiral. Niki thinks she is angry about the decision not to go to back to visit Ukraine right now, given the war, and that she is worried about her mother and grandmother.

I am worried about her. I think she is depressed, among other things. I do not feel we can just sit back and wait for her to change her attitude. We talked about waiting her out and not pushing her into therapy, but I think things are worse and we need to take responsibility and get her the help she needs, but cannot yet understand or accept.

As Richard aptly put it, "It's almost like waiting for the fever to break." I agree, and have been waiting for the upward swing that in the past has followed her downward turns. This has lasted longer than previous times. I am waiting for "the break" where she usually will get emotional and realize how she has been acting and tell us something about it. That release hasn't happened yet, and she is wound up pretty tight right now.

Also, our au pair, Anastasia, has been in Ukraine for two weeks for her grandfather's funeral. She will return Sunday, May 5. I expect Paulina will probably be rude to her at first, and then go to her as a confidante. I am hoping that Anastasia's return may bring about the "break" we are hoping for.

We are not sure what to do to help her. She affects everyone around her with her negativity. Please let us know any suggestions that you have that may help.

Thanks!
T.J.

Unfortunately, Lindsay's only response was to wait and see how Paulina does when Anastasia returns, which didn't help. I continue to worry that if we keep waiting, it will be too late to get Paulina the help she so clearly needs.

December 22, 2013
Today would have been a pretty good day, except for what happened around eleven a.m. Niki had finished taking a bath, as I asked her to, and went to go in her room to get dressed. Paulina was still sleeping and would not allow Niki to turn on the light. Niki came to tell me, and I went to assist.

Paulina was in a particularly feisty mood. I went to turn the light on, while explaining that it was eleven a.m. and Niki needed to get dressed. I told Paulina she could either put her head under the covers or sleep somewhere else, but it's Niki's room, too, and she has every right to put the light on to get dressed.

Paulina physically grabbed me and pushed me away from the light. She shoved Niki and me out the door. (She is strong!)

Niki followed me to my room for a moment and told me to call Richard.

I said, "No, it's okay. I can handle it."

Then Niki reported that Paulina had moved away from the door and had gone back to her bed. I opened the door, turned on the light, and instructed Niki to get her clothes.

Paulina came at me again. As we fought to get near the light switch, I tried to think of martial arts techniques, and how to get her away. She grabbed my wrist and shirt and threw me to the floor!

Mortified and scared, I left the room and texted Richard, who came in and fortunately backed me up. He stood between her and me, with my back to the light switch. She was fighting and threatening me and saying she can't wait until I die and maybe she'll just kill me.

At that point, the doorbell rang. Richard told me to go down and see who it was. He took over standing in front of the light switch, blocking Paulina, while Niki got dressed. (It was a delivery of books I ordered.) I came back upstairs and went to my room.

Somewhere in there, I think before Richard came in, I'd asked her if she would like me to call the police for her this time. She said, "Sure. I'd like them to come." I told her that if they came, they would take her to a place where she would have to get up every day at six a.m. It would be far worse than here! I believe that's when Richard came in the room.

Niki was very sweet. She came and hugged me while I was crying in my room. She brought me my water bottle "so you can breathe." (I didn't know I needed water to breathe or that I wasn't breathing!) Poor Charlie was frightened by what was going on. Apparently, Eric didn't really know what was happening.

After things settled down slightly and Richard spoke to Paulina, I asked Niki to leave and Richard to stay for a minute. I told him, through my tears, that I was tired of not knowing who would try to hurt me next. I thanked him for coming and backing me up, and told him I felt safe with him standing between me and Paulina.

He wouldn't hug me. He barely touched me. He told me I should shower and calm down. Then he left the room.

At some point he told Paulina that if she wanted to go to the mall with him, she should apologize to me. She dutifully walked in, said "Sorry I threw you down," and had turned around and started walking out the door before the words, dripping with attitude, were even out of her mouth.

I told her that that was not an apology and I would not accept it unless it was sincere.

She came back and said it again, with the same tone of voice, with a hand on her hip. I again told her that that wouldn't do it.

She did it a third time, this time in front of Richard. I thought it was a bit better, but still done out of wanting to go to the mall, not because she meant a word of it. He thought it was okay.

After she walked out, I tried to explain to him, with him cutting me off, that I would think she was sincere if she offered to help with something to try to right the wrong. At first, she refused, saying that she would not do anything I asked. He told her he was asking. (It was nice to have him back me up.) Ultimately, at his request, I wrote out one big category for her to do. I basically said I wanted her to clean up - all clothes, shoes, books, dishes, and food from wherever it was in the house. She finally did most of that and they left without saying good-bye.

I haven't seen or spoken to her since we arrived back home this evening.

This school vacation is off to a great start.

CHAPTER 25
Reactive Attachment Disorder

I first heard of reactive attachment disorder (RAD) at an adoption conference. I listened to the description and dutifully took notes, but I couldn't conceptualize what it was or how it could impact my family. I've since read up on it and believe that both of my daughters suffer from it. When I rated each of them on the scale provided, they scored pretty high: Paulina, 42 out of 70; and Niki, 54 out of 70. Apparently, A score of 40 – 50 should be further evaluated. A score above 50 indicates a high probability of RAD based on DSM-IV criteria.

Todd Friel, host of the show *Wretched*, describes it by saying, "For children with RAD, authority is the enemy. They crave chaos and control. When you discipline a child with RAD, they provoke you to get a response out of you because they want chaos, because that brings them peace. They are not willing to be helped and want you to fail as a parent and give them up."

For Paulina, it means she cannot form an attachment to me, seemingly due to what I represent about the mother she wanted love from, but cannot get. For Niki, she has shallow attachments to lots of people, but not deep attachments to anyone. When a brand-new babysitter came, she hugged her immediately and told her she loved her, but she wouldn't hug me. It remains a painful daily reminder of the shattered hopes I had for my relationships with my children. I had no idea at the time how much worse it could get.

On February 7, 2016, I wrote this letter to my friends about RAD:

For any of you who know our current situation and really want to try to understand the experience of parenting children who are adopted, PLEASE, watch this video. All of it (24 minutes). It focuses on Christian families and church, but it is exactly the same here (http://www.youtube.com/watch?v=5ypmGTGG-N7A&sns=em).

This man pinpoints what goes on in my home with frightening accuracy. While these things don't happen for every adoptive family, they happen often. This is so to varying degrees, regardless of religion, amount of time, love, patience, or skill in parenting.

To be clear, I love my girls and always will. Despite my current situation, I would never, ever "send them back," as some have suggested. I love them all the more because I can see underneath their behavior, however awful it may be.

Like the narrator, I would not tell people not to adopt. We even took online and other classes that talked about RAD (reactive attachment disorder). However, we could not have known or been prepared for what was to come. There was a course we took called "Eyes Wide Open." It was pretty good, despite leaning toward issues with younger children. What might help prospective parents to make informed decisions about adoption may be to create a video of a household experiencing these issues and the fallout from them.

I have always said, adoption is not for the faint of heart, from the application process through parenting these children. The journey continues and we are on it together, even if my children claim they don't want me to be a part of it.

One more note, for the well-meaning friends, family, and acquaintances who want to be empathetic by relating stories of their children or challenging teens: Please don't compare your situation to ours. Yes, everyone faces challenges. Being a parent can be tough, no matter where your children came from. Just un-

derstand that what many of us experience is not remotely close to "typical teenage behavior."

Just be supportive, not judgmental. Hold yourself back from offering advice, unless we ask you directly. Call us. Watch our kids for a bit so we can get a much-needed break. Please don't criticize us when we take it. It's survival. Just be there and listen if we want to talk and try to recognize when we've had enough of hearing about the wonderful things your children are doing. We want to know and support you, too; it's just hard to hear 24/7.

Don't advise. Just listen. Learn. Support.

Thank you.
T.J. Kyri

CHAPTER 26

Paulina's First Boyfriend in the United States

April 28, 2014

Paulina now has her first real boyfriend here, Miguel Martinez. She is fifteen. He is seventeen, and came from Mexico about two years ago. He is a shy seventeen, not a worldly seventeen. I told her that seventeen is the outer limits of acceptable years older at this age. I am really happy that she is with him because she is happy whenever she hears from him or spends time with him. When she is happy, she is more often nice, to me and everyone else. If he doesn't text her, she gets grumpy.

She asked me today, while I was in her room and she was getting something in her closet, "I'm not saying I would now, but would you be mad if I had sex?" I calmly responded that "mad" is not how I would describe it. I told her that she had to be aware of the consequences, and that if she got pregnant, her life would be changed forever. That being said, I am glad she is on birth control pills, mostly to regulate her period and acne, which she is very good about taking.

I told her that no matter what age she is when she decides to have sex, fifteen, eighteen, or twenty-six, it should be with someone she loves. She should never be with someone who pressures her to do anything she doesn't want to do. She told me that Miguel asks before doing anything. She was very giggly when I asked about the last movie they saw. She didn't seem to remember what it was about. I would bet they spent most of the time making out, and I'm not sure what else.

In thinking about our conversation, I am impressed that, although she won't directly admit it, she cares what I think and seems to be looking for guidance. I love that she tells me important things and even asked for my opinion on a very important subject. It's one more quality about her that gives me hope that her future will be a bright and positive one.

CHAPTER 27

The Toll on Our Marriage

When we set out to adopt the girls, Richard and I were experiencing the normal highs and lows of marriage. We would fight and make up, as we were used to doing. We did not plan to get divorced. No one in my family had ever gotten divorced. I had only one friend who was divorced, and she didn't have children. I taught conflict resolution for a living and lived it daily. I was used to managing conflict in my marriage and my family. I didn't like it, but I felt I should be able to handle it. Fighting was just our normal way of living, and adoption was the next step in our family plan. I took vows in my marriage and during the adoption process, and I intended to stick to them.

During our adoption journey, we got along better than ever, relying on each other's strengths to accomplish our unified goal. Once we got home with the girls and began to blend our new "Kyri Family of Six," the problems between us intensified. Although we had realized our dream of adopting daughters, there's no way we could have been prepared for the nightmares that became our daily reality.

We were not naive. We took classes, read books and blogs, and went to conferences to prepare ourselves and our existing family as best we could. We knew there would be unspecified challenges in bringing two older girls with a traumatic history to our country, and into our lives.

When I thought about taking my daughters shopping and doing their nails, I was not under the illusion that it would be a perfect fantasy. I knew there would be difficulties helping them adjust, teaching them everything from the alphabet to sitting down at a dinner table as a family, where food was plentiful. I expected squabbles between siblings and some power struggles.

What I could not have predicted was how they could seize upon the lack of unity between Richard and I and pit us against each other to re-create the chaos that had enabled them to survive in Ukraine. I could not have imagined that Richard would be drawn into taking their side over mine at every turn, invalidating me as a parent.

Paulina was used to being in a parental role, both for herself and for Niki. She strongly resisted all attempts I made to parent them. I believed that our children needed boundaries to establish safety. I believed that if you punctured your new phone with a pen multiple times, you should have to earn its replacement. Richard wanted to provide them with everything they had been deprived of in Ukraine. He bought them everything they asked for, and replaced everything they broke, even if they'd done it intentionally. When Richard and I disagreed, he became the favored parent because he always said "yes."

Paulina resented everything I represented as a mother. She desperately wanted her birth mother to love her, but her mother could not show her love appropriately. When I tried to gently love her, she pushed me away, hard, literally and figuratively. Her birth father was not much of a presence in her life, so she didn't seem to feel as much hatred toward Richard as a father figure. Plus, he gave her everything she wanted. She even commented on this to me once, saying coyly, "I have Richard wrapped around my finger. He will do anything I ask."

She was right, and manipulated our family to get everything she thought she wanted, which included not relating to me as her mother.

Paulina treated me with utter disdain, when she would speak to me at all. When we would pass each on the stairs, her frequent greeting to me—"I hope you get hit by a bus and die!"—would often be met by me with "Love you too, sweetie!"

How else do you respond to such a venomous statement that you know comes from a place of deep pain you did not cause? Despite my outward smile, I told my friends, "If I ever wind up dead, it was probably my family. Not sure which one."

Richard and I both thought that our love for each of our children, in our own ways, would be enough to keep our family together.

It wasn't.

PART III:

THE
DIVORCE

CHAPTER 28
Stay or Go

This section includes journal entries, notes from my phone, texts, e-mails, letters, court documents, and my commentary on the entire experience of the end of my marriage and the impact it had on me and my family.

Affection was waning between Richard and me, now that the adoption process had been completed. I tried to get him to go out with me, find a new hobby together, anything to reengage, but he refused. He seemed angry all the time and would turn away from me. We were hardly spending any time together, and when we did, we fought. He continued to be nasty and berate me in front of the children, and I'd started to wonder if staying in this marriage would actually be more harmful for me, or for them?

Our sexual relationship was just one more parallel irony. He thought I hated sex and didn't want to have it. I wanted to enjoy it without pain, but didn't know how. Eventually, I didn't think I could. Yet, still, I would try to engage him. I would try to suggest fooling around, at least so that he could come and be in a better mood. In the past two to three years, he had consistently turned me down. As we lay in bed, I would try to get him interested. He would say no, and just roll over and go to sleep. That evolved into him not sleeping in our bed—first, randomly, and then, regularly, because, as he put it, it was too painful to think about not getting sex. I got used to the rejection and eventually stopped trying.

Richard had consistently brought me to orgasm externally, but sex was always something to get through, not enjoy. The best part was that he was quick, so the pain didn't last too long. While Richard would have liked me to enjoy it, and we tried so many ways to make it better, he was inexperienced and so was I. He would start to do something I'd like, then change it, despite my clear instructions to the contrary, to my incredible physical and emotional frustration. I couldn't trust him to know what he was doing, because even though he could get me to come, he didn't know what would and wouldn't make it work. He would get annoyed at my suggestions. His insecurity seemed to make him feel inadequate if I described what I wanted. It was as if he felt he was supposed to know, but didn't, and any ideas I expressed made him feel like he was being told what to do. He didn't understand that having sharp nails and an unshaven face made the pain worse. He didn't set the mood, despite my suggesting music or a game. If we took a bath, it meant there was the expectation of sex that would annoy him if not acted upon.

It wasn't just the sex, or lack of it. In the days before our marriage, a friend had given us great advice, which, I believe could have potentially changed the outcome of our marriage. He told us that the key to a happy marriage was for us to go out once a week, as a couple. He had his wife choose how she wanted to spend each Thursday night with him, alone or with friends, but she knew she could count on his company and companionship, consistently, at least one day per week. Richard would not commit to this.

Even at a marital retreat in Vermont years ago, they suggested that we needed to go out once a week with each other, and go away together once a month. This advice also went unheeded.

After the adoption, it got worse for many reasons. When I suggested going out, he would say he didn't want to do that until things were fixed. I pointed out that spending time alone together would be a way to connect and fix our relationship. I repeatedly asked him to find a new joint project. We worked well together through the adoption. We needed some way to get back that joint focus. He said no to classes, films, sports, and anything else I could think of. Ultimately, he was saying no to staying together.

While we did go out on occasion, more and more, invitations to events went unanswered. Being the social person that I am, it was hard to know there were parties and events going on without me. Eventually, I decided that I was done waiting for him. If I wanted to go out or go to an event or show, I'd go myself, or with friends. I did, and do, and I love it!

April 14, 2012: Letter to Richard
With the fighting between Richard and I intensifying, I tried putting my thoughts down on paper and wrote him this letter:

Obnoxious comments you've made to me:
This was a mistake.
You are not ready for this.
You can't give her what she needs from you.
You are self-centered.
You are acting like a two-year-old.
You are unequipped to handle this.
Sorry, but you signed up for more.
Act like an adult.

If I were to dare say even one of those comments to you, you would be screaming at me. To continue to berate me will not change anything about me, other than how mad I am at you. I deserve to be treated with respect, most especially by you. I expect to be supported in trying to teach respect, responsibility, and flexibility to all our children. When we disagree, we MUST not do it in front of the kids.

I think much of Charlie's behavior, though not all, is related to the insecurity he feels when he sees us yell and fight and me cry. Niki was also scared by what she saw yesterday morning and asked me about it. They want to know why their daddy made their mommy cry. Me too. Again, and again. THAT is not a good environment for them.

I never claimed to be a perfect parent, and this is very difficult. There is only so much I can take of "no," refusals, and attitude in a given day, from anyone. Maybe there are other people who could hear that all day long and not react. I am not one of those people. I try my best to be patient, but it is not unending. I am the parent these kids got, like it or not. I am a good parent, whether you or they think so or not. All four of them would be in a worse place without me and the parenting skills I possess. You can continue to try to knock me down, but it really won't change anything.

I expect a sincere apology from you, preferably written. You were wrong to continue to say so many bad things about me as a parent and as a person. I am not a bad parent or a bad person. I don't need to be perfect to get respect from my husband. That is what needs to be modeled for our family. I hope you are able to do that.

After giving him this letter, we tried to have a conversation. Eventually, like so many of our fights, we just dropped it and continued on with the day-to-day routine of tolerating each other and trying to raise our family.

In July of 2012, Richard and I had another, particularly vicious fight where he screamed to the kids, "I'm tired of dealing with your fucking mother!"

That was a last straw for me. He had called me a "fucking bitch" to the boys years before, and I had warned him that if he ever did that again, I would leave.

Following his tirade this time, we stopped speaking for several days.

Faced with the dilemma of sticking to my earlier word about leaving if he cursed at me to the kids, versus the reality of our extremely needy family, I sought the sage advice of one of my best friends, Arya. I stepped outside of Niki's gymnastics practice one day for a soul-searching conversation with her. I told her about our recent fight and what Richard had said. I told her that I didn't want to leave the marriage, and wasn't sure I could if I tried, knowing how vindictive Richard could be.

213

Arya asked me how I would feel if someday a boyfriend of Niki's spoke to her like that?

That clicked for me. I realized that I needed to be setting a good example of how partners should treat each other.

We agreed that I should write him another letter:

July 23, 2012
Dear Richard,

I have spent the day figuring out how it would be if I leave you and this relationship, and that makes me very sad. The last time you cursed at me, I warned you that if you did it again, I would go. Apparently, either that has no effect on you, you forgot, or you couldn't control yourself. Cursing at me, particularly in front of the children, is simply unacceptable. It is abusive. There is nothing that I did or could do to deserve to be abused.

You may argue that when I "berate you," as you call it, it justifies your response. It does not. There is no justification for abusive language toward a spouse. Even when you do things wrong, I may say to the kids, "I don't know why Daddy just hung up on me," but I do not disparage you. I do not call you names in front of them. Telling them that you are "tired of dealing with your fucking mother" is simply crossing a line that I cannot be party to.

I have always felt that staying in this relationship until the kids are grown was better than subjecting them to divorce. I have spent the day thinking about their future. I need them to know how to form healthy relationships, and this just isn't a good model. It breaks my heart to see Charlie cower under a table when you yell and tell me he loves me because I protect him from you. It is hard to explain to Niki not to cry, and that Daddy will come back. It's hard to comfort Eric when he sees you leave a restaurant and not come home. It makes me sad to have to reassure Paulina that we can still get home if you decide not to come back with the car. Your responses hurt not just me, but more importantly, your children. They watch what you do and learn from you. What will their relationships be like when they grow up? How would you respond if one of Niki's future boyfriends cursed at her?

It is fine to be angry. You need to learn how to control that anger and express it in appropriate ways, to me, and especially, the kids.

I do not want to be part of a relationship where I am disrespected and disregarded. I understand that it's a two-way street. It needs to be dealt with, intensively, right now, or the relationship will not continue.

I made a mistake many years ago, when you threw the Benzi box against the windshield and broke it. I took the car to get it fixed for you. You needed to take responsibility for your actions then, and you do now.

I am not the Devil. It is troubling to me that you have the ability to keep talking long enough to turn things around until it looks like everything is my fault. It is not. I am not perfect. I do criticize you. You do make mistakes. You don't listen when I speak. Half of your unplayed messages are from me. Walking out of the room and hanging up when I am in the middle of a sentence, which happens several times a week, is a clear indication of your disregard for the value of what I have to say. I need a relationship that values me, what I bring and what I think.

I am strongly thinking about taking a break and trying some time apart. As sad as that makes me, it may be a positive thing for everyone.

Perhaps we should go someplace, privately, to discuss whether or not this relationship can continue.

Upon reading this letter, Richard agreed to go for a drive to discuss things. We wanted to go to the local park, but it was raining, so we just sat in the car. He tried to steer the conversation to my reaction—saying that I would not stay and listen to him yell at me in the moment. I insisted that I would not discuss my response until we had sufficiently discussed his actions. He finally agreed.

It was a loud and teary conversation. Ultimately, he apologized for cursing at me in front of the children and agreed to try to not do it again. We talked about trying to use a silly code word between us when things got heated as a signal to make sure we were not in earshot of the kids. I think we came up with "broccoli," though it rarely worked. Ultimately, we agreed to keep trying to make our marriage work and find a new therapist.

October 8, 2013: Kiss and Fly
Every fall I get a chance to travel, to attend the Association for Conflict Resolution conference in whatever part of the country it is held. This year I got to fly to Minnesota. As I waited for my flight, I made this journal entry:

It was nice that he offered to drive me to the airport. I can't show my hesitation, knowing we will fight about something. Just thank him. I did. I needed to talk to him about what my friend told me in relation to her daughter and ours. She was concerned about Paulina's behavior and I thought Richard and I should discuss it. That was it. After previous silence, that was the spark. His opinion stated as fact. There can be no other. I offer, "I can see how you would see it that way. I see it differently." His response, "I can take out a gun and blow someone's head off. That is expressing an opinion too, right?"

He says, "Let's just drop it. We can't talk about it." Silently, I think to myself, "Add it to the list of things we can't discuss." With hope, I suggest that we shouldn't allow someone else's issue to cause us to fight. He responds, "It's our issue too." More silence on the ride.

When we arrive at the airport, he gets out and gives me my bags. I hug him, looking for his reaction. He hugs back. I tell him I love him, which I do, though I say it more because I should. I try to kiss him. He pulls away and says no. "Okay," I think, though it hurt.

As I roll my bag to the door, he comes up from behind me, kisses me, tells me he loves me too, and says, "Have a good flight." I turn for just a moment to look at him as he hurries back to the car. I have tears in my eyes, trying to make sense of his inconsistency. As I go to the kiosk to add my bag, I steel myself and focus on enjoying my freedom as a traveling professional.

I long for someone who truly loves and appreciates me.

CHAPTER 29
Midlife Crisis

Things continued to deteriorate between us. It felt as though Richard was having a midlife crisis. I began to wonder how long they typically last and if I could hang on long enough to move past it.

We argued in our new therapist's office about needing a new car and what type to get. With four children and their friends to drive around, I wanted to replace our nearly ten-year-old minivan. He wanted a Porsche Boxster, a two-seater.

After many rounds, including him storming out of the therapist's office, she ultimately helped us draw up an agreement that allowed him to get the Porsche, while I tracked how often a bigger car would be useful. She taught me an important technique that I have used many times since, called, "Don't return the serve." Since Richard was adept at baiting me into arguments via text, phone, or in person, she taught me to say, "I'm not returning the serve," which acknowledged that I knew what he was doing and would not be party to it. I would say that and then not give him a counterpoint, so the argument would stop. It was very effective.

Even with the written agreement, he would not accept the fact that I'd agreed he should get the car. To show him I was okay with it, I called his bookkeeper, Tatiana (the one who spoke Russian and helped translate with the girls), and asked her how I could get the $75,000 so I could buy him the car. I had always called her in the past when I needed money to pay our joint bills and she would transfer whatever I needed, often $10,000 at a time. In trying to buy a car for Richard, I became aware for the first time that Richard had complete control over our finances. Apparently, he had to approve every transfer Tatiana made to me. While Richard would often chastise me for things like spending $50 on shoes for the kids, he rarely said we couldn't buy something. I felt quite fortunate to be living a somewhat extravagant lifestyle where we could buy what we wanted. Even then, I was always conscious to not overindulge. I was happy shopping at stores like Target, never knowing or caring what brands I wore.

While I was somewhat concerned by this development, I still wanted to show Richard that I was okay with him getting a Porsche, as we had agreed in therapy, so I created a gift certificate with a picture of a Porsche and his picture on it for Father's Day. Shortly after that, he purchased his red, two-seater Boxster.

He drove it around with the top down and kept it parked in our driveway without a cover, no matter the weather. He ignored the fact that children were supposed to be age thirteen or one hundred pounds to ride in it, and regularly took it to drive Niki and Paulina, mostly separately, to school. Sometimes he squished them together in one seat.

Our au pair Anastasia had come from Ukraine in May of 2012 and was a welcome support. At twenty-seven years old, she was tall and beautiful, with thick, long black hair that cascaded around her shoulders as she helped me around the house and with the kids. I was grateful for all of her help, which allowed me to spend individual time with each of the children and also to return to work.

With complete trust, I allowed Anastasia to go with Paulina and Richard to Salem, New Hampshire, for Halloween. A few months later, when Richard asked about taking Anastasia with him on a business trip to Chicago, I believed him when he said she had a friend there and had never been, so that was fine, too. A couple of my friends were leery, but I saw no reason to be suspicious. Even when Niki told me she saw Daddy and Anastasia kissing, I explained it away, saying they were probably just close.

In hindsight, this affair was happening under my nose, in my own house, in front of my kids, but I was too trusting to believe that my husband would do something as clichéd as have an affair with our au pair! Proof of his midlife crisis was right in my face, but I was too naive to believe it. I foolishly thought that the vows we took meant as much to him as they did to me. I was wrong.

We grew even further apart. In addition to Richard alternately fighting with me and ignoring me, he stopped consistently sleeping in our bed. He often alternated working long hours in his office in Manhattan and in his home office, which was a separate structure above the garage, which we used for storage. Sometimes it felt like he lived in his home office, except there was no plumbing, so he was forced to come in the house to use the bathroom. I started keeping track on my phone of how frequently he wasn't sleeping with me.

CHAPTER 30
Where Are You Sleeping?

From: T.J. Kyri's iPhone
Subject: Bed

11/18/13. Richard slept on the air mattress in his home office: (At least ten times, probably more, before I started tracking.)

11/22/13. Richard's text: "I have thoughts about sleeping in my own bedroom. Just don't feel safe expressing them." He ultimately slept in our bed.

12/5/13. We were going to watch the end of a movie, but the remote wouldn't charge, so he couldn't get it to play. I had a headache and was tired, but was willing to watch it. He put on the middle of a Nicholas Sparks movie. I watched for about fifteen to twenty minutes. There was a scene about a boy running away from his dad who gets stuck in a storm on a bridge. I didn't want to watch a suspenseful scene and my head was hurting. I told him he could continue to watch it. He sarcastically grumbled, "It was great to watch a movie with you. I'm not going to bed at ten p.m." He left and ultimately slept in his home office.

12/6/13. I told Richard this afternoon that I had work to do tonight. I came down about 10:40 p.m. to find the TV on and Richard in his home office. I told him I was going to bed. He said he wasn't sure whether he would sleep in our room or his office.

12/11/13. I wake up and realize Richard never came to bed. My first thought is picturing him lying on a floor somewhere, having had a heart attack, like his father. If he at least told me he was sleeping elsewhere, I wouldn't worry. I wouldn't even mind. I haven't checked around or texted him. I thought he would be coming in, since I asked him to bring up toilet paper and he did, around midnight. He said he was going down to eat a bagel and didn't return to the house until eight a.m.

12/12/13. No reason I can tell. Just never came to bed.

12/17/13. I texted "Good night" at 11:30 p.m. He texted back "Good night" at 11:50. I asked if I should leave a light on for him or if he was sleeping elsewhere. He replied that he would sleep in his home office. Another night with thoughts running through my head. Door will be left unlocked, since I'm not going back down to lock it. No alarm set because who knows when he will want to come back. I hope he is up on time to deal with the kids. I have to leave for work around 7:30 a.m.

12/20/13. We met with Julie Stone, a new therapist for Niki, at six p.m. I wanted to go to dinner after. Richard wanted to go home. He went straight to his home office and didn't come in until this morning. Anastasia had taken the kids to the diner. The house was a mess. Carmela pooped in the kitchen and it was left for me to clean. The deciding factor was when I went to use the bathroom downstairs and it had not been flushed. I took my iPad and went out to eat by myself at Karuta.

12/21/13. Today I went to the funeral for my friends Kim and Nathan's baby, Grace. Richard said he was going to take the kids to California Pizza Kitchen (CPK) when I got home. (It was almost three p.m. and he'd never given them lunch.) I asked if he wanted me to meet him there and he abruptly said, "No." I said okay. Charlie didn't want to go, so I came home to stay with him (rather than get a manicure). When Charlie found out he couldn't play with Jonah, he then wanted to go to CPK. I asked Richard if he wanted me to drop him off or join him. He said I could stay. I did, then I went with Niki to the bookstore and then to see *Frozen*. I barely saw or spoke with Richard when I got home, at almost nine p.m. He went to his home office when I got home. After getting the kids to bed, I texted him, "Where are you sleeping tonight? Should I keep your light on or off?" He responded, "Not sure. You can shut off the light." Another night of not knowing what to expect. I am planning to write in the journal I keep from my third pregnancy with Collier, but he could walk in at any moment, shut the light off, and go to sleep. This means that he would be annoyed if I stay up with the light on. I think he probably will sleep in his office. At least I will have the freedom to do what I want. (He did sleep in his home office.)

12/22/13. I barely saw Richard today (Sunday), except when he intervened when Paulina was hurting me for trying to put the light on at eleven a.m. so Niki could get dressed. He took the girls to the mall. I eventually took the boys to Sportime USA, then dinner. As soon as he came home from dinner with Niki, he said hi and went to his home office. He texted me "Good night" at about 10:30 p.m. He is in his office again. When I kissed Niki good night, she asked if he was sleeping in his office again. I said I think so.

12/23/13. Richard apparently saw a coin collection late, went to his office in the city to drop it off, and joined Anastasia and her friends nearby. I don't know when he got home, and I figured he wouldn't come to bed here, so I didn't argue too much, when Eric begged to sleep with me.

12/24/13. Christmas Eve. Our second year celebrating. Richard was somewhat helpful with setting the table and as-sisting with dinner. I brought up the pros and cons involved with picking a date for Eric's bar mitzvah with him and Eric. He interrupted me, then got mad at me for wanting to fin-ish, since he claims I've already discussed it. He muttered something, cleared his plate, and left the table. When he returned, Niki ordered him to sit down and try it again without interrupting. (She would be a great mediator!) I began again and she stopped him when he interrupted again. We are leaning toward February 7, 2015. He left at the end of the discussion. I guess he's sleeping in his home office again.

12/26/13. Another night with him sleeping in his home office. He did come in for part of the day and spent some time with our friends, Michelle and Adam, who came for lunch with the girls. Last night, he slept in our bed. He actually had something interesting on TV about brain games. I would have watched longer, but he turned over and went to sleep.

12/27/13. I spent the day at my parents' house with Eric, Niki, and Charlie. We swam and had dinner and the three of them slept over. (First time for Niki.) Richard took Anastasia to the city today and worked. Paulina stayed home and slept. I got home about 10:30 p.m., after helping to get the kids settled at my parents' house. I tried to find out when Carmela was last out. Paulina wouldn't tell me. Richard didn't know. I took her out myself and told Paulina if she couldn't be responsible, I couldn't leave her home alone. (She'll be fifteen in one week!) Richard walked in, walked out, and texted me good night about fifteen minutes later. I wonder if he realizes how many days he has not slept here?

12/28/13. Richard did a nice thing in watching Rosalie so Terri and I could see *Les Mis* at a small theater in Westchester. I preferred going with her, though I had asked him. It is interesting that he would rather watch five kids than see one of his favorite shows with me.

As I pulled up to the house, I saw the light on in our bedroom. I thought, Oh yeah, I guess since he's watching the kids he'll be sleeping at the house. Nope. I didn't even have my coat off before he left to go to his home office. It's now 12:05 a.m., so I guess he's sleeping there again.

I am conflicted. I really like not having the pressure and stress of having him around, but I'm not sure why I'm still noting each time he's not here. I think I am gathering proof of abandonment if we ever get divorced.

12/29/13. He slept in our bed because he had to get up early for Boston.

12/30/13. Richard was out until one a.m. with Anastasia and Paulina in the city. Came home, slept for a couple of hours in his office at home, before leaving at six a.m. with Paulina to get Zoe from the bus station in the city. Went back to his home office to sleep midday, 12/31, as I prepared for our New Year's Eve party. He disappeared without a word, around ten p.m. Didn't respond to text at 11:45 p.m. Said later that he fell asleep. No one knew where he was.

12/31/13. He is sleeping in our bed, probably because he let someone use the air mattress he's been sleeping on in his office. Happy New Year.

1/2 and 1/3/14. Anastasia is in Aspen and Zoe is staying in Paulina's room. Richard spent the last two nights in Anastasia's bed, having sleepovers with Niki. I wish he would just say he's not going to sleep in our bed anymore. Then I could relax and do what I want to at night.

Last night, Charlie begged for a sleepover with me. I said to ask Dad. Dad said yes. Initially Richard was going to sleep here, I think, but then said he would go up and have a sleepover with Niki. I liked how huggy and snuggly Charlie was. Charlie seemed happy that Richard didn't stay. He said what he really wanted was a sleepover with me.

Tonight, when I tucked Charlie in, he asked Dad to come in so we could give him double kisses. Richard gave him a kiss, said good night, and walked out. Charlie turned to me and said, "You see, that's why I like when you kiss me good night. Daddy gives me a quick kiss, then leaves. You stay and give me lots of snuggles and kisses everywhere." Melts my heart.

1/8/14. At this point, it seems not even worth it to write about the reason or fight of the day. Richard seems to have decided to no longer sleep in our bed. Now that Anastasia is back, he can't sleep in her bed. I think he slept on the couch yesterday. Tonight, he says he is sleeping in his office in the city. That's good, because he was on a rampage this morning.

There was no point in continuing to track Richard's comings and goings or where he slept. None of his actions were based on paying any mind to me. It was all about him and his inability to talk about or deal with the frustration he was apparently feeling.

Fortunately, he was physically in the house early Monday morning, January 13. At four a.m., I apparently had food poisoning with diarrhea and passed out. I weakly called to him for help. He was in the kitchen and thought I was telling one of the kids to get out. Paulina was up, but apparently thought I was a ghost. He came up after a few minutes and called an ambulance. Fortunately, he handled everything and cleaned up.

While at the hospital, I thought about what would have happened if I'd been alone. I was grateful he happened to be there, but he easily could have been out. I pondered what I would have done. I couldn't have called an ambulance for myself at that point. I felt, at once, taken care of and alone.

Things continued to deteriorate, both in our relationship and with the kids. At different times, Paulina, Eric, and Niki would sometimes have violent outbursts, leaving me physically fearful. Every time I thought about possibly leaving Richard, I grappled with the reality that I still needed his physical protection from my own children at times.

Plus, how would I manage all four of these super-challenging children on my own?

Occasionally, he would give me reason to think that he still loved me. Sometimes, he would sleep in our bed and want sex. What was I supposed to make of that? You ignore me, berate me, abandon me, and, when it's convenient for you, the light is supposed to switch on for us to be amorous?

As I wrestled with how it felt to be in a marriage where my husband regularly refused to sleep in our bed and yet on occasion still wanted sex, I wrote the following journal entry. It was not something I could share with him, at least not without another fight, but it captured how I was feeling.

June 3, 2013, 9:21 a.m.
Which part of you
Wanted sex from me?
Was it the part that doesn't speak to me?
The part that won't kiss me?
The part that won't hug me?
The part that won't go out with me?
The part that won't sleep in the same house, much less the same bed, with me?
Please, tell me which part was thinking about sex.

CHAPTER 31

The Beginning of the End

Neither of us was sure if our marriage could be saved. We'd tried so many therapists, books, retreats, but nothing seemed to work, as the fighting continued. Our last-ditch effort was marital mediation. I had heard about it at an Association for Conflict Resolution conference a couple of years before. I located someone in New Rochelle who seemed to have a good reputation. The focus was supposed to be on saving the marriage. Instead, our marital mediator seemed to be a divorce mediator in disguise. This was evident as I reviewed the agreement to mediate, with the language all about divorce. My legal and mediation training made me question her skills, but we were already sitting in her office, so we proceeded with the session.

Richard began, as usual, and continued droning on as I looked longingly out the mediator's window. Her office overlooked New Roc City, with a bit of shopping, an arcade, bowling, a movie theater, and a local residential hotel. I looked at the hotel and thought how nice it would be to escape my family's abuse and just stay there for a little while. Snapped back to reality, we finished our session, no better off than when we'd arrived.

It was a snowy February day, and the drive that would normally take fifteen minutes was taking forty-five. As we crawled along the icy road, the defeat from our session set in. Richard was driving, and as we stopped at a light, he turned to me and calmly said, "We are not making each other happy, and I think we each deserve to be happy."

"Yes," I agreed.

He continued. "I think we should see other people."

Whoa! I thought. Somehow, I wasn't expecting that. My

first thought was, If he has sex with someone else, we're done.

Then the reality of the idea sank in. My head continued processing this concept.

Wait. We're done. This is my get-out-of-jail-free card, ten years early. I don't have to wait until Charlie turns eighteen and goes to college. I can start my life over now!

My sadness and excitement wrestled with each other. Was this the end of my marriage? Was this just a break? How long before he would start seeing other people? What about me? What about the kids?"

As my mind processed this huge new concept, all I could do was silently nod.

We drove the rest of the slow ride home in silence, both lost in our own thoughts about how our lives were about to change.

What I was too naive to know at the time, was that Richard had suggested we see other people so that he could essentially have permission to date the person he was already having an affair with: our twenty-seven-year-old au pair, Anastasia! I wouldn't learn about their affair until months later when admitted to kissing her when they were alone on one of their trips. To this day, I still don't know when it officially began, or how far it went when, but in hindsight I was far too trusting.

When Anastasia told me she was quitting, later that same month, she claimed it was because Eric had hurt her finger during one of his fits. I cried in my office as she told me, wondering how I would manage without her, still not suspecting the truth.

With Anastasia gone, we needed a new au pair. We did a thorough search through an agency and were thrilled to find Bernadette. We needed an older, experienced au pair, who could drive, speak English, and handle the complex needs of our children. Bernadette had been an au pair previously and had spent time in the United States. She even drove a bus for a special needs camp. She sounded perfect, so we worked with a couple of temporary au pairs, while we waited for her to be available.

CHAPTER 32
Rebirth

Five months. That's all it's been. Yet so much has changed in less than half a year. The last time I sat on this train to Vermont, I was beginning the journey of the original concept of this book, which was to be titled, *Mission Adoption*. Over the eight days I spent at that writers' retreat, I had many conversations about the state of my life, my marriage, and my family. There were many unknowns. Wishes and hopes that danced near the fringes of my current reality.

But I wouldn't act. Once again, my double-decade struggle for some agency in my relationship gave way to the desires of others. The irony of power and control being sought by both sides, each thought to be won by the other.

In the end, power leads to loss. We were losing at the endeavor of marriage.

Surrender leads to gain. As we acknowledged that our efforts were not improving our situation, we began to find moments of happiness apart. But it would be five months before that began to make sense.

When Richard had suggested that we see other people, part of me felt he had done what I couldn't do. I suppose I had felt that if I initiated a separation or divorce, if he disagreed, then I would suffer for it. With permission from him, it was okay.

Ironically, he seemed to want permission from me, though at the time, I didn't understand why. I was happy to oblige. We would each have the freedom to be happy. To find others that could do what we could no longer do for each other. I was elated! My life could begin anew. I tried to let my excitement override the sadness and regret I felt for all the failed efforts we'd made to try to keep our marriage and family together.

Shortly afterward, I signed up for Match.com and Jdate. I was anxious to get back in the dating game at age forty-five, rather than fifty-five. At times, I had thought we might get divorced when Charlie turned eighteen, but now I was free sooner than expected.

I longed for companionship, for appreciation, for calm conversations and connection. I was vaguely aware of how I longed for sexual intimacy, the hint of a spark present when I would see an attractive man, though it was fairly easy to put it out of my mind, since I was used to its absence.

I created my dating profile and wrote this poem to describe what I was looking for:

It's time for me to start anew,
Perhaps with someone just like you.
Quiet dinners in or out,
Broadway shows or walk about.

Listening and talking with one another,
(I'm not seeking a new big brother!).
Smiles, laughter, optimism.
Chivalry, not chauvinism.

Respect is what I'm looking for.
Intelligence and not too poor.
If you give a great massage,
I'll be thrilled, that's no mirage.

Board games can be fun to play,
A great connection, any day.
Movies, music, hanging out,
Lots to do, I have no doubt.

Romance truly seals the deal,
Please no liars, just be real!
If you enjoyed my try at rhyme,
Contact me to chat sometime!

I briefly corresponded with a few people and tried a few events. My second event was an intimate wine-and-cheese tasting, just one block away from Richard's office. To my surprise, I connected with someone right away. He kissed me in the park that night and I felt like a giddy schoolgirl, my leg rising in the air with desire. He reignited a passion that had long ago died. We saw each other for about a month, and I slept over a few times.

There were things about him I liked and admired and there were things that I didn't. He was a true bachelor, having never married at the age of forty-eight. He was a lieutenant commander in the Air Force, as well as a US marshal. A most unusual choice for me, as someone who has dedicated their professional life to teaching non-violence. I felt protected around him. Honor was clearly something he took very seriously. Most importantly, he asked me to tell him what I liked and then remembered and did those things, anything from stroking my hair to kissing my neck. Requesting my guidance and then observing it really turned me on. It was so refreshing! I told him that I would tell him if he crossed a line to something I didn't like. He said that would be too late. He said abuse was common in the military, and he didn't want to be anywhere near that.

On the other hand, his home was a mess, dusty, with things left out. (Not that mine is neat.) He had virtually no food in the house, and when I asked about breakfast, his response was that if I wanted breakfast, I would have to bring it next time. I was a bit put off by that remark, but made note of it.

He was a very private person, being clear that I would not meet his family or friends, nor he mine. He was definitive, yet it was not really an issue because I knew this was not going to be a long-term relationship. He voiced his concern about Richard still living in the house, yet was still extremely helpful in trying to figure out where I could safely leave my car while I went straight from his place to Woodloch Pines, a beautiful resort in the Poconos, to celebrate my parents' fiftieth anniversary.

One of my biggest concerns was that the last time I'd been with him at his place, I had tried making advances to him on the couch. He was not interested at the time and put his hands on my arms and gave me a slight push off of him. He certainly hadn't hurt me, but I was a bit shocked by it. While I wasn't fearful, it did make me think about the fact that this was a military man who is strong and trained to kill, if need be. I tried to reconcile that action with the honor described above. Ultimately, I couldn't.

For a variety of reasons, we mutually decided not to continue to see each other. The conversation about it was actually pretty easy and straightforward, which I truly appreciated.

The evening before the last time I stayed over, I went to a speed-dating event. (Since this concept has been known to raise eyebrows, I offer the following by way of unneeded explanation. I am willing to try anything at least once, and I looked at it as a social networking opportunity, never mind a night out.)

Again, to my surprise, I connected with the first person who sat across from me. We easily began speaking before they told us "the rules." When the facilitator called time for the men to move on, we were still conversing. I suggested that he stick around at the end to hang out. He readily agreed.

While another guy bought me a drink and a schoolteacher took my card and then came back to give me his number, Damian was the only one there that I wanted to spend more time with. He made me laugh and the conversation flowed smoothly.

After the event, he took me to Katz's Deli for a late-night dinner. I let him drive me back to Grand Central where we continued talking about our lives for about an hour. He said he wanted to make dinner for me at his place the following Friday. I agreed, then got worried that I was going to some strange guy's place, whom I hardly knew, alone. I struggled between logic and instinct. Ultimately, I followed my instinct, which said that I was comfortable with him and could trust him.

Bernadette, my new au pair, knew where I was and I was in contact with her. Damian and I had a great time together, and I loved having a guy cook and clean up for me! I got naked with him pretty quickly, as I was beginning to rediscover my sexual hunger. We enjoyed exploring each other in new and exciting ways. Since discovering my newfound freedom, I had been experimenting with sexy clothes and undergarments. When he requested I get a Brazilian wax and a corset, I did so without overthinking it too much. My visit to Romantic Depot felt empowering, rather than demeaning, which in and of itself was a change.

For the first time in my life, I was with someone who understood the importance of foreplay and getting me to relax, without alcohol or even lubricants. Damian's soothing words encouraged me not to worry, not to focus on negative past experiences, just to enjoy allowing him to please me in the moment. He showed me he understood what I was feeling and how my body reacted to his. He made me believe that he was there to please me with sex. He had a strong desire to teach me to have not one, but multiple, internal orgasms. I looked into his eyes and trusted him to take care of me in more ways than one. He succeeded, and so did I. It was an incredible experience!

I discovered that being able to trust someone enough to give them control over my body, knowing that they have the right experience and good intentions, can be mutually beneficial. I pondered and shared with my therapist my new interest in steamy romance novels, which progressed to Fifty Shades of Grey and a similar series in the same genre.

Again, this was an area previously unexplored. It's not that I'm into S & M or its iterations. What appealed to me was not the man hurting the woman, but the care taken of her afterward. Now I think there is more to it than that. There is something to be said for submitting yourself to someone else for

YOUR pleasure. In the past, I could not trust that this would be done, because whether I gave directions to Richard or allowed him to follow his instincts, I would often end up frustrated. It's not that Richard couldn't bring me to orgasm; it's just that it often took a while, and he couldn't understand why. He never allowed me to guide him to bring me pleasure. The fight for power continued in the bedroom and ultimately left us both unfulfilled.

The military man made me come, fully clothed, in my car in five minutes. There was no pretense or fight for control. Just his interest in pleasing me, and it worked. That was impressive!

Damian took his time to teach me something I had never before experienced. Again, it was based on his desire to please me, not control me, and without the fear or insecurity that I was controlling him with my requests.

I was enjoying my "sexual rebirth," as Damian called it, and I reveled in my newfound freedom. I was grateful to our new au pair, Bernadette, who was extremely supportive and encouraging of my new ventures. She seemed more than happy to watch the kids at night, so I could go out and experience a new part of life.

Little did I know at this point that her kindness was an illusion. At the time, I was enjoying the "whole new world" blossoming around me. I couldn't wait to see what would grow in my new garden.

Here is a poem I wrote a bit later, reflecting my thoughts about divorce and dating:

Goldilocks Grows Up

When she was small, she wandered around.
Traipsed through the forest to see what she found.
Porridge and beds and bears she did try.
Perfection she sought, though one may ask, "Why?"

Then as she grew, she settled on down.
With the one she thought best, from her very own town.
Comfort she had, at least from outside.
But inside she found, almost daily, she cried.

Still, she moved forward, she'd made her clear choice.
She never realized, she was losing her voice.
As her family grew bigger, the fighting got worse.
Sometimes, she felt as though this was a curse.

She stayed and she stayed, thought it best for the kids.
Until she discovered a secret of his.
The interest he used to have for her waned,
While he transferred affection to one from Ukraine.

Trust had been broken and misery grew.
The extent of deceit, no one really knew.
Decisions were made to alter her fate.
Desire from others did percolate.

Where would this new road in life really lead?
Strange, though exciting opportunities indeed!
Some were too hot or too cold, not just right.
None yet resolved her ultimate plight.

Well into adulthood, Goldie now pondered:
Is this the time now, really to wander?
The bears often growl, and so, instill fear.
But deep down inside, her strength does appear.

She stays on the high road, her back to the storm.
Enjoying, exploring, seeking out a new dawn.
And when she so happens upon the right chair,
She'll let comfort embrace her, then home will be there.

Key Dates in Our Divorce Process
This is an overview of the order that events occurred. Details follow.

February 2014: Since neither of us is making the other happy, Richard suggests that we agree to see other people. Marital mediation with Diana Pope.

April 6, 2014: Richard admits to kissing Anastasia.

May 24, 2014: I tell Richard that cohabitating and seeing other people isn't working. We need to get divorced. He agrees.

July 2, 2014: We jointly tell the kids that we are getting divorced.

Summer 2014: We try divorce mediation with Connie Monroe, without attorneys. When I ask about the status of finding a new place, Richard tells me, in mediation, that he has already purchased an apartment in Manhattan for $1.45 million.

I hire Jack Massimo as counsel.
Richard hires Clive Johnston as counsel.
We return to mediation with Connie Monroe and the attorneys for a couple more sessions. She cannot manage the flow of conversation. Jack, as a trained mediator, tries to assist in the process.

November 3, 2014: Pendente lite (temporary support agreement) signed, giving me $12,500 per month for maintenance and child support.

November 5, 2014: Richard moves out of the marital home and into his NYC apartment.

May 7, 2015: We officially file for divorce.

May 2015: I speak with Bernadette about some of her deceitful behavior.

Summer 2015: Mr. Brunt is assigned as the attorney for the children.

September 2015: I become aware of more details of Bernadette "fanning the flames" and turning the children against me.

November 3, 2015: After begging my attorneys to let me fire Bernadette (which they didn't want me to do for fear it would be seen as making a unilateral parenting decision), I finally let her go.

November 9, 2015: Niki throws a fit, cuts her arm, Paulina takes a pic, Richard picks her up at midnight, and doesn't tell me until nearly two hours after I call him the next morning.

November 13, 2015: WORST DAY OF MY LIFE! First court appearance. I am ordered to leave the house by 2:00 p.m. on Monday, November 16.

November 16, 2015: I move into a local residential hotel until March 1, 2016. Thanksgiving destroyed.

November 23, 2015: Follow-up court appearance "to make sure I was out on time."

Thanksgiving 2015: The thirty people coming for Thanksgiving from five different states are forced to scatter and not be together. Mom and Dad host some of us. Only Charlie is with me. Uncle Benny passes away.

March 1, 2016: I move into a rented furnished house.

April 2016: I host Passover, with financial support from Mom and Dad.

October 5, 2016: I finally get my Honda Pilot.

November 7, 2016: I begin working full-time at Lehman High School.

November 2016: I host Thanksgiving.

December 2016: Aunt Judith passes away.
My attorney, Bart Lazio, demands payment of more than $100,000 from tax refund awarded the week before but not received by me. He suddenly withdraws as counsel. I have to file a brief, pro se.

May 2017: Richard and I try mediation again with new mediators.

June 2017: I hire my third attorney, Beth Zinger.

August 25, 2017: I move to a new rented home on Victory Street.

December 27, 2017: We sign and submit our mediated settlement agreement, thus avoiding a trial, scheduled to begin January 3, 2018.

January 30, 2018: Divorce decree signed by Judge Ringwald. We are finally, officially divorced.

CHAPTER 33

The Divorce Process Begins

Saturday, April 6, 2014 was a relatively normal afternoon, until Richard approached me, saying he wanted to take a walk and talk to me. My tension heightened, knowing his unpredictable moods, and fear crept in, making me not want to be alone with him. I reluctantly agreed to walk with him, as long as our dog, Carmela, joined us. As we started our walk, on that warm, spring day, it became evident that he was in a soul-bearing mood.

He began by explaining that he kissed Anastasia on one of their trips. Shock, anger and resignation fought each other for control in my head and heart. I didn't know what to say, what to ask, what to believe. He continued, with remorse, explaining that they were spending more time together, but never admitting when the infatuation or affair began, nor how far it had gone. I didn't ask. I didn't want to know—didn't want to acknowledge the fool I had been for trusting him and being blind to the signs of what he was doing right in front of me.

He did the teary thing. I did the stoic thing. We rounded the corner, winding back up in front of what was now our tainted home. There was nothing else to do, but go back inside and silently figure out what to do next.

Richard and I tried the "live-in-the-same-house-separately" thing for a while, though I quickly came to feel that he was an intruder in my space. It felt like he was lurking, me still on edge, never knowing when he would be home or out, in the basement or our bedroom. I would come home from a date and he would be in the bathroom, brushing his teeth.

It began to feel strange to see each other naked when either of us showered. When he came home from being out, I had no idea where he had been, or with whom, though I no longer had

241

the right to care. This marriage needed an official end. I wanted him out. I needed to begin to move on with my life without living in his shadow.

On May 24, 2014, after we were able to have a civil conversation regarding Paulina's challenges with school, I told him there was something else we needed to discuss. I told him that I wanted a divorce. With a somewhat heavy heart, he agreed.

It still amazes me that with all the fighting we did, our most civil conversations seemed to be around us moving on with our lives. Something to ponder. Perhaps we both already felt defeated in our failed attempts to keep the marriage alive? There was no more power left to struggle for. We were now both powerless, at least in terms of our relationship as spouses.

We decided to try divorce mediation, and I searched for a mediator with a good reputation that I didn't know personally from the field. Connie Monroe was on the board of the state mediation council, so I thought she would be well qualified. Richard and I went to our initial meeting together. She struggled to try to balance the flow of conversation with Richard's dominating presence.

I asked him about the status of looking for an apartment so he could move out. He nonchalantly responded that he had already purchased a $1.45 million apartment in Manhattan. I was stunned. Not only had he found an apartment (and was still living with me), but he had spent $1.45 million of our marital assets without consultation! I silently fumed and completed the mediation, politely making a follow-up appointment, which I promptly canceled when I got home.

By now, I realized I needed an attorney. I had no idea what our finances were. I knew he was deceitful and revengeful, but I had no idea how far he'd go. I also knew he loved our children and I believed he would not do anything intentionally, financially or otherwise, to hurt them. I thought that would extend to me as their mother, but again, I was wrong.

I hired Jack Massimo, a mediator and attorney. Richard hired Clive Johnston to represent him. The four of us returned to try mediation again. When Richard became teary in the session, which he often did, garnering sympathy, Jack stepped in to manage the situation, when Connie couldn't. Sadly, it became clear that this mediation would not work, and similar to finding the right therapist, it would be years before we would try it again, with someone else.

We began the court process, initially seeing court referee Audrey Murphy. She was a strong, opinionated woman who had little patience for us and our bickering, or our lives. We tried to figure out parenting plans and amounts Richard would pay me for maintenance and child support, once he moved out of the marital residence on November 5, 2014.

At first, Richard covered the bills as he always had, probably feeling a bit guilty about his affair and expensive new apartment.

One day, I was doing some shopping at the Westchester Mall and happened upon a new store, Peloton. I had been taking spin classes at the Jewish Community Center of Mid-Westchester and was intrigued by this indoor spin bike. At first, I just peered in the window. Then I went home and did some research. The next time I went in and tried it out. Wow! I loved it right away, with the dynamic instructors and the precise way to adjust the resistance, from zero to one hundred, as opposed to just how it felt between a seven and a ten.

I went home and called Richard.

"I don't have to ask you, but I want to get a Peloton bike, and I want to make sure we have the money."

"How much is it?"

"Two thousand dollars, plus $39.99 per month."

"Wow! That sounds like a lot! How do you know you'd use it?"

"Well, I already pay $1,000 for the gym each year that I could stop. This I would have for a long time. I think if it were in the house I would use it more often. I'm not asking your permission. I just want to make sure we have the money."

"I guess so."

"Good."

I called up and ordered it right away.

Within a few weeks, two attractive men arrived in the black Peloton van, carried my new pride and joy into my bedroom, and set it up. I was ecstatic! I tried my first ride and was surprised by how hard it was, yet I was proud that I completed it. I began taking more rides, having to just go a few steps from my bed to the bike. I tried a few instructors and liked them all, though they really challenged me physically. I had thought I was in decent shape from spin class and martial arts, but this was different.

I remember one of my early rides; I could barely catch my breath at the end. I unclipped and made my way down the hall between the kids' rooms. Red-faced, I lay down on the floor, exhausted. Sweet Charlie came over empathetically and placed a pillow under my head.

Soon, I tried Christine D'Ercole and was instantly hooked! She was the most positive person I had ever heard. I really connected with her words of wisdom and enjoyed moving to her great taste in music. She quickly became my favorite, and I rode her live rides whenever I could, finding strength in her words. Later I learned she was a world-class cyclist, having won numerous medals in track racing. She was also someone I could relate to, since she was about my age, divorced, and raising a daughter the same age as Paulina. Yet, despite her fame, she seemed so down-to-earth and real.

I also loved Jenn Sherman's rides, with her great taste in music. I especially loved her Sunday morning rides and still do them whenever I can. There's also Hannah Corbin and Denis Morton who also bring great energy to the rides. Now they've added a London studio, so I can add Ben Alldis and Sam Yo to my favs, with their great accents. I also do Peloton meditation, often before I go to sleep and find Aditi Shah, especially soothing. Members have created strength challenges that I count among my accomplishments. I often set monthly challenges for myself for the number of minutes or miles or classes and find that if I set that intention, I almost always achieve it.

In the early days, Peloton fans created the community beyond the bike. They made Facebook pages and car decals, jewelry, and even tattoos. Eventually several dedicated members decided that riders should descend on the "Mother Ship," aka the Manhattan Studio, and the first Home Rider Invasion (HRI) was born. I believe I was at the very first one, with about fifty people.

Peloton exploded in popularity and soon the company took over the main "Official Peloton Member" Facebook page. Now there are hundreds of groups on Facebook and Instagram. They began improving their merchandising and respectfully gave independent members the chance to finish their sales before enforcing their copyright. They sponsored their first HRI, which morphed into "Homecoming" events of three thousand people that sold out in minutes to fans around the world.

Peloton has changed thousands of people's lives, earning them the tagline of "more than a bike." People have gone through illness, loss, births, marriages, crises, and celebrations with tons of hands on their backs. I came to rely on the bike, the instructors, and the members to give me the internal and external strength to manage everything I was going through. My bike became my most prized possession, and every time I moved to a new place, I would explain to the movers, "This is my Peloton; you wrap it completely so NOTHING happens to it."

245

I attended several of Christine's "Wordshops," which were inspirational workshops built around her mantra of "I am. I can. I will. I do." I have many garments with her amazing inspirational quotes. She begins most rides with "Drop your shoulders. Drop your baggage," encouraging me to release my tension and focus on the ride. She tells you to "Change your chatter" to rid yourself of negative messages.

With all the challenges I've gone through and continue to go through, Christine's positive words always motivate me to move forward. Now they have yoga, meditation, strength training, stretching, and more, and I do most of it. While I don't ride every day, I have done something on that bike nearly every day for several years. As of this writing, I'm on a 149-week streak, meaning I have done something on the bike for 149 weeks in a row. I had never done any exercise this consistently. It's amazingly motivating. (I know this probably reads like a commercial, but it really is that great. Talk to almost anyone who has one and you'll likely see the same passion. My Peloton and its community have gotten me through the toughest times in my life, and I know it will continue to do so. Getting the Peloton at the beginning of the divorce turned out to be one of the smartest moves I made.)

As the divorce progressed, Richard's generosity evaporated. The lawyers decided, without me understanding the implications, that what I received each month would be half child support and half maintenance. Each month, I would have to try different approaches to get him to pay. He was supposed to pay by the first of the month, when my rent was due, but he often never got around to it. I would try to ask nicely, and then I would foolishly try to get him to empathize with my zero bank account. At times I would have to ask my lawyer to contact his lawyer to contact Richard to tell him to pay, wasting even more money for their time. I was grateful that he paid, but it was whenever he felt like it.

CHAPTER 34
Evil Au Pair, Bernadette

I had come to rely on Bernadette to help me with the kids, the house, and rebuilding my life. As I started dating, I would tell her where I would be as a safety precaution. She encouraged me to enjoy myself, offering to watch the children overnight on occasion, so I could stay out. Her supportive words helped me believe I could trust her.

Once again, I was wrong. So very wrong to be so trusting.

Our housekeeper, Gabriella, initially worked for us at our first house, beginning around 2003. Her role expanded to babysitting the kids and helping me with parties. Her family would celebrate events with us, and when we moved to the bigger house, she cleaned regularly and helped me with virtually anything I needed. She worked with our family for fifteen years and I trusted her completely.

One day she called me and asked to meet me, outside the house. She said she needed to speak with me about Bernadette and didn't feel comfortable doing it in the house.

We met at a diner and I took careful notes on her concerns about Bernadette:

- Bernadette is no good for you or the family. Don't trust her.
- She is convincing Eric to move to the city with Richard; Charlie too.
- Eric told her that Charlie should finish fifth grade and not have to go to Woodlands School, but should live with Dad in the city.
- Bernadette asked Eric, "Did you tell your dad yet that you want to move in with him?"
- The kids are now repeating that I am a control freak and that they like it better when I'm not around.
- Bernadette showed Gabriella texts from Richard telling her he's lonely.

- Richard and Bernadette decided to call Gabriella and pay her separately without my knowledge.
- Bernadette wants to move in and watch Eric from Richard's house.
- Bernadette often complains to Gabriella about work.
- She tells Gabriella and the kids that I'm going out "every night with different men."
- She shows the kids texts I send her.
- She has a secret credit card from Richard (which explains why she was always buying food and not asking for reimbursement).
- Excessive shopping.
- Richard asked her to stay through the summer, and will pay her.
- She is pitting the kids against me.
- Bernadette complains to Gabriella: "Why should I have to do T.J.'s laundry? It's not in the contract."
- She complains to Gabriella: "I can't go out because T.J. is out all the time."
- She's depressed because she has too much to do.
- Leaves kids alone.
- Tells Richard there's no food in the house.
- Convinces the kids to order food so she can order and feed her boyfriend, Bruce.
- She was making plans to move to the city and stay with Richard at least through the summer.
- Shares private info with the kids to pit them against me.
- T.J. is good with other kids, but not her own.
- Told Gabriella that I grabbed the kids, getting physical with them.
- Speaks badly about Richard; Friday late, disorganized.
- Richard is calling Bernadette every night to see if I am sleeping at home.
- Bernadette speaking to Richard by phone and text for extended periods of time.
- Apparently, once when I planned to take the kids out,

Bernadette and Paulina promised Niki a bag of Takis (chips), if she said she didn't want to go with me. She actually paid Charlie $5 not to go with me.

- Bernadette apparently promised to buy Niki a purse if she was mean to me.

I listened to this extensive list of concerns and my head started to spin. There were small things that I could explain away, like her ordering food and not asking for money back, but this list was extensive, specific, and alarming, coming from a trusted source. I vowed to pay closer attention to interactions with Bernadette.

After a night out in March 2015, I came home and started making the following notes of all the things that seemed amiss, and then Gabriella met with me again, confirming and adding to what I discovered:

- Someone slept in my bed.
- Condom found.
- Bike used.
- Paulina and Bernadette in my room.
- Bernadette and the tutor, Renee, speaking outside for twenty minutes.
- Bernadette sees the kids' texts, not sure about mine.
- Bernadette was telling the kids I'm spending Richard's money and that the money should be for them.
- She told Gabriella not to come.
- Made Charlie cry over grades.
- Richard called Gabriella directly to tell her not to come.
- Bernadette said something like there is no money to pay her. She said she'd come anyway.

By now I was convinced that Bernadette was plotting against me, though I couldn't understand why. I knew I could no longer trust her and needed to get her away from my kids. She was planting thoughts in their heads and telling them lies about me. With the existing drama of the divorce, she was fueling the fire that was already starting to burn out of control.

Long after the divorce, this pathological liar actually stole checks from Richard and fraudulently cashed one of them for two thousand dollars. She also told a landlord that she and her boyfriend were Richard's foster children! No one believed me when I tried to show how delusional she was, and my family insisted on keeping in touch with her until these events transpired, in 2020. Finally, they saw that I was telling the truth and that she'd been lying and manipulating everyone all along, but it was way too late by then. There is actually now a warrant out for her arrest for the check fraud.

CHAPTER 35
Romance Amid Chaos

I had met John on Jdate in October of 2014 and dated him for four years (though I almost didn't go on a second date). He was Italian, but had converted to Judaism for his wife, whom he divorced. She was not allowed to see their son, due to mental health concerns, and was out of the picture.

I cared about John and his son deeply. We were a bit of an unusual pair, with me being very outgoing and him being quite introverted, but at the time, we were both good for each other. For the first time, I felt safe, cared for, and listened to. We had lots of good times, and I truly appreciated being with someone who made me laugh instead of cry. He had a gorgeous back-yard with a deck where we'd often sit and talk, soaking up the peace that nature affords.

On my forty-sixth birthday, John took me to dinner, before going to see Carol Burnett live at the Westchester Coun-ty Center. I left my car at his house and he drove. As we were approaching the theater, I got a call from Bernadette, telling me that Eric was throwing a fit and trashing the house, tossing pillows everywhere. I asked her if I should come home, which meant either John would have to take me (and his being there might add to the situation, since no one had met him yet, even though I'd been seeing him for six months at that point), or he'd have to drive me back to get my car in Chappaqua.

Bernadette insisted that it was not necessary for me to come home. She felt confident in her ability to handle the situation. She mentioned something about Eric opening the knife drawer, but that he wasn't acting in a threatening manner.

I told her to call Richard in the city. When she tried, he didn't answer his phone.

I went back and forth with her, assessing the situation, feeling very torn. On the one hand, I wanted to be there for Eric and the other kids, even though I knew my presence might exacerbate the situation, since I never knew how Eric was going to respond.

Eventually, we decided she would call Renee, his tutor. Renee had a good relationship with Eric, and as a special ed teacher for thirty years, had specific training as to how to handle these things.

I kept the phone on my lap throughout the show and kept checking it to see if I would need to leave. Both Bernadette and Renee assured me via text that they had gotten the situation under control. They suggested that I not come home that night so that Eric would have time to clean up the house the next morning, when he was in a different frame of mind.

Because it was my birthday, I had already planned to spend the night at John's home, so that's what I did.

When I came home the next morning, I spoke with Bernadette, Eric, and the other kids about what happened. Things were calm at that point and I was glad it ultimately worked out the way it did.

A few days later, I wrote this poem to John.

Finally Happy

Finally happy.
After years of yelling, fighting, crying,
I found someone who makes me smile and laugh.
He knows how to instantly relax me.
When I'm stressed, he listens and tries to make it better.

Finally safe.
I feel protected. Taken care of.
There is someone I can count on.
He'll be there. He'll help.
He lets me be who I am and doesn't try to change me.

Finally supported.
Not a fifth child, he can take care of himself.

Of course, he remembers his keys and phone.
He's checked the times and parking.
Arranged everything. Made sure of all the details.

Finally cherished.
To make me happy is his pleasure, not a chore.
Something needs to be done, he does it, without being asked.
Socks are off the floor. Toilet seat is down (usually).
Garbage is out.
Just to make it easier for me.

Finally appreciated.
Thank-you's and kisses and hugs and texts, all show me how he feels.
Plus, words—he tells me how glad he is to have me in his life.
Smiles and sighs reveal his pleasure.
Poems, cards, e-mails, and books, carefully chosen to demonstrate what he thinks of me.

Finally respected.
Asking my advice. Following some of my suggestions.
Trusting my ideas. Welcoming me into his world.
Matching my intellect. Holding the door. Carrying my bag.
Treated as an equal, recognizing and building on my strengths.

Finally, truly loved.
Thank you, John, my Sweet Knight.

~ T.J. Kyri
April 19, 2015

`As has been a tradition for many years, I held a party for the Fourth of July at my home in 2015. I had two and a half drinks total throughout the eight hours of entertaining.

Most of the guests had left by about ten p.m. At this point, my kids had been getting to know John and his son for the past few months. Richard had stopped seeing Anastasia and started seeing Karen. At the end of the evening, I asked each child, individually, how they would feel if John and his son spent the night. They each said they were fine with it. I then asked, specifically, if they would feel more comfortable if he slept on the pullout couch downstairs versus with me. Again, each child individually confirmed that they had no problem with him being in my room with me.

It had been a long and tiring day and I was pretty exhausted. I also wasn't feeling that great. (I was a little headachy and my stomach was a bit upset.) After making sure the house was cleaned up and all the kids were settled, I just wanted to get some sleep.

But that was not to happen for a while.

In short, I was woken up repeatedly, about twenty times, more than I have ever been woken in my life, including when my kids were infants! I got texts, phone calls, knocks at the door, each occurring just after I'd finally fallen asleep again.

It started around eleven p.m., when Bernadette took Paulina and her friend, Alan, to McDonald's, and then to drive him home nearby. Shortly after, Paulina contacted me, asking if she could spend the night at her friend Lacey's. Though I told her I preferred to know in advance, I said I'd allow it, since she'd done the right thing in contacting me.

About midnight, Niki knocked at my bedroom door, waking me again, saying something about feeling uncomfortable with John there. I got up, spoke to her sleepily, and ultimately told her that if she was uncomfortable with it, the time to tell me was when I'd asked, not after everyone was asleep. She said she wanted to go to Richard's apartment, where he was with his girlfriend. I asked how that was any different, and she replied that she knew Karen better. I pointed out that she had actually known John longer and had spent more time with him. Had I felt better, I probably would have made up the bed downstairs, as I had offered to earlier, for John or me to sleep there. At that point, I simply told her I was sorry she was uncomfortable, but that at this hour, he and his son (who had already been asleep for about an hour and a half) were staying. I told her she needed to go back to sleep.

Instead, she called Richard, and apparently lying for effect, said that she thought John and I were having sex. (Absolutely and completely untrue!) She asked him to come and pick her up. He texted, then called me a short while later, once again rousing me from the sleep I was trying so desperately to get. He claimed that I was drunk, which was utterly false. He said he was coming to get Niki. I told him that was unnecessary and advised against it. Ultimately, rather than continue to argue with him, I said, "Do what you want." At one a.m. he came and got her, but did not take her medication for the next day.

The next morning, he returned to take Charlie to breakfast, but left Niki in his apartment, and still didn't take her medication with him. Through lots of lying and deceit on the part of Richard, Paulina, Niki, and Bernadette, I learned that Bernadette actually took Paulina to the city by train around midnight that night, after I'd allowed her to stay at Lacey's. Paulina, Bernadette, and Karen may or may not have been at Richard's apartment with Niki that night, or the next morning.

I found it amazing that Richard was able to come and go as he pleased, take the kids at any hour without telling me, not give them their medications, and yet somehow accuse me of being drunk and having sex that night, yet this was how it was.

CHAPTER 36
Lawyer Up—Spiral Down

Throughout what became a four-year divorce process, using mediation and the courts, I ended up hiring three different attorneys and we had four different judges, two mediators, and one court referee. Richard and I also thought it would be a good idea for the kids to have their own attorney, so they wouldn't have to choose sides between us. The court appointed Don Brunt, whom we had to pay. I couldn't have known then that he would become one of the few people in this world I actually hate. He had no idea about the inherent challenges of our blended family with significant special needs. He listened to what the children told him and took it at face value. When they said they didn't want to live with me, he brought a petition to the court to have me removed from my home.

Paulina propagated the ultimate transference. With the abuse, abandonment, and resentment she felt toward her mother in Ukraine and at us for taking her from everything she knew, she figured out how to have me feel much of what she endured. She wanted to escape her abusive home in Ukraine and desperately wanted her mother's love, but she couldn't have them at the same time. By having a powerful attorney working at her disposal, she accomplished ripping me from my home and family and everything I knew and loved. The difference was, I would have chosen to live with the abuse, so as not to lose what I loved. She rightfully chose to escape abuse, but could not win her biological mother's love, which she craved. Since she couldn't have that, sadly she denied herself any love at all. To this day, she struggles to understand that she is worthy of love. She doesn't know how to be vulnerable enough to accept it, although it surrounds her.

I had hired my original attorney, Jack Massimo, because he was also a trained mediator. I still had hope that we could attempt to make this a somewhat amicable process. He was able to step in and try to assist with our early attempt at divorce mediation.

I wrote him this e-mail after one of our appearances before court referee Audrey Murphy in October 2015, which unfortunately had no impact on his representation of me for my case:

As a conflict resolution specialist, on one hand, I feel I am defending what I do (explaining why I go to conferences). On the other hand, I find it ironic that I am so enmeshed in the field of conflict resolution, yet I cannot get the other party in my conflict to engage effectively in alternative processes, to the detriment of our children and ourselves.

Somewhere in this case, I want it made known that I am the kind of person who surrounds myself with positive images and messages. My career involves sharing that mentality and knowledge with others, for their own improvement and the trickle-down effect when they utilize techniques with students and peers.

In contrast, for years, Richard had a sign in his office saying, "All Customers Are Liars." He reads books such as The Joy of Hate (really, he does). I used to have a Post-it note near the door in our old house that said, "Do you have your keys, phone, wallet, good attitude?" It didn't help. He often forgot many of those things.

October 30, 2015: Update to Friends and Family about Court

Hi all,

I just wanted to update you all as to how things went today, meeting with the court referee. Thank you for all your positive thoughts. The good news was that they did not allow an emergency hearing. Meaning that the ref did not try to set up a meeting with the judge to hear the case on an emergency basis.

The bad news, though not unexpected, is that the ref allowed the kids' attorney to file a motion with the court to change custody and residence. This means that the kids' attorney is asking the court to have me move out and Richard to move back in. As a result, the court will appoint either a forensic psychologist or psychiatrist, who will spend the next few months interviewing everyone, which will be both emotionally and financially draining.

Note that I tried to avoid this, but Richard would not even return my text, much less talk to me about how we could do this without so much court intervention. This makes me sad, to drag the kids through all this, so unnecessarily.

Keep us in your thoughts. It's going to be a bumpy road. Thanks.

T.J.

November 1, 2015
I felt Richard was setting me up, doing as he pleased and taking the kids when he wanted to, sometimes even without my knowledge, much less consent. Richard took the kids when they were supposed to be with me, and I kept a record of our text exchange:

R: Kids want to come into the city. I can drive them back tonight.
T.J.: They have HW. At least Niki does.
RL   I know, she is telling me about that. Were you planning on helping her?

T.J. If she needs my help. Sometimes she works more diligently independently, if no one interferes. It depends. She told me yesterday that she would do it when she came back today.

R I am taking Paulina, Niki, and Eric to the city. Will take Niki's HW. Will drive the girls back tonight

T.J. I allowed you to take them to lunch on [my] weekend. I did not say you could take them to the city. Every time they are with you, they come back more obnoxious to me.

At that point, they arrived at the house.

Niki came in. I said hello to her. She ignored me in a huff and ran around the house, gathering things. I asked what she was doing. She told me to shut up.

Charlie and Eric had come in at that point. Charlie said they were going to Dad's. Niki retorted something like, "Nice job, idiot!" I started to text Richard, when he walked in. He started yelling at me in front of the kids, and after the fifth time of me saying it, I finally got him to at least come into the kitchen. The kids could still hear us fighting, but at least it wasn't right in front of them.

I told him again that I had allowed him to take them to lunch. I never said he could take them to the city afterward.

He threw his hands in the air and said, "Fine! I'll leave them here!"

I said, "You've put me in an impossible situation. If I say no, I'm the bad guy and they will continue to blame me. You never should have said they could go to the city today."

He responded by yelling that all I said was that Niki had homework. Somehow it was on me to say more. I reminded him that he did not respond further after that. He said, "She'll bring her homework."

I'd been considering taking them to the movies, but regardless, they spent time with him and were back to being mad and not speaking to me. There was nothing I could say or do that would compensate for what he said to them when they were with him.

Charlie did not want to go with them. At his request, I arranged for a playdate to come to my place. The rest went to the city.

As Richard left, he texted: "More fake conflict. The nonsense will only stop when you want it to stop."

I continued to be amazed at how he could turn things around and make it look like everything was my fault. He simply should have brought them back after lunch. This was just one more example of his gaslighting. At one point I decided the way to stop it was to "wet the wick." Here, he was trying to make me think what was happening was my fault. If I didn't respond, it would extinguish the argument. I tried to do that as often as I could. Other times, when he would try to bait me into an argument, I would say, "I'm not returning the serve," as our therapist taught me. These were two ways I tried to prevent him from dominating me.

Later that day, Niki called me from Richard's apartment to ask me to allow her to get a free ringtone app. I asked her what she thought I might be upset about, and compared the way she was speaking to me now versus earlier.

She said she was sorry and that she'd been in a bad mood from a stomachache. I told her to ask Dad for some medicine if her stomach really hurt, but that wouldn't justify her treating me the way she did. I reminded her that this was at least the fourth time this week that she'd been nasty to me in front of others and then apologetic when she wanted something from me. I told her that if she could be nice to me for the next couple of days, then I would let her get the app.

She retorted with an attitude, "Well, then I'll just call Don Brunt and let him know that you have parental controls." I said, "Fine. Please do. He should know that I have parental controls on your phone." She said, "No, he'll just say that you should get your fat ass out of the house!" Then she hung up on me.

I could not parent like this. I am a good parent, and they could threaten, but they couldn't prove otherwise. Teenage children cannot be left to decide what kind of boundaries are placed on them. I am pretty liberal, but that is why children have parents.

I sent this note to my attorneys, highlighting texts between Richard and I and asking their advice about how to handle Paulina:

More texts to be aware of:

R: FYI, I am not comfortable having Gabriella watching the kids. She allows Niki to do whatever she wants. And Niki will take advantage of that.

T.J.: Gabriella has worked with us for more than twelve years. She was trying to protect Niki from Bernadette, who adds to her hating me. Contrary to what you think, she was asleep in the basement and went upstairs at one a.m. She did not first go to sleep at one a.m. I'd also like to know who removed the lock from the basement door.

Another text from me to Richard:
Bernadette will be leaving soon. Gabriella is helping me while I look for a replacement. Pro Au Pair has au pairs that specialize in working with children with special needs. I think that will be a better fit for our family. I have been looking to change Niki's psychiatrist from Dr. Frederico for a while. He is very hard to work with in getting her prescriptions renewed. He doesn't do e-scripts and doesn't return calls promptly. I've had to go to his house to get scripts so she doesn't run out.

I looked online for a new psychiatrist for Niki under our plan, so it will be much cheaper anyway. I have tried to reach her, but haven't been successful yet. Her voicemail had been full. Let me know if you have any issue with this, as I will try again to reach her this week.

I'm wondering if I should consider a PINS mediation or case with Paulina, and also whether we should countersue Richard, because as much as I feel the children should have a relationship with both parents, I remain concerned about his mushrooming control over their feelings toward me and his lack of ability to co-parent and communicate about their well-being.

Please let me know your thoughts.

Thanks.
T.J.

November 13, 2015: That Fateful Day

"Don't hit a tree" was all I could think as part of my reeling brain directed my hands at the wheel, eyeing the inviting trees lining the sides of the road. It's the only time I could recall thinking I wanted to die. Probably because I felt like I already had—like I'd been shot at close range by an army conspiring to bring me down.

But I don't die easily, inside or out. Through my tears, I dialed my therapist. She talked to me until I could make it home, twenty minutes from the courthouse. Later, John came over to support me and my therapist made a house call, given the dire circumstances. Normally, I am an emotional eater, but I could not bear to eat anything until well into the evening, when John convinced me to have some mashed potatoes.

The events of that fateful day—literally, Friday the Thirteenth—of November, 2015, remain surreal to me even now. I've gone over those events in my mind too many times, and there is just no making sense of it. Reading the transcript transports me back, reliving how people with power, but without an ear to listen, can so easily strip the essence of who you are, destroy your family, and, all in a day's work for them, topple what you've worked so hard to build, like a child's tower of blocks. But there is no one to cry to about your tower's destruction. Not when it was the person in authority who toppled it, then forbade anyone from helping you to pick it up.

It was the first time we were seeing the judge. The children's attorney, Mr. Brunt, brought an Order to Show Cause that the court referee, Audrey Murphy, allowed, asking that the children be removed from my custody.

The concept itself was absurd. How do children get to tell a court that they don't want to live with the person who takes care of virtually their every need? They lie. Then they are supported by others in authority to make their lies seem true. Add that to the other side being silenced and you have the opposite of justice—injustice!

We walked into the large courtroom. There were two oak tables facing the looming judge's bench, where he sat perched above us. As I took out my pad of paper and pen, the court officer instructed me to take my water bottle off the table. My attorney, Jack Massimo, spoke first. The judge interrupted virtually every thought he tried to get across, and made him dance around the issues to answer every question the judge had, the moment it popped into his head. Patience was not taught in his law school!

I had disagreed with my lawyer's strategy when we'd discussed it in advance, but it was just another time that I had to put my trust, falsely, in someone else. Someone who seemed to know the system that I did not. He tried to argue that the allegations that I was a bad mother were false, but if they were found to be true, they weren't emergent, and if they were found to be emergent, they could be corrected.

This seemed like faulty logic to me from the start. How could we claim to fix something that we were claiming wasn't true? Unfortunately, the judge saw the argument as incongruently as I had. Sadly, it was the only thing we agreed on.

Richard's attorney, Clive Johnston, spoke next. He laid out the arguments for why the children felt they should live with his client instead of me. He spoke of me not being home, not being there for them, traveling, not providing food, not helping with their homework, not providing a computer for them to do their homework, and then the biggest blow: Niki was cutting herself.

If those things were true, painted on a clean canvas, they might have been reason for the judge to consider exploring alternative arrangements. At the very least, to speak to the children and possibly get us some services if I was the unfit mother being portrayed. Even if they were true, there was no drug or alcohol abuse. All the children were healthy. Three of the four were in school, while we were dealing with Eric's issues of school refusal and an uncooperative school district. All were well-clothed and trying to adjust as best they could to the crazy circumstances of a difficult divorce, while being a recently blended family of teenagers through adoption.

But they weren't true, and no one cared to hear the counterpoint to any of it. This court date had been set prior to the events of that week, which served to strengthen the false picture that was now being painted in indelible ink.

Clive Johnston went on to describe how Niki was cutting herself, implying that it was due to her unhappiness at having to live with me. Ultimately, Richard produced a picture, that I had never seen, of her arm with some light scratches and a bruise on it. Apparently, Paulina had taken the picture and Richard had saved it for a surprise attack on me, to prove his point that I was an unfit mother.

The judge questioned me pointedly, demanding immediate answers to his yes-or-no questions, without allowing any explanation of context. Every time I tried to help him understand any of what had actually happened, he cut me off, just as he'd cut off my attorney numerous times before.

The judge had heard enough, but only of what he wanted to hear. He made his ruling: He ordered me to pack up my life and vacate my home and family within seventy-two hours! The mild objections of my attorney were barely noted. My attorney's efforts to say that I had nowhere to go went unheard.

Flippantly, the judge asked Richard if he would like to give me $25,000 or $50,000 to get myself resettled. Guess which he picked? $25,000. Then his attorney had the gall to ask that the monthly maintenance amount of $12,500, that was recently paid, come from that. Thankfully, the judge declined that request.

I was left feeling helpless and afraid, incredulous that in America, a person and her family could be treated like this. I went to law school believing in the justice system. I helped fight for people who had no money or power. Now, I was the one on the other side of the table, with my voice, my dignity, and my family being stolen from me. My meager attempt to control the tears pounding at the back of my eyes failed miserably, as the life I had built was instantly destroyed.

These men had no understanding of the issues of adoption, no understanding of developmental stages of teens, no understanding of children with special needs, no understanding of reactive attachment disorder, no understanding of cutting and what it does and doesn't mean, no understanding of transference of feelings from bio-mother to adoptive mother, no understanding at all of what it is like to want nothing more in life than to be a mother, to go through the incredible process of adoption, only to be torn from the life you had worked incredibly hard to build—not only from the children you adopted, but from your biological children, too!

By now, I could no more control my tears than any other part of my life. Upon being dismissed from the courtroom, my attorney and his assistant ushered me outside so my wailing would not disturb others.

Throughout the ordeal, I had held a stone in my pocket that said "Strength." A woman in the hall, who had apparently been through a similar ordeal, tried to tell me to be strong. The strength I could usually muster wasn't available to me. Instead, I felt like my legs were cut off at the knees.

There was a small patio outside the courthouse where the slight November chill did little to dry my eyes. Without empathy, my attorneys pressed me about where I would go, imploring me to move in with my parents. As one who is not easily angered, I felt simultaneously enraged and depleted. I alternated between yelling at them and crying so hard, I could barely breathe.

"You need to move in with your parents," they said.

"They live in a senior development in New Jersey. I need to be in Greenburgh with my children."

"You need to find someplace immediately."

"No! You need to go back in there and fix this! How could you have let this happen?"

"I tried to speak, but the judge wouldn't let me—and you didn't tell us about the cutting."

"Are you kidding? Do you have any idea how many things go on in my family on a given day? I told you about the fight Niki and I had, and about Richard taking her without telling me. I told you what you needed to say to the court. I didn't know she actually cut herself. I checked as best I could. How dare you insinuate I did something wrong here!"

"Don't yell at me. You need to calm down and find a place to live."

"I have a place to live," I said. "With my family! What if I refuse to leave?"

"We cannot advise that. You could be arrested."

"Great. Then let's call the papers and let them report on this travesty! Throwing a mother out of her own home!"

"Where will you go? Do you have a friend you could stay with?"

"No! This is crazy. "

"Then stay with your parents."

"Will you drop the parents thing? They live in a fifty-five-plus community. I'm forty-five years old. I am not allowed to live there. Plus, they are in New Jersey. My kids are in Greenburgh. Richard's the one who moved an hour away to the city. I am not willing to be that far from my kids. I'm the one who told him to stay in Greenburgh so they could be near both of their parents."

"Well, then, find a place near Greenburgh."

I thought back to the day when I'd stared longingly out the marital mediator's window at the residential hotel below, wishing to escape the daily abuse at home. Little did I know that eighteen months later, that's exactly where I would be. Defeated and depleted, I relented and said, "I guess I could go to a residential hotel temporarily, until this wrong can be righted in court."

"Great. It's decided."

I thought I would be at the hotel from the date I left my home on Monday, November 16 at 2:00 p.m. until our return date of November 23. Instead, I remained there for three and a half months, never again to live in my marital home, never to return to the family and life I had painstakingly built, without a soul to help me pick up the pieces of my world, so carelessly toppled.

Living at a local residential hotel was incredibly demoralizing. Only Charlie would stay over on occasion. Having no money to compete with Richard's fancy dinners didn't help encourage my children to spend time with me. Most of the limited shopping I did was at Dollar Tree and Target. During my time there, I was repeatedly bitten by bedbugs. All the hotel did was change my room and give me a roll of quarters to do my laundry!

When I went to pick up Charlie from my former home, the girls would not allow me to even pet our cat, Sparky, or our dog, Carmela. They would rip the animals from my arms, leaving me completely empty. I was denied the opportunity to see or hold Carmela for nine long months, and I never got to spend much time with Sparky before he passed away. It was a horrendous time.

Months later, I would get to describe my version of events of that fateful day, not to the judge, but to the court-appointed psychiatrist who evaluated our family.

Here is what I wrote:

Hi, Dr. Strauss,

In answer to your question about why I was forced to leave the marital residence on November 16, 2015, the short version is that Don Brunt, the children's attorney, brought an Order to Show Cause, to change custody and residency.

As timing would have it, several days before we appeared before Judge Wickett, Niki went back and forth, as usual, between being sweet and nasty. Ultimately, she fought with me about walking the dog, after agreeing earlier to do it. She had a raging fit, screaming, kicking, and throwing things at my door. Richard contacted me saying she was cutting herself. I immediately went into her room, where I found her sobbing under her blanket, talking to a friend. I saw no evidence of her cutting herself.

In court, Richard produced a picture on his phone that I had not previously seen, apparently taken by Paulina, showing some very light scratches and a black-and-blue mark. (Less than a week later, there was virtually nothing there.)

The judge interrogated me and was quite displeased to learn that I did not pull back the covers to check on her. While in the moment, I didn't think of that, having seen no evidence of weapons or blood, I still think that if I would have tried to approach her, she likely would have kicked me in the face.

Based on my responses and lack of opportunity to explain the backstory, Judge Wickett immediately ordered me to vacate my home.

If you would like more details, keep reading; otherwise disregard the fuller explanation below.

Here are the events that, from my perspective, resulted in the order of Judge Wickett (the original judge) on Friday, November 13, mandating that I vacate the marital residence by Monday, November 16, 2015, at 2:00 p.m.:

- *For several weeks, the children call Mr. Brunt (their attorney) and Richard anytime I ask them to do normal things, like chores, go to bed, turn down music, etc. Richard believes everything they tell him and, in my opinion, rescues them when they call. Paulina and Niki repeatedly taunt me that things will be great when they get me out of the house and I am "left with nothing."*

- *Mr. Brunt brings an Order to Show Cause to change custody and residency.*

- *Richard has all the children the weekend of November 7–8. Niki is not given her medication consistently (apparently not at all on Sunday).*

- *Niki refuses to do her HW and refuses to go to bed, and is still up at 11 p.m. Sunday night, 11/8. I predict to her that it will be hard for her to get up the next morning, which it is. Niki wasn't ready to leave when she needed to be. I told her I was taking Charlie, who was ready, so he wouldn't be late, and she should start walking. I would pick her up on my way back. A neighbor saw her walking and texted me that she had picked her up.*

- *I picked up Niki and Charlie after school. We discussed what occurred the night before and she understood that I would take her phone as a consequence. Upon her request, I allowed her to text her friends to tell them not to contact her on her phone for four days. Then she handed over her phone willingly.*

- *Both Niki and Charlie were in a good mood and we had a mini family meeting when we got home about walking the dog. Charlie agreed to walk her in the mornings and Niki agreed to walk her either after school or before dinner.*

- *After repeated requests, delays, and leniency on my part, Niki promised to walk Carmela when her show was over in three minutes, at 8:30 p.m. I agreed and said she needed to walk her, then go to bed. After the show, she came to me in the laundry room and told me she was tired and would not walk Carmela. We had an irritated discussion about keeping promises, after which I said, Okay, if you are so tired, go straight to bed. She went up stairs, called Richard on the house phone, and told him that I was making her walk Carmela alone at night and that she was scared and I refused to go with her. None of that happened!*

- *Then she called her friend, Rosalie. When I went into her room to get her off the phone and to bed, she got very agitated and ordered me to leave her room. When I didn't, she tried twice to physically push me out the door. I told her that if she put her hands on me again, I would call the police (which has happened twice before, including in therapist Julie Stone's office).*

- *I left the room, without the phone, and unplugged the cord in the hall. I went into my room and locked the door. (Meanwhile, Charlie was taking a bath in my bathroom.)*

- *This enraged Niki and she began kicking my door with all her might and throwing numerous things against it, taking off chunks of paint, while screaming, which I have a recording of.*
- *When Charlie finished his bath, I told him that his sister was throwing a fit and that it would be safer for him to*

sleep in my room. He agreed, despite not having his favorite blanket.

- *Niki started to calm down and asked if she cleaned up the mess she made, if she could have the phone back. She did clean it up and then figured out how to reconnect it herself.*

- *She apparently called Richard and Paulina, then called Rosalie back.*

- *Shortly afterward, Richard called me and said that Niki said she was cutting herself.*

- *I immediately went to check on her and found her on her bed, sobbing and talking to Rosalie. I saw no evidence of any weapons or blood at that point and went back to my room to tell Richard.*

- *Richard wanted to pick her up and I asked him not to, saying that she was calming down and just needed to go to sleep.*

- *Charlie suggested I pick up the other line to hear the conversation, which I normally don't do, but did in this case. I learned that Niki had called Paulina, who ultimately came back to the house after 10 p.m. and took Niki with her to Paulina's friend, Lacey's house. I could not have physically stopped either of them from leaving, so I contacted Lacey to ensure that they were there.*

- *When I went downstairs, since now I had to walk the dog again, I saw poultry shears on the steps and the dish washer opened with a knife on the counter. I saw no blood on either object. While it was unusual to find poultry shears on the stairs, it was not unusual to find a kitchen knife left out.*

- *The next morning, Paulina returned home to get ready for school. Niki did not. Concerned, I contacted Lacey,*

Rosalie, Richard, and Niki's teacher. After a couple of hours, Richard finally told me that he had picked Niki up last night.

- *He decided to keep her in the city and out of school Tuesday, November 10. (Wednesday 11/11 they were off for Veterans' Day.) He took her without her ADHD meds and refused to take her school books. I have a recording of a heated conversation we had regarding what she needed and when he would bring her back.*

- *Despite the apparent urgency, he did not take her to be evaluated, nor would he let me. On Wednesday, he took her to Lindsay, but apparently, he did most of the talking. He mostly spoke about a traumatic encounter Niki experienced, when she saw her biological father on a bus when Richard took Niki and Paulina back to visit Ukraine earlier in the year, which was important, but not what this situation was based on.*

I believe the children have been greatly and unreasonably empowered, primarily by Richard and Mr. Brunt. In contrast, I have been consistently undermined and excluded. Furthermore, Bernadette has been enabled and encouraged to usurp my role as their mother. I truly hope you can be instrumental in righting this egregious wrong.

Thank you.
T.J.

The day after court, I wrote the following letter to my attorneys, Jack and Amelia (Amelia was the associate attorney working with Jack):

Dear Jack and Amelia,

I understand that you felt blindsided by not knowing about the cutting incident. Please note that I was impressed by and appreciated the powerful opening you made. Please understand that any omission on my part was certainly not intentional, and obviously I am suffering the greatest consequence from that situation and need not be reminded of it. In trying to provide you with documentation of the myriad of layers to this situation, I truly regret that the events of that evening apparently failed to include Niki trying to cut herself, which was part of what led up to Richard taking Niki without my knowledge.

Frankly, with the multitude of incidents and behaviors I am constantly juggling, as my psychologist puts it, "living from crisis to crisis and consistently putting out fires," I understand that this situation seemed dire to the judge and to you. Rest assured, I don't take it lightly, but I also feel I acted appropriately, as evidenced by the fact that Niki was fine. As I mentioned to you afterward, which was not mentioned in court, I unfortunately have had experience with kids cutting, since Paulina did the same thing at age thirteen. Being new to that behavior at that time, I did Internet research and learned that cutting is not an attempt at suicide and is rarely, if ever, serious. Rather, it is a cry for help. Help that I have been actively barred from providing. In Paulina's situation, I immediately found a Russian-speaking therapist in NYC (for $450 plus parking), that I took her to the very next day, straight from school.

In this situation, when Richard decided to keep Niki home from school that Tuesday, my first question was whether he was taking her to our adoption therapist, Lindsay. He responded that Lindsay was in Brooklyn and he would be unable to do so. I implored him to let me take Niki to either Julie (with whom she has a relationship) or Evelyn, her former therapist. He refused. The "urgency," he claimed, did not match his actions by waiting a day, not letting me take her, keeping her from school, where there is a psychologist, and then, when he did take her to Lind-

say the next day (at a time that kept Niki from her tutor), he dominated the session, while she apparently cowered behind the couch, as he spoke about an incident with her meeting her dad on a bus in Ukraine, back in July.

I contemplated calling the police, who have been called to subdue her tantrums twice before; the first call was made from her psychologist, Julie. Although she's trained in restraint techniques, she and I, combined, were unable to restrain Niki in Julie's office. The police wanted to take Niki to a hospital, but knowing my daughter and the traumas she's been through, I knew that she was calming down at that point, as she was last Monday, and that escalating the situation would only bring back the scary memories of hospitals in Ukraine.

There are many incongruities here. Cutting is just one part of institutional behavior, which we struggle with daily. Further, it was exacerbated by Richard not giving Niki her meds much of the weekend before this occurred, on Monday. Without living my life, it is hard to comprehend that this incident was one element of an insane week. I regret that I did not act in the way the judge felt would have been prudent, and I regret that I failed to inform you in advance.

The only thing that changed in that courtroom was the judge's strong opinion that I did not act the way he felt, in hindsight, that I should have acted in order to ensure the safety of my daughter. I am not discounting that an option would have been to pull back those covers, yet even having done so, nothing would have changed. I could not have prevented Paulina from coming back, or Niki from leaving. I ensured their safety by confirming their whereabouts. Of note is the fact that I also kept Charlie safe from Niki's violent tantrum in forcibly trying to kick my door down and throwing things at it.

Honestly, I feel, as I did before Friday, that in the long run, taking me out of the home so suddenly not only re-traumatizes my girls, who have already been abandoned, multiple times, but it also gives them a power greater than their developmental age (quite different from chronological). This further harms them by removing the safety of boundaries that these children naturally rebel against, but desperately crave. As I've said, contrary to Mr. Brunt, my role is not to be their friend and give them what they say they want, but to do what I feel is best for them. In my opinion, I provide stability, extensive knowledge of special needs and adoption, boundaries, consistency, and, most importantly, unconditional love.

In addition, the judge's actions have also been detrimental to my kids. I have always been a strong advocate for all of my children's needs. Until recently, Eric and I have had a very close relationship. He has grown up knowing that he can ask me about anything on his mind, and I will try my best to address it. He is a child with complicated issues and needs. At the moment, he is closer to his dad; however, when he is allowed to be with me for a period of time, parts of the "old Eric" shine through. While I am more flexible about where he lives due to his schooling, I do have grave concerns about him continuing to receive negative messages about me from Richard. Furthermore, I have concerns about Richard's ability to administer his medication properly. (When I was at the house the other day, Eric asked me to check his meds. He had refilled them himself, since Dad didn't know how. That is a parent's job, not a job for a thirteen-year-old boy.)

Charlie, as the professionals have noted, is the most "level-headed" of my children, despite being the youngest. He is honestly enjoying some "Daddy time," because he is often ignored by him. However, he has told me that he would prefer to reduce the amount of conflict that he experiences and would prefer to live with me.
Be that as it may, at this point, I need you to fight aggressively for my interests and not lay additional blame on me for any unintentional omission on my part. I do not want to wait in a hotel

room for dates to pass as papers are filed back and forth. I need this egregious wrong to be righted ASAP. I look forward to discussing our unified strategy tomorrow.

Sincerely,
T.J.

Since we were to return to court the following week, I wanted to be clear with my attorneys as to what I expected from them, and wrote this e-mail:

Hi Amelia and Jack,
In further preparation for Monday, since I don't know exactly what to expect, I wanted to tell you what is important for me to achieve.

1. *Prove that what I did is no worse than how Richard parents our children.*
2. *I am not a threat, in the least, to them.*
3. *I should move back into the house.*
4. *Under NO circumstances is Bernadette to be alone with my children; coming to my home; driving my car. Richard is absolutely forbidden to rehire her in any capacity! This is nonnegotiable!*
5. *The girls have broken into my office three times. I have changed my code, yet they have somehow managed to get in there and go through my things. The other day, they appeared to have tried to break the deadbolt lock. What are my rights here? It seems like breaking and entering to me. This is my office and I expect it to remain that way. (Yesterday, 11/21, at the end of the evening, Niki taunted me, saying it's no longer mine because I don't live there anymore. This was after spending a nice day together, swimming at my parents' place. Her attitude did a 180 when I brought up how upset I was about them going into my office.)*

276

6. *We need an affirmative defense that explains the*
   children's behavior toward me as a result of:
   A. *Richard's alienation;*
   B. *Bernadette's alienation (and being paid by Richard);*
   C. *The nature of them being recently adopted;*
       i. *Niki: Trauma disorder and ADHD (impulsive, among*
          other things)
       ii. *Paulina: undiagnosed conduct disorder (refuses*
           therapy; saw Lindsay a total of approximately ten
           times in three years);
       iii. *Still in touch with their family in Ukraine (which*
            often throws them into a tailspin after speaking with
            them);
       iv. *The strides they have made since joining our family*
           less than four years ago;
       v. *Their preexisting conditions and behavior toward me*
          does not make me a "bad parent";
       vi. *Explain the cutting incident:*
           a. *I had knowledge of how to handle it from when*
              Paulina did it at age thirteen.
           b. *Not a suicide attempt, but a cry for help.*
           c. *I checked on Niki and ensured her safety. (No*
              blood, calming down in bed, contacted Lacey to
              make sure she got there.)
7. *Richard didn't tell me he picked her up that night, when I*
   expressly told him not to.
8. *I had to ask four people, including Niki's teacher, where*
   she was.
9. *Richard responded, about one and a half hours after I*
   asked, that he had her.
10. *He kept her out of school Tuesday.*
11. *Refused to take her school books with him.*
12. *Richard claimed the situation to be urgent, but:*
    A. *Didn't take Niki to see Lindsay on Tuesday. (Said she*
       was in Brooklyn, so he couldn't take her. He took her

Wednesday, instead of seeing her tutor.) According
to Lindsay, (because I called to find out how it went),
she was fine. No cuts broke the skin. Apparently,
Richard spoke for most of the session and geared it
toward seeing her father on a bus in Ukraine. While this
is an important issue, worthy of discussion, it occurred in
July. The pressing issue was why she got so upset that
she tried to break down my door and cut herself.

B. *Richard would not allow me to take her to Julie or*
Evelyn for assessment, on Tuesday, which I strongly
suggested.

C. *RICHARD DID NOT GIVE NIKI HER PILLS SUNDAY,*
which likely greatly contributed to her behavior on
Monday.

13. *At a minimum, I should be allowed to have the kids over*
night. Richard suggested it and I told him I was not
allowed. Charlie and Niki both asked and I had to say
not yet.

14. *I should be allowed to spend time with them in the house.*
As a practical matter, the kids shouldn't have to choose
between spending time with me or playing with their
friends in the backyard (which is what Charlie wanted to
do when we got back from my parents; instead, I had to
spend $30 at New Roc arcade to occupy him, Niki, and
his friend). Richard has his apartment, so he doesn't have
to be at the house. I also miss the dog and cat. I don't
want them to destroy the hotel room, but my cat seems
to be missing me. He has slept with me on my bed since
Richard stopped sleeping with me.

15. *We should absolutely be allowed to make plans with our*
mutual consent. I recall the judge having an issue with
this, yet it was fine this week. I went to Niki's gymnastics
Thursday. Took Charlie to dinner Friday. Saw a potential
new school with Eric Tuesday.

16. *It should be noted how unnecessarily disruptive this has been for my entire extended family for Thanksgiving.*

November 23, 2015: Return Court Date

During the return court session, the subject of my employment came up. Rather than ask me directly, though I was sitting right there, the judge asked Richard's attorney when the last time I practiced law was. Of course, he'd never asked me and would have no idea, so he made it up, saying, "It's been a few years."

Furious, I nudged my attorney. "Can I answer that?"

"No."

"Well, then, you answer it."

"Shhh."

"But I've never practiced law a day in my life!"

"We can't speak now."

Mr. Johnston added that with my law degree, I should be making $100,000 per year.

The judge asked Mr. Johnston if he would hire me.

"Well, we're not hiring now."

The judge then suggested I get a job at Target. Literally. He actually said that.

What a fucking mockery! No one would let me speak. Just a complete disregard for the business I've had since 2003, since I didn't make nearly as much as Richard. My profession as a conflict resolution professional, serving on boards of international organizations, irrelevant. No one thought to inquire as to what I gave up or put into the kids, Richard's business, or the marriage. It was months before I was allowed to correct this false impression that I was ever a practicing attorney, and that was with the third of the four judges that were involved in our case over the years.

Once again, I summarized the court's ruling for those who cared about me:

Hi all,

I wanted to give you a summary of what occurred today, November 23, 2015, in court. Fortunately, it wasn't as bad as last week.

- *The good news is that we have a return date for a status conference before the judge, on December 16 at 9:30 a.m. (At least we don't have to wait until the new year.)*
- *I still cannot have overnights, but if the kids' attorney speaks to them and they want to, then it's possible.*
- *I am supposed to see the kids either Saturday or Sunday every week. I will probably get to see them more often than that, but Richard controls it.*
- *The judge said that Richard needs to look for a new au pair and report back on his progress on December 16. In the meantime, Bernadette can be in the house, but not stay overnight.*
- *The guest room is to remain locked.*
- *I had to say the code to my office lock in open court, because Richard claimed that work needed to be done on the heating system from there. He is not to allow the kids to be in there. (No faith that will happen.)*
- *He was told to cancel a trip he had planned for next week. Honestly, I'd be fine with him going on the trip, but he and the kids' attorney are (amazingly) not fine with the kids staying with me for those three days. He'd rather have Bernadette. The judge said no. Said he can't have it both ways.*
- *They also revoked child support, but kept the maintenance for now.*
- *My attorneys have to file their answer to the original claims by 12/1.*

So, for now, I am trying to deal with the current situation. I know you all want to know about me looking for an apartment. I have a plan of how to do that, but I really have to take this one step at a time. Please understand that my life has been turned upside down. I am fully aware of the entirety of the situation, including financially. Please just support me, where I am, day by day. Feel free to check in, come hang out, or invite me out. I am dealing with all of this as best I can and will continue to do so.

Thanks for your understanding and support. I rely on it.
T.J.

CHAPTER 37
New Attorneys

When Mr. Brunt's application to the court was successful and Mr. Massimo was unwilling to let me speak in court or do so effectively on my behalf, I let him go. He gave me a final bill of about $2,000, which Richard questioned and refused to pay. I tried to explain that the services were valid. Enraged, Richard countered, "I will make it my life's mission to destroy Jack Massimo!" I didn't despise Mr. Massimo; I just didn't think he was adequately representing me as firmly as I needed him to. I would have paid him, if I had the money, but I didn't at the time. I called his office and explained the situation. Fortunately, Richard did not follow through on his threat, but he didn't pay either. When I saved up enough money, I paid Jack, but asked him not to tell Richard that I did so, so it wouldn't be held against me.

I sought a new attorney who would give me an edge and found Bart Lazio, a former judge, who was now with a high-profile law firm. He and associate attorney, Mallory Canton, worked on my case together, though she was cheaper and I mostly met with her. I had to borrow $25,000, which my parents had to wire to me from their vacation in Florida, in order for them to accept my case. I begged both Mr. Massimo and Mr. Lazio to depose Richard, to expose what he had been hiding, financially and otherwise. Both counseled me to wait, which I felt enabled Richard to sell and hide assets.

Meanwhile, I spent months searching for a place to live that was near my children. My attorneys pushed me to get a one-bedroom apartment, but I wanted room for the children to be able to stay over, and I wanted them to be close to their school. Apartments were mostly downtown, where they would be zoned for a different school, and were expensive for very little room. I wanted a house that they would want to be in that could feel like home.

Finally, I found a fully furnished house to rent from a former neighbor that was nearby and big enough for the kids to stay with me. I had gone from having everything in our home, to having nothing in the hotel, to now having someone else's things that I could use to provide a temporary home for my family. I went from expensive sushi dinners on random weeknights to chicken nuggets for $1 from Dollar Tree and taking extra food from the breakfast buffet to stretch to lunch and dinner.

I was so grateful to have furnishings that I could not afford to buy. Old couches, chairs, dishes, silverware, pots, and even a television! All I had to buy was a bed, which I was thankfully able to finance. I was so delighted when my new landlord bought me a new shower curtain, that in keeping with my attitude of looking at the positives in my life, I revised the lyrics to "These Are a Few of My Favorite Things" to reflect all that I now had.

Charlie and Niki had regular sleepovers and would take turns sleeping on the pullout couch they left me, while the other slept with me in my bed. I couldn't afford to buy them furniture, but they accepted the situation as best they could. Eric would come for events or spend some time with me if I took him out. He only slept over once, when our friends were there. Paulina wouldn't even see the house, as she still wasn't speaking to me.

I stayed there from March 1, 2016, until August 31, 2017, while our case dragged on. I had hoped it would come to a close more quickly and I would receive a settlement that would enable me to buy a house of my own. But the dates kept getting extended.

There were lots of challenges throughout the years of the divorce. So many fights, with Richard and others pitting the kids against me. It seemed like parent alienation, among other things. In my research on the issue, I found this statement citing child psychologist, Richard Gardner, who specialized in parent alienation syndrome:

Any change in custody should be based primarily on the symptom level of the alienating parent. In mild cases, there is some parental programming against the targeted parent, but little or no disruption of visitation, and Gardner did not recommend court-ordered visitation. In moderate cases, there is more parental programming and greater resistance to visits with the targeted parent. Gardner recommended that primary custody remain with the programming parent if the brainwashing was expected to be discontinued, but if not, that custody should be transferred to the targeted parent. In addition, therapy with the child to stop alienation and remediate the damaged relationship with the targeted parent was recommended. In severe cases, children display most or all of the eight symptoms:

1. *A campaign of denigration.*
2. *Weak, frivolous and absurd rationalizations.*
3. *A lack of ambivalence.*
4. *The "independent thinker" phenomenon.*
5. *An absence of guilt.*
6. *Support for the alienating parent.*
7. *Borrowed phrases and scenarios.*
8. *Rejection of extended family.*

and will refuse steadfastly to visit the targeted parent, including threatening to run away or commit suicide if the visitation is forced. Gardner recommended that the child be removed from the alienating parent's home into a transition home before moving into the home of the targeted parent. In addition, therapy for the child is recommended.

I shared this information with my attorneys, but they never brought it up in court. I kept trying to gather proof of what was happening and developed my "Purple Sky Theory." It was as if Richard would say the sky was purple. Then Paulina would agree that it was a lovely shade of lavender. Niki would concur, noting the fuchsia color. Eric would comment on the grape color he saw. Bernadette would add how nice the violet appeared. Mr. Brunt might have noted the plum color. All would feed off each other, concurring on the absolute truth that the sky was purple. The problem was that the sky was blue, but only I seemed to see it.

February 19, 2016: Journal Entry
I planned to Eric to see the movie *Race*. Charlie called me, crying, saying that he wanted to go with me, but Richard said he had to clean his room.

When I arrived at the house to get Eric, Charlie was very upset and still teary. Paulina was lying on the couch, under a blanket. Niki was barking at me to get my #$@!% face out of there. Eric was in a good mood and seemed pleased to be going with me. He was ready when I arrived. After trying to comfort Charlie, Eric and I left.

When I dropped Eric off at home, Charlie was still sad, though his room was clean and he seemed happy that we would have dinner together on Sunday. Niki was very rude, yelling at me to leave. Paulina was actually cleaning and had garbage bags piled in the front hall. (In the past, when Paulina cleaned, I would have to go through all of her bags of garbage, since she would throw out perfectly good school supplies, clothes, shoes, toys, or anything she didn't have a use for, even if it wasn't hers.) She did not want me to go up the three stairs in the entryway, to hug Charlie, as she continues to try to "defend the house from me," especially if Richard is not there and Bernadette is.

February 21, 2016: Journal Entry
As I was getting ready to pick the kids up for dinner, Charlie called me, upset, because he thought that he and I were spending time alone together. I reminded him that this was making up for time I was spending with Eric, and that

Eric said it was okay for him to come along. He seemed sad. I asked about his underlying interests, and why it was important for him to spend one-on-one time with me tonight. He said he hadn't seen me. I told him I always want to see him and reminded him that he stayed with me Monday and Tuesday nights. I proposed the idea of him sleeping over tonight, if Dad said it was okay. He liked that idea and put Richard on the phone with me. Richard agreed.

Charlie is here now, asleep. I will take him to school tomorrow. He asked which room will be his in my new house. I described the second bedroom with the pull-out couch. I think he wants to live with me, at least part-time, if not full-time, partially to escape the chaos of the house and being yelled at by everyone. (He is their scapegoat. If someone doesn't want to do a chore, they berate Charlie until he does it. He is the most compliant, but hates being bossed around. I think he acquiesces as the path of least resistance and the quickest way to avoid a fight.)

Paulina was out when I dropped Eric back at home. I went up to say hi to our cat, Sparky. Niki was upstairs and was getting ready to go to sleep in Richard's bed, as she often does. While nothing inappropriate happens, I still think it's not a great idea, especially since she was sexually abused in Ukraine. I brought her stuffed animals to her and gingerly went over to her on the bed, not sure how she would respond to me. She let me tickle her feet and give her hugs and a kiss. I told her that if she wanted to have a sleepover at my hotel and have breakfast there, she needed to do it this week, since I was moving into my new home on March 1. She asked nicely and genuinely what they had available for breakfast, which I described. She seemed interested. We'll see if we can make it happen this week. Hopefully, I will at least see her at gymnastics on Thursday.

Once again, when I am able to speak to and interact with Niki, without Paulina or Bernadette around, she drops her defenses and I am, fortunately, able to reestablish our relationship. She continues to switch from being callous, obnoxious, and rude to me, to being warm, friendly, and loving, often in the blink of an eye. This child, as well as each of the others, desperately needs significant, consistent, therapeutic intervention!

The courts continue to dictate our every move, without regard for any facets of our lives. At one point, the court referee, Audrey Murphy, set a return date for us on a day when I was scheduled to start a training session for thirty people that had been coordinated between the six schools within Lehman High School.

When I asked if we could change the date and tried to explain why, she insisted, "You will appear in court!"

I couldn't help the tears of frustration. They wanted me to work, but were acting in ways that could make me lose my job.

"Stop crying!" she demanded, with a demeaning disregard for me and my life.

CHAPTER 38
"Dr. Strauss, I'm a Good Mother"

While being represented by Mr. Lazio, the court made us hire and pay for a forensic psychiatrist, Dr. Conrad Strauss. We might have gotten a forensic psychologist, who would have been cheaper, but the court decided that since Eric saw a psychiatrist and was on medication for his ADHD and other issues, it should be a psychiatrist who met with and assessed us and wrote a report with recommendations for our family.

The process of meeting with Dr. Strauss was a logistical nightmare. He divided his time between New York and Arizona and only saw clients two days a week, during school hours. We had to turn our lives and our children's lives upside down, just to meet with him. Everything had to be done in person, forty-five minutes at a time, driving to and parking in Manhattan.

Dr. Strauss wanted the kids to come with me when he was seeing us together, which was complicated, since Paulina was not speaking to me, and Eric and Niki often followed her lead in being nasty to me.

This is a text exchange between Richard and me, showing Richard's responses to me regarding getting the kids to the forensic psychiatrist on Tuesday. I shared this exchange with John, whom I was dating at the time:

R: I am going to have all the kids in the city Monday night, in order to make sure they are there with you the following morning. I am sure if the situation was reversed, you would not lift a finger to help me. Why do I think that? Experience

T.J.: Actually, I would like to take the kids myself. You can take Paulina.

R: Take them all.

T.J.: I will be at the house Tuesday at 7:45. Please have everyone ready. You can take anyone who won't go.

R: Spoke to Strauss yesterday. He apologized for not relating the plan himself. Matter is already settled. Kids will stay in the city Monday night. We talked about me working it out. That is what I did.

"He is setting me up," I texted to John, "I have no chance. They will walk in there with Richard and either not go with me, make a scene, or be so obnoxious toward me. It scares me."

When I actually arrived at Dr. Strauss's office, Richard came in with the kids and they were antagonistic toward me before we even stepped foot into the doctor's inner office. I had to sit there quietly in a small room with the four of them and Dr. Strauss and listen to them mercilessly berate me in front of him. Then I had to not seem defensive while trying to show this man with the power to control the future of my family, that I was actually a caring, loving, fit mother.

I prepared lists of my strengths as a mother for both Dr. Strauss and my attorneys.

For Dr. Strauss—What I have done well as a parent:

- I try my best to give natural consequences whenever possible and practice positive discipline.
- I have taken PMT (Parent Management Training), along with participating in many workshops and webinars and reading countless books and articles on parenting, discipline, adoption, opposition, ADHD, and numerous other topics. I take notes on virtually everything I attend.
- During the marriage, I tried to share materials with Richard, but he would rarely, if ever, read them. The only exception was the adoption conference, which we attended together for several years, but he has opted not to attend for the past two years, though I have.
- As a trained mediator, I use my skills more with my

family than I will in my profession. I have successfully deescalated numerous arguments between the children, with myself, and with other friends and potential bullying situations. Yet, it is hard to be neutral when you have a stake in the outcome.

- When Paulina stopped speaking to me, I reached out to Paulina's therapist and school, speaking with her advisor, house principal, and school psychologist. They did not want to get involved because the one thing Paulina is doing is going to school. (Last year, she was cutting classes frequently.) The house principal, Mr. Brandwein, said that he has worked with challenging adolescents for many years. Paulina stands out to him as one of the toughest. He and the school psychologist agreed that "No one will be able to get Paulina to do anything she doesn't want to do."
- Parent–child relationships are difficult, and I have four tween/teens. All four of them go to school regularly, well dressed and well fed (note annual checkups: normal height and weight). These are children with a variety of special needs, emotional, educational, and otherwise. I have always been a strong advocate for them, doing the lion's share of work to try to meet their multitude of needs. Just some of the ways I've done so include:
- IEP meetings: attendance, prep, follow-up
- Regular contact with teachers (way more than the average parent)
- Research doctors, make and take them to numerous appointments, get and administer prescriptions, deal with insurance companies, immense follow-up
  o Stay highly educated on various issues affecting them through webinars, workshops, books, articles, etc.
  o Endless research for appropriate placement for Eric, educational lawyer, Dramatic Pragmatics (social skills therapy), cognitive behavior therapy, cog med computer

program to help with his ADHD, speech, occupational therapy, social skills, and psychological support
- Fostering relationships for playdates, even going to Connecticut, Pennsylvania, and Florida to enable children to maintain friendships

In response to allegations that I was not available to my children, in part, I said, "Far from absent, one of the main reasons I have an au pair is to enable me to spend one-on-one time (Mommy-and-me time) with each child. I will often take them out before or after an appointment or activity. In addition, my children will ultimately benefit from the active role model that I am. Running my own business for twelve years, being vice president of an international conflict resolution organization where I was just honored for my contribution to the field, co-president of our neighborhood association, and currently president of a state-wide dispute resolution association. Many parents work and do volunteer work. I am proud that even though I am not a full-time, stay-at-home mom, I am there for my children and provide proper care when travel is necessary."

For my attorneys:
- Note that our society is fond of saying, "Take care of yourself," yet when I try to balance that and truly need respite from these challenges, I am blamed for doing so.
- My future relationship with my children is second only to my strong maternal desire to raise them to become happy, productive, contributing members of society.
- Clear expectations: Shoes belong in your room; bedtime, etc. (usually stated in the positive).
- Clear and consistent consequences: If shoes are not removed by a specified time, you will be telling me that they are unimportant to you. (Dr. Emily Becker-Weidman from Center for Family Development: What I do with

belongings is a perfectly reasonable expectation and consequence.)

- Poor choice—not bad person; don't like behavior, do love you.
- Still love you no matter what!
- Adapting physical affection—scale it back, but still try, small touch, tickle.
- I identify feelings for them—It's okay to be angry; it's not okay to throw something.
- Daily: "Good morning, good night, welcome home, can I get something for you? I like your _____, great job on _____."
- Time "In"—Safe if separate—"I am here and am happy to talk to you when you are calmer."
- Continue to try to get them to therapy consistently.
- Endless advocacy—IEP, ESL, advocate, tutor.

During the months that it took for Dr. Strauss to meet with our family, our case continued to move at a snail's pace. He finally issued his fifty-two-page report to the court in July of 2016, which is summarized below, to the extent I was allowed to.

July 21, 2016: Summary of Dr. Strauss's Report
This report was viewed by me under the strict supervision of my attorney, who was only allowed to have one copy in her office (for the two attorneys to share). She had to sign an affidavit that she wouldn't let any copies be made. I had to have my phone put away and I couldn't take notes on my computer. Nothing could be written verbatim, nor could page numbers be referenced. I was allowed to take some handwritten notes, which she reviewed before I left. I asked why there was that much protection, when we had paid him for this report? She basically said the courts hold this information to a high standard, particularly before a divorce is finalized.

With all that being said, below are my general observations about the main points and recommendations in Dr. Strauss's report.

- His overall recommendation was for joint custody and co-parenting.
- The report agreed with me that all four kids needed quality therapy ASAP and that, while I should consult Richard, I should have the final say on therapy. He noted which of the current therapists were qualified, in his opinion, and which ones we should see vs. replace.
- Bernadette has an unhealthy relationship with my family and should leave immediately. (This was emphasized in several places.)
- He thinks that all the children should spend time with me, even if they are silent, and that Richard should not "rescue" them if they contact him to complain.
- The allegation of me having no food in the house, except Weight Watchers food for me, was repeated by the children, Bernadette, and Richard. He said he has no way of knowing about food in the house and that I strongly denied that to be the case.
- He intimated that my spending excessive time in my office was a factor in the decline of my relationship with Paulina and Niki.
- We all recognized that, at age seventeen and a half, Paulina could not be forced to do much. As such, she should live with Richard. Due to their history, Niki would likely want to stay with her sister.
- Parenting time should be on a flexible, established schedule, particularly with Eric and Charlie.
- He mentioned how most of Richard's claims against me were based on unsubstantiated statements from the kids.

Again, I updated my friends and family. It's worth noting that part of what helped me get through the whole situation was the ongoing support I received from my friends and family, even though none of them had experienced anything like it. It was easier to keep them informed as a group than to have to relive the experience by repeatedly explaining it individually. This is what I wrote to update them about the findings of Dr. Strauss's long-awaited report:

7/21/16

Hi all,

I just wanted to give you a quick update on my case. The forensic psychiatrist, Dr. Strauss, finally issued his report. I was allowed to review it today, under the strict condition of being supervised by my attorney to ensure nothing was copied. I was allowed to take notes, as long as they weren't direct quotes. Here is a brief summary of the key points:

1. *He firmly recommended joint custody.*
2. *All kids in therapy immediately, with me having final say on therapists.*
3. *Bernadette must leave immediately, as she is detrimental to our family. (Our new au pair started last Thursday, but, contrary to what we were told, can't drive, so we are now in re-match. Amazingly, I found someone locally, who seems ideal. Richard is reluctant and only wants to work with Au Pair in America. We'll see.)*

Court was rescheduled, ultimately for August 4 at 9:30 a.m. That's all for now. And so, it goes . . .
T.J.

CHAPTER 39

Arms Open through Repeated Rejections

I worked as a consultant for Morningside Center for Teaching Social Responsibility for many years. In the fall of 2016, my colleague, Luisa Cruz, called me up and said, "Hi, T.J. My job today is to get you to say yes to what I am about to offer you. We want you to become the restorative practices coordinator at Lehman High School."

Most of my work for them was per diem, so I inquired further.

"How many days? What's involved?"

"No, T.J., this is full-time, with benefits. There are six high schools within Lehman High School. With your experience, we are hoping you can get the six principals to work together to create a more restorative and collaborative building."

"Wow. Full-time? With an office in a school? Let me think about it."

Given my financial situation, it certainly sounded appealing, but my life was in complete turmoil, and the court schedule was so unpredictable. Ultimately, I called her back and explained my situation. Since they knew the quality of my work for the past twenty years, they were understanding and flexible. They were willing to give me the time I needed, so I accepted. I ended up working in that position from November 2016 through June 2018, when the contract ended.

April 17, 2016: My Birthday
This is a text exchange between me and Niki as I checked in on her doing her homework so we could go to a movie. She had spent time with me for my birthday yesterday, and the movie was the plan for the end of my birthday weekend.

T.J.: What's the status of your HW?
Niki: I'm done.
T.J.: Tell me what assignments you did.
Niki: Fuck off.
T.J.: I love you.
Niki: I don't care, good-bye. I will never love u.
T.J.: Try to think about your response compared to how big a problem this is. Responses should match the level of problem. An appropriate response might have been to say, "Mom, I did the science, except I didn't understand #8. I did all my math, see. I'm still having trouble with the project," or whatever the actual situation is.

Yelling, screaming, blaming, and cursing had the result of you staying home, which disappointed both of us. We discussed that you and Charlie had to get your work done before the movie. I checked his work before we left. I asked you to list what you did, but there was no response.

All I did was ask to see what work you did so we could go have a nice afternoon. It makes me very sad that it became such a problem and now you're not here. I was really looking forward to having a nice afternoon with both you and Charlie.
Niki: I don't care about Charlie. He's a brat like u.

April 26, 2016: Repeated Rejections
I texted the kids and Richard to see if any of the kids wanted to spend time with me. Richard has to ask Niki for me since he took her phone and I have no way to contact her directly. Charlie responded to the group text that since he will see me tomorrow, he didn't think so, but he loves me a lot. No response from Richard at all, which means he probably hasn't asked Niki. Eric had said "Okay," which I was happy about, until I called him and he clarified that "Okay" was in response to a different text and he didn't want to come.

I hung up and played a game of Solitaire on my phone, which I often do as a distraction when something upsets me. It became hard to see the cards as my tears continued to fall. Several tissues later, I pondered how to keep trying, after repeated, random rejections from my kids. How do I maintain the stamina to keep making the effort to connect with them? It kills me inside, like a fire-tipped spear, searing my heart, time after time. What will become of the scars it creates?

How is it that virtually no one—not the kids, the attorneys, the courts, or even Richard—sees how random their treatment of me is. Three of the kids came to both Seders. They were helpful and participated. They hugged our relatives, but did not willingly hug me. Somehow, I have more understanding about it with Niki. She and Charlie were happily here for Easter. Last weekend, I spent nearly the whole weekend with her, and it was my birthday.

Eric, I just don't understand. He's like a rusty wheel that turns only once it's oiled. Slowly at first, and then the rust melts away and it's well in gear. Until his brain is warmed up and reconnected with me, he is so cold. Once I can get him talking, about virtually anything (and I usually can), he and I can have such insightful conversations! Often, I don't get to interact with him long enough for me to oil his brain sufficiently to get it moving smoothly. It's so frustrating! Everyone believes it's my fault, that they treat me the way they do. However, there is rarely a precipitating event.

Even when there is, or was in the past, the things they get mad about are normal family responsibilities, usually requested, using positive language, giving them minor choices, etc. All the good parenting stuff that I teach and try to utilize. The intensity of the negative responses I get (to put it mildly) is unfathomable! Who speaks to their parents the way my children do? Who is so completely disempowered to correct any misbehavior? How can their father take their side over mine so often?

Everyone likes to be in control, yet how is it that children have so much control, that they can actually, successfully, oust their parent from their home and family? The world is upside down. I don't know how or if it will ever be righted. The "Perfect Storm" that sealed the fate of our family continues to wildly rock our boat. Will there ever come a time when the seas will be calm? What will it take? We can't control Mother Nature any more than we can control our own lives.

Those who know me, know that I try to focus on the positive. To a fault. Sometimes to my own detriment. I deeply believe that this is my choice, and that if I allowed myself to get sucked into the downward spiral, I would be useless to everyone, including myself. So, I get my feelings out through reading, writing, talking to friends, using my Peloton, and trying to take care of me. My oxygen mask is on. I only hope others will allow me to assist with theirs, so we can all breathe freely again.

June 12, 2016: Thirty Minutes from Walking Out to Yes, Movie!

I want to write about the conversation Richard and I had with Niki this afternoon, regarding specific times and dates for access, meaning when we would set a schedule to see each other. He agreed to bring her to meet me at Cosi. I stopped what I was doing and walked over.

She walked in with an attitude and acted annoyed to be there. She wouldn't look at me or talk to me. Note that nothing happened, that I am aware of, to cause her to be mad at me, since I'd left her birthday party last night. When she went to order, she didn't understand what the cashier was asking her (type of bread, side), so I clarified it for her. She looked to Richard, then to me, and accepted my clarification.

She went to sit at a two-person table and Richard offered to get an extra seat, which he did. Niki seemed immediately agitated, stating, "Even Mr. Brunt says I don't have to talk to her if I don't want to!" Then she got up and walked out of Cosi and sat at one of the outside tables.

I looked at Richard and said, "Are you going to talk to her, or should we both go?"

We both joined her outside. Although I feared she might get up and go back in, she didn't.

I told her that she wasn't in trouble; we both just wanted to talk with her together about she and I spending time together. I reminded her about the nice time we'd had yesterday, before her birthday party, when I took her for a haircut, then curled her hair.

She repeated that she didn't want to speak.

I said, "Okay. No one is going to force you."

I really wanted to walk away at that point, but I knew I couldn't. I just had to stay there and take it and keep trying to chip away at her angry shield.

I turned to Richard and said that the two of us should just speak to each other. We started speaking about how it made sense to create a schedule so the kids would know times they would see me. I said that, while it should be fluid, with the kids being able to go back and forth more or less when they wanted to, it would be helpful if there was some consistency.

He started to say Wednesday, but I corrected him to say Tuesdays and Fridays after school/camp, and they could stay overnight, if they wanted to.

Niki was slightly engaged in the conversation. Richard brought up my next-door neighbors, who Niki likes to play with. I then focused on the cat-sitting job that their mom asked Niki about, since she loves animals. Previously, Richard had told her no, and I told her I would speak with him. She tried to speak to him, belligerently, and I stopped her, explaining that there was no need to yell; that wouldn't get her what she wanted. I further said that when we want something, we have a conversation, back and forth. This was a good opportunity for me to explain it to him and have her see me advocate for her. Once he found out that it was only about a week and that I would do the transportation, he agreed. This lightened her mood.

The conversation moved back to the access schedule for Tuesdays and Fridays, with overnights when she wanted to. She didn't quite say yes or no, and Richard said he had to get going, as it was almost four p.m.

I said, "Wait a minute—I was going to see if Niki wanted to see a movie with me this evening."

Interested, she looked at me and asked, "What movie?"

I said to hang on a minute while I checked my phone. We talked about seeing *Alice Through the Looking Glass*.

Ultimately, I picked her back up at 6:30 p.m. and took her to see the original *Ghostbusters*. We had a nice time and her laughter told me she enjoyed the movie. She let me put my arm around her as we walked out to the car. When I dropped her off, I asked her about the Tuesdays and Fridays. She said, "Sure."

I wish it were that simple. Unfortunately, I realize that it will still be an uphill battle for me to overcome her angst each time, but at least it's potential progress.

I just wish her responses to me would not be so arbitrary. It's so hurtful when she is mean to me and so nice when we get to just be mother and daughter together. I hope she will soon go back to therapy to help her sort out her very mixed-up emotions, since Richard pulled her out of the last therapist when she said she didn't want to go.

Later that summer, I had made arrangements with Richard to pick Niki up from camp, where my colleague, Talia, worked. I met her about the time we were adopting the girls, when she contacted me about wanting to learn about the field of conflict resolution. I mentored her and ultimately, she joined my company. Over the years, we became friends and she knew a lot about my family. As I spotted Niki and pulled my car up, she threw a fit in front of everyone, screaming, "I don't have to go with you! You can't make me! I'm calling Mr. Brunt!" Talia and the camp psychologist tried to talk to her and calm her down.

I tried to explain. "Niki, remember we talked with Dad and decided I would pick you up today?"

"I'm not going!" she protested.

"Well, Niki, I'm not sure what else we can do at this point, since the bus already left and Dad is at work in the city. How about you come with me and I can drop you off at Dad's?" Starting to calm down, she relented. "Well, I'm sitting in the back and you are taking me straight to Dad's."

"Okay."

There was nothing more I could do. Embarrassed and defeated, I couldn't and wouldn't force her to be with me. The car remained silent as I drove and dropped her off at my former home.

August 4, 2016: Summary of Court for Friends and Family

Hi all,

Finished court for today. Went pretty well. The judge reluctantly agreed to give Richard two more weeks to find a new au pair (the last two didn't last a week), then Bernadette is OUT! The judge was quite fed up with him.

The attorney for the kids and the judge agreed to have the judge meet each child, as we requested, probably in August. Unfortunately, the judge wants Mr. Brunt there, but at least my attorney added the potential for them to be seen without him afterwards, if necessary.

The judge seemed to understand that flexibility is needed in an access schedule, which I've been saying, but my attorneys keep saying we need a baseline to be ordered. He said they could file the motion. He also told Richard directly that when he isn't available, he and the kids should call me. If I am available, I should do what they need/want. (Again, I keep saying that but Richard doesn't do it. We'll see if that changes.)

The judge acknowledged the need for each child to have therapy! He did not quite give me final decision-making authority and encouraged using in-network providers, but left open the idea that we may need to go out-of-network.

301

Arrangements have been made for me to get a new Honda Pilot, since my 2004 Sienna leaks in the car when it rains.

I was finally allowed to speak briefly about my financial situation, which is improving somewhat with more work early in the school year than I have ever had! He now knows I have never practiced law. He seems to want me to contribute, yet told Richard's attorney that it may cost more in lawyers' fees to make the motion than I would be able to add. He said my lawyers could file the motion to increase maintenance.

Finally, although he offered trial dates in September that opened up, it doesn't look like that will happen. He said the next available time is in the new year.

What a system! Richard was pissed! Good day overall and no tissues needed.

A couple of weeks later, I was dropping Charlie's friend off, after taking them to see *Pete's Dragon*. Niki appeared and asked Charlie to go to the car so she could speak with me alone. I greeted her warmly and was met with her harsh, threatening tone.

She admonished me, saying something like, "I know what you're doing, trying to ruin everything, and you better stop it! I'll be talking to the judge soon, and when he finds out what you've done . . ."

She went on to talk about her life in Ukraine, and how her parents fought. (Actually, I believe it was her mom and her boyfriends. I don't think she was with Niki's father long.) She again mentioned the incident in which she was thrown toward a mirror as a baby, something she has told us many times before. She was almost certainly too young to actually remember it, and was likely told about it by Paulina and possibly her brother, Nikolai, and/or her mother. She has brought it up many times over the years and sometimes embellishes the details, likely because she doesn't recall what actually happened. There is little doubt that something traumatic occurred, but we will probably never know exactly what.

She then flipped the conversation back to "What do you have against Bernadette? What did you tell the judge about her?" saying, "She was like a sister to me." She then threatened that she had put all the pieces together and my plan wouldn't work once she talked to the judge. I tried to reflect what she was saying and then said something like, "I know you think you have figured this all out, but it's not the way you think it is. I never even got to speak to the judge about Bernadette." She stormed away, saying, "Just wait until I speak to the judge!"

I got into the car with Charlie and we called to Richard across the street to let him know that we were coming by the house so Charlie could get what he needed for the beach the next day.

When I came in and, as usual, asked to see Carmela, Niki scooped her up and refused to give her to me or even put her down to go to me or Richard. Finally, Richard convinced her to put Carmela down and she came right to me.

I briefly mentioned to Richard about the hotel reservations I was trying to make to stay Friday and Saturday for my best friend, Susan's son, Keith's bar mitzvah, to avoid the morning rush and drama. Niki initially protested, saying with intense attitude, "I can't be with her for two days!" I reminded her that we just had a wonderful time at Woodloch resort with my extended family, all together for four days. She immediately softened, saying, "Well, I'll only go if I can listen to music in the car." I said sure, that would be fine.

She mentioned that Richard was apparently considering giving her phone back, although there didn't seem to be a specific plan. Richard brought up that she was talking to a boy on Snapchat on Charlie's iCloud account, while at Woodloch. She fully denied it and was indignant with Richard for "accusing her of something she didn't do."

It left me feeling sad that my kids get away with threatening their own mother! Worse yet, it's based on a series of falsehoods.

This kid was pounding on the door, begging for help to sort all this out. The clock was ticking as she moved toward her teenage years, without the support she desperately craves.
I wrote this poem about what I was going through at the time:

Raised by Love—Apart

Texts unanswered.
Phones to voicemail.
Attempts at connection,
So often fail.
Contact missed.
Deepens the void.
Do they purposely avoid?
Moments lost.
Chances fade.
How, really, will they be raised?

Tears that form
In both my eyes.
Most every time,
That I drive by.
The injustice
And the shame.
How could this be?
It's not a game!

Four children, we proudly say.
'Til they say, "Mom, you cannot stay!"
Mothering's a trying task.
One that is supposed to last.
Harder still with different factors.
Wondering if to them it matters?
Needs are special,
Not unique.

Adopting older
Family we seek.
Add to that, the teenage years.
No wonder there are many tears!

Days have passed,
The months go by.
Few days there are,
Where I don't cry.
My main life goal, to be a mother.
Stolen from me, by another.

Externally, I try my best.
To be there, despite my separate nest.
Each time they take a little part
Of my shrinking, broken heart.
The daily torture I endure
'Cause I'll love them evermore.

~ T.J. Kyri
November 30, 2016

Attorneys' Fees
In another cruel part of the court process, Richard was supposed to pay my attorneys' fees, but refused. It became a vicious cycle of my attorneys not being willing to file a motion for the fees, because they were owed fees. In November of 2016, the judge decided that I should receive half of a sizable tax refund that was expected from the IRS from our joint return. My attorney, Bart Lazio, without warning, issued a letter to me mandating that I pay him the balance owed to him—of over $100,000—in a week's time, or he would drop me as a client.

I had not yet received the tax refund, so I could not pay him. My bank account hovered at zero as my credit card balances piled up for the first time in my life. Lazio brought an action against me for failure to pay, even though Richard was supposed to be the one paying. Lazio would not discuss the matter or return my calls, completely indifferent to the fact that I had not yet received the money he was claiming I was supposed to pay him with. I later learned that what apparently drove his demands was the fact that he was leaving his firm. His bonus would be based on his earnings, and so he wanted my fees to count toward his bonus.

The result was me having to file a motion pro se, meaning on my own behalf. I had only a slight concept of how to do this from my law school days twenty years earlier, given that I had never practiced law. Fortunately, one of my law school friends, Gordon Holmes, who now lived in Florida, and Sebastian Kakoulli, a lawyer whom I was starting to date in addition to John, spent many hours helping me draft and revise this document.

I updated my friends the night before court, which was also Eric's fifteenth birthday.

January 24, 2017: Update on Round Three of Judges and Attorneys

Hi,

Here is an update about my case. Apparently, I will be taking a personal day tomorrow to attend court at 11:00 a.m. The court ref would not grant an adjournment and required Mallory (my associate attorney) to call me to let me know that I have to be there. I told her to meet me at 10:30. Bart (head attorney) may be there later, if at all, as he has something else to attend to.

No one cares that I was supposed to start a five-day training of staff from all six schools tomorrow, which I now had to postpone on less than a day's notice! It seems it is a discovery con-

ference to set dates for depositions, etc. This makes no sense, since they will be setting dates with attorneys that have just withdrawn from my case—but since when does logic play a role in justice?

Oh, and by the way, we have a new judge. Judge Geller supposedly pissed someone off at the courthouse and was moved out of White Plains. We now have Judge Heidi Wallace, who signed the order to show cause, that my attorneys filed, to withdraw from my case. She set a return date of February 9 to appear before her. If I don't have new counsel by then, Mallory will have to represent me. Gordon said I should ask Ref. Murphy for a good amount of time to retain new counsel and allow them to get caught up on my case. Not likely I will get to speak much anyway, nor that my opinion or request would be at all considered, but you never know.

Do I sound pissed and sarcastic?! This is an insane, wholly unproductive, demeaning, expensive process. "Due process" feels like a sham. I'd love to know when in this "process" I get my "due"? Maybe it should be "dues process," since I feel like I repeatedly have to pay my dues.

Rant over.

Stay tuned.
T.J.

On my own in court the next day, since my own attorney was now against me, the judge reviewed what I had written and had Mr. Lazio and I step outside the courtroom to negotiate. In the hallway, I calmly but firmly negotiated a final price of $90,000, which Richard was then ordered to pay and eventually did.

The tax refund did not materialize until months later, after several rounds of contradictory letters from the IRS as to whether or not there would be a refund at all. When it finally came, it ended up getting deducted from our agreement, so I never saw the money anyway.

Somehow, I continued to try to stay positive, writing this poem a couple of months later:

Choose Positive

Some days spiral, way down low.
It's hard to smile, frowns just grow.
At those times, it's hard to see,
What the next day just might be.

Each morning we receive a gift.
We choose whether our spirits lift.
To hear the birds or hear the rain.
Or do we focus on our pain?

The choice is ours, each day to make.
Each moment, in fact, we give or take.
While sorrows are a part of life,
It's how we choose to deal with strife.

We can't be happy all the time,
We're learning from our daily grind.
Accepting of life's downs and ups,
Reflecting on our own hiccups.

Challenges help make us wise.
The universe seems strange sometimes.
We may never know why things occur.
Seasons change, become a blur.

Rising in the face of doubt.
We choose whether or not to pout.
The way we craft our situation,
Determines despair or celebration.

It seems that others' lives are great.
Know that thought, is our mistake.
We cannot know another's tales.
Just little bits of their details.

Appreciate all that you have.
Give thanks to all, but do not brag.
Be positive in what you say.
You have the choice, every day!

~ T.J. Kyri
March 8, 2017

Despite my efforts to try to stay focused on the positives and what I had to be grateful for, I felt constantly sucked into my family's conflict. I dreaded communicating with Richard, yet we needed to speak frequently, between everything going on with the kids and court. With every text, call, or conversation, I would have to fluidly figure out how to respond, trying to be assertive, yet keep the peace.

March 13, 2017: Texts with Richard
R: Paulina will go to community college. All the lawyers are taking our kids' college money. Very sad.
T.J.: We can stop the money drain together. Did you meet with Mr. Westin [Paulina's advisor]?
R: The damage is done. It is too late.
T.J.: We both know that Paulina's choice of college has little to do with the divorce.
R: She came to me and wanted to go to community college. Why? The cost of the divorce. And you know what? She is right. It was all about the cost. Plain and simple. Ask her. She was worried that she would have to take out loans.
T.J.: I can understand the frustration. There are many financial options, both for college and our case.

R: Your last lawyer, 90k down the drain. What did they produce for that money? Nothing that I can see.

T.J.: We can easily take out a mortgage if need be, to pay for college and other things.

R: You can understand the frustration? You are creating legal fees that needed to be paid. With zero to show for it. Who will pay the mortgage payment? You? I am out of money.

T.J.: We both have legal fees. I do not want to be baited into a text fight. When you would like to constructively sit down and decide how to avoid paying another half-million dollars of our children's money just to get divorced, let me know. We can still try to find someone to help us work much of this out.

R: Niki's college education? Eric's? Charlie's? We sat down with a mediator. Once. After that, you brought in a lawyer.

T.J.: I hear your frustration. I'm not going to continue this blaming text exchange. So, don't be mad when I don't respond. If you can just tell me you want to try to work this out, I'll be all ears.

On May 9, 2017, I wrote to my friends again to update them on the end of Richard's honeymoon period with the kids:

In other related news . . . Richard is quite fed up with the daily battle of getting Eric up and dressed for school. He has missed many days because he simply refuses to go. I understand Richard's mounting frustration—mostly because I've been there!

Then an interesting thing happened as he was ranting to me this morning, while I drove to work. In addition to him threatening to either put a gun to his head or jump off a building (which he used to threaten regularly), he said he's done. He can't take it anymore; it's too much to handle all four of our kids and work (welcome to my world!).

Then he actually said, "You can move back in. I'm going back to the city! I can't take it anymore."

While it is amazing that the honeymoon is finally over for him as a full-time dad, this presents challenges for me. I have been contemplating what I really want to ask for. Still not completely sure. I wish everyone and everything were not so unpredictable! We'll see what happens with the rest of this process.

CHAPTER 40
Return to Mediation

So, as I began to look for a new attorney, Richard and I discussed returning to mediation, with a different mediator. I remained concerned about finding a mediator who could manage our truly "high-conflict divorce." I had gone to a restorative justice conference at Lehman College in The Bronx and saw a colleague of mine, Penelope (whom I later went to work for). When I mentioned needing a mediator, she suggested a team approach with Tom Waters and Joyce Glasser. I had served on a mediation committee with Tom about ten years earlier, but hadn't seen him since. He was a financial specialist. Joyce was a parenting specialist and therapist. I talked to Richard and disclosed my connection to Tom. Ultimately, we agreed to work with them and met in Joyce's home, about twenty minutes from ours.

Being intimately familiar with the process and practice of mediation, I had never known any case that proceeded as ours did. We met for three hours at a time, usually twice per week for months. Their fees were almost as much as the attorneys we were already paying. There were numerous issues to discuss, and at one point, I brought chart paper and markers to chart out our issues and decisions.

As we sat on Joyce's couch in her living room and she made us tea, we developed guidelines for how to conduct ourselves during the mediation and made an agenda at the beginning of each session. Most of the time, the agenda was co-opted by Richard. He would insist on relaying details of situation after situation, proclaiming its relevance to whatever we were discussing. Often, Joyce would try to redirect him back to our agreed-upon topics, to no avail. If she said anything that disagreed with his point of view, he'd raise his voice and respond in a patronizing way. Several times, our sessions ended with Joyce telling him if he couldn't stop yelling, he would need to leave her home, and he did. At times, she suffered from migraines triggered by his behavior.

Mediation is supposed to be a safe place where the parties have equal voice and can talk through issues, with the help of a neutral third party, in order to make decisions in their own best interests. Contrary to the tenets of mediation, many a time I'd sit curled up in a corner of Joyce's couch, trying to distance myself from Richard's hands that flailed precariously close to my face, making me cringe. If I tried to interrupt his tirades, I would be admonished as well. Tom weighed in mostly when the topics veered toward financial issues.

As a mediator myself, I hope never to have clients as difficult as us. To date, no one has even come close.

Meanwhile, court was proceeding, so I had to find a new attorney, which was especially tricky because I still couldn't afford much of a retainer. With this complicated case dragging on endlessly, I knew I needed a tiger who could put Richard in his place.

Later that spring, I eventually found Beth Zinger. Walking into her office, I was struck by her tight red curls and the fact she was wearing high heels when she greeted me firmly, yet kindly. When I explained my situation, I was eternally grateful that she agreed to take on my cause. She explained that she rarely took on a case like this without a substantial retainer up front, but she was willing to do so, based on the likelihood that she could get Richard to pay, eventually.

Unlike my other attorneys, she agreed with my idea to depose Richard right away. She was shocked that this had not yet occurred in all this time. We were right. When he was finally deposed, it became apparent that his games would now cease. His attorney had to pull him out several times to counsel him not to expound upon his answers and further incriminate himself. He couldn't help it; he just had to keep talking, but this time it was to my advantage.

In contrast, when I was deposed by his attorney, I followed my attorney's instructions perfectly, answering only what I had been asked in as minimal a way as possible, and not allowing any room for conjecture. Afterward, she said I was a model client, and she wished her other clients would do so well at their depositions.

After the first day of the deposition, Richard called me before I'd even made it home, to discuss a settlement. Finally, we had some real terms to discuss in mediation!

Moving - again.
Eventually, my landlord said she wanted to put the furnished house I was renting on the market, and that I would need to find somewhere else to live.

After much searching, in August of 2017, I found a beautiful new home that was a bit more than I had been paying, but would allow the kids to each have their own rooms, and Charlie and Niki could walk to their middle school. Since I was now working full-time, I was able to afford basic furniture so the kids would feel comfortable in their own space. My relationship with Eric was starting to improve a bit, but I wasn't sure if he would be willing to stay with me. When I took him to see the house, he loved it right away and claimed an area between the main floor and the basement as his room. I had considered using it as an office, but was thrilled to move my home office to the basement, if it meant that he would be with me. I moved in as soon as I could and all three kids stayed over for periods of time.

Meanwhile, we were spending hours each week over the course of months, chipping away at parts of a mediated agreement. I started to feel pressured to accept the terms being suggested and my attorney, Beth wasn't pleased that I was still mediating, for fear I was being taken advantage of. Despite her concerns, I persisted, feeling at least at times I had a voice, whereas in court, I had none.

One of the basic elements of most types of mediation is that the mediators do not make suggestions, but leave all decision-making to the parties. They will reality-test what the parties come up with, but should not impose their own opinions on the parties involved. They can provide information but cannot counsel as to the law. Especially in a case like ours, all agreements would eventually be reviewed by our attorneys, before being submitted to the court to be "so ordered."

I did not feel I could adequately represent my interests in mediation and was unclear as to my legal rights. I repeatedly asked for sessions with my attorney present, but Richard and the mediators felt that would destroy the process, so they wouldn't allow it. I was left to fend for myself, only checking in with my attorney after certain sessions.

The court process moved along under her representation and we were now locked in to trial dates to begin on January 3, 2018. No one wants to go to trial, especially in a divorce. The amount of money, paperwork, and animosity created is not beneficial for anyone. We went to extra mediation sessions over the holidays and finally reached the best agreement we could, which was submitted to the court for approval on December 27, 2017. With the submission of the mediated agreement, our trial dates were canceled.

On January 30, 2018, the court accepted our mediated agreement and we were finally, officially divorced. I went from constantly being berated to being liberated. It was a huge weight off my shoulders and it meant that I could now have a more equal say in what happened with the kids, since we had joint custody.

Richard paid me some of what we agreed to, but as of June 2022, there are still parts he has not complied with. I was supposed to be allowed into the marital residence within thirty days of the divorce being finalized to get my remaining things. We explicitly agreed that no one else would be present—no children or nanny, so as not to make it even harder on anyone. There never seemed to be a time for that to happen.

Finally, I took a day off work, and while the kids were in school, I made a first attempt to get my things. I gathered the children's old school portfolios which I had created each school year for each of them and went through a few other things in the attic, before Paulina appeared.

When I protested, reminding Richard that we'd agreed that no one else would be home, he once again admonished me in front of her. "What, so I should tell her to leave her own house?"

"Yes, until I am done," I said. "No one is supposed to be here until five p.m."

He refused to do so, leaving me exasperated and in tears.

I packed what I could into my car and still have not been given a day to come back alone.

I have tried many times, in many ways, to ask him when I can retrieve the rest of my belongings. He has given me bits here and there, but I have resisted going back to my tiger attorney to force him to follow through with the agreement and pay what remains. Every time I gear up to do that, we have another crisis with the kids. There always seems to be something that prevents me from pushing the envelope to force him to pay.

We still have four very needy, complicated children. We live close to each other and speak several days a week about issues with each of them. I know that getting Beth involved again would only exacerbate the situation. The last time I mentioned to Richard that I needed him to pay and was trying to hold off getting her involved, he retorted, "Let's get your twat Beth involved so I can knock her the fuck out."

I feel like I am trying to maintain our relationship so we can best handle all we need to for our children. I'm not sure how or when the remaining terms of our agreement will be resolved, if ever.

CHAPTER 41
Dark Tunnel to Sunshine

With the divorce finally behind me, I reflected on my journey, writing this poem, six months later:

Dark Tunnel to Sunshine

Plunged into a deep, dark well.
Tears would well up, but I couldn't.
Anger would well up, but I couldn't.
Fear would well up, but I couldn't.

Indignation would well up, but I couldn't.
Helplessness would try to engulf me, but it couldn't.
Pain would try to surround me, but it couldn't,
Because joy would bubble up within me to counter it.

Craters in the ground beneath me would try to trip me,
But I stepped carefully, steadying my footing.
The turns in the tunnel would try to confuse me,
But I learned to expect them, so they became less daunting.

I crawled, so I could feel my way,
Until I recognized a crack of sunshine.
More confidently, I moved toward it.
I enabled the sounds ahead to guide me toward the mouth
of the tunnel.

After time, I found a ladder, with support.
Rung by rung, I climbed toward the brightening sunshine.
Now I stand, proudly, on solid ground, having journeyed
through

People, feelings, circumstances that, in their darkness,
Enabled me to grow into the light.

~ T.J. Kyri
July 20, 2018

I was now able to start moving forward in rebuilding my life. I had a steady job and was seeing a couple of different people. I was always very up front that I did not want a boyfriend and would not date anyone exclusively.

Initially, I enjoyed my time with John. He was the calming presence I needed during the turmoil of the divorce. As a single dad, I think most of the time he appreciated the maternal influence I offered to him and his son, who was about the same age as Niki and Charlie. They even hung out together on occasion. We spent two summers joining them at their local pool. Being in his house gave me the purpose I was missing in my own family. I could cook and straighten up and occasionally provide some parenting advice. I needed to manage a home and was happy doing it for him. I will also never forget his kindness in cleaning out a spare room at a moment's notice for me to store my things, when I had to leave my home so abruptly.

A mutual friend introduced me to Sebastian within a month of meeting John, and I saw him on and off during the same four years. I liked Sebastian. He'd never been married and had no children, but he was still living with his long-term girlfriend, albeit, apparently more like roommates on different floors of a house in Greenburgh. He was also eight years older than me; a bit more than I would have preferred. Sebastian was classy, dressed well, and was very sociable. He was born in England, but grew up mostly in Syracuse, New York. I liked his bit of European flair, though he wasn't Jewish. He was president of an in-house lawyers' association which sponsored lots of fun events, which we often attended together. He would take me to nice dinners and interesting places. I could take him with me to events and not have to worry about babysitting him. Still, neither of us was fully available, so we enjoyed each other's company only casually.

Years earlier, I'd randomly had my palm read at a fair and the woman told me I would meet someone I'd known twenty

318

years ago. While I doubted it was true, I secretly hoped it would be my old high school friend, Tristan Fields (who I've never been able to find).

Instead, I received a random Facebook message from someone I didn't recognize. All it said was, "How've you been the last twenty years?" Thinking it was a prank, I dismissed it, but Marty Picard found me and texted me in 2016. I realized he was someone who used to work for Richard, whom I took a liking to before we were married. I used to call him from pay phones and talk to him, often complaining about Richard, his boss. We liked each other, but never did anything, given the circumstances. When Richard found out there was an interest between us, he understandably fired Marty. I felt bad about it, especially since nothing ever happened.

We reconnected by phone in 2016 and soon he came to see me. Within minutes, he said, "Come here." Curious, I came closer to where he was standing in my living room. He leaned over and kissed me passionately, saying, "I've been wanting to do that for twenty years!" I was a bit shocked, given that we'd only just reconnected, but I'll admit to being flattered by the affection.

Just as I had with John and Sebastian, I told Marty very clearly that I was seeing other people and was not looking for a serious relationship. He was in the process of divorcing his wife and said he understood, but would like to see me. For a while, I focused on Marty and John, even telling Sebastian to leave one night after taking me out, since the thought of me being with Sebastian made Marty uncomfortable.

In all, I was amazed that anyone would be interested in a forty-five-year-old woman with four kids, but they were. Honestly, I enjoyed the attention and the distraction from everything else going on in my life.

Marty and I dated for about a year, while I was still seeing John and occasionally, Sebastian. He lived a bit far away, and the spark we had rekindled had faded. Eventually, we

319

decided, mutually, to end it. We remain friendly today, with no hard feelings.

Sebastian had finally moved out of the house he shared with his girlfriend of fourteen years and moved to Hoboken. He began to date other people, and when one of them wanted to get more serious, it dawned on him that what he wanted was to be with me. We started seeing more of each other, though I was still seeing John.

By the summer of 2018, things between John and I were waning. I didn't want to hurt his feelings by breaking up with him, but eventually, he broke up with me. Again, someone did what I couldn't do, though the circumstances were completely different. While I was a bit surprised, I knew it was probably for the best for both of us. I only regret that he chose not to keep in touch. I imagine it was probably too painful to watch me move on with my life. He is a great guy, and I truly hope that he has found someone who makes him happy.

Around this time, Richard finally sold his apartment in the city, which allowed him to pay me the shares he owed me from the apartment and the marital residence that he now occupied. This enabled me to buy my own home, which thankfully I could do outright, because I wasn't working long enough to qualify for a mortgage.

Eric had helped me look on Zillow and I had a wonderful real estate broker, Gwen Radlin, who showed me many homes, but unfortunately none of them were quite right.

One day in late August, Eric found something that had suddenly come on the market as "For Sale by Owner." I contacted them right away, and since they were shomer Shabbos (meaning religious, so they don't conduct business on Friday night or Saturday), we made arrangements to see the house on Sunday at two p.m.

I had gone away with Sebastian to Pennsylvania for the weekend, and he drove us back Sunday morning, picked up Eric, Charlie, and Niki, and we all went to see it. We all loved it immediately! It was within walking distance to the high school and a long walk to Richard's house. (I kept telling Eric: Location, location, location!) It had a huge kitchen and a gorgeous walk-in closet. It was perfect!

While we were seeing the basement, as the last stop, I asked the owner to give me a minute with Sebastian and the kids. She did, and I asked them what they thought. I got eight thumbs up! I went upstairs and told them the kids and I wanted this house to become our home. I told them we would go above asking price if necessary (which was the kind of market it was at the time). We made arrangements to be back in touch the next day.

That night, I happened to have a few friends from shul over for a rare get-together. I excitedly gushed about the house. When I told my friend Casey about it, she realized she knew the owner and texted her right away to put in a good word for me. The next day, I put in a bid above the asking price, as two other families did, but I got it! I was elated! Finally, things were starting to turn around for me.

I started spending more time with just Sebastian and he bravely helped me move in November of 2018, which was a long, nightmarish day.

I settled into my new home, a home that was truly mine. I was free to decorate it any way I liked and had budgeted for some new furnishings. The kids felt comfortable and helped make it our new home together—all except Paulina, who wouldn't come see it. The others wouldn't follow a set schedule, but spent time with both me and Richard. The kids alternated whose house they slept at. Niki spent some time in her new room and would go out with me, but mostly lived with her dad.

Meanwhile, my friend Joanie Webber, who had adopted Paulina's friend, Zoe, moved from Pennsylvania to Thailand for her husband's work. As soon as I found out she was in Thailand, I told her I was coming to visit. My plan was to take the kids for an amazing international vacation, now that I could afford to do so. Initially, Eric, Charlie, and Niki seemed excited to go.

Then one day, as I was looking into flights, Richard said, "I don't think the kids want to go with you to Thailand."

"Really? What makes you say that?" I asked, surprised.

"Talk to them," he replied, as he often did when he already had, and I needed to catch up on the conversation.

I called them and one by one, they confirmed they no longer wanted to go. Niki didn't want to go on a long flight. Charlie wanted to spend the break with his friends. Eric didn't want to go if Charlie didn't.

Exasperated, I texted Sebastian to see if he wanted to join me, though I would have gone alone if no one did. He was out at an event in the city, having a good time.

He texted back, "Sure."

"Really?" I confirmed. "You can get the time off of work and want to go?"

"Yes. That would be great."

"Okay!"

We booked the flights and left on February 14, 2019. I had been talking to my therapist and friends about becoming exclusive with Sebastian. We had been seeing each other on and off for five years and were getting closer in our relationship. I thought about what to call us, since "boyfriend/girlfriend" felt juvenile. I had been calling him my "partner" for a while, always appreciating how helpful he was to me. He would do the dishes and take out the trash without my asking, and he didn't even live with me.

I never liked combining holidays with other events, but since we would literally be on a plane for twenty-four hours on Valentine's Day, I decided I would give him a card and gift on the plane and ask him to be my boyfriend. That's exactly what I did, and he said yes!

We had a wonderful, memorable trip together! I truly love him, and love being with him all the time. We were supposed to travel to England and Cyprus, where he is from, in April 2020, but COVID-19 put those plans on hold. Since we are both working from home now, he mostly stays at my house. I miss him when he goes back to Hoboken once every week or so. He is kind, loving, patient, and always treats me with the utmost respect. We talk all the time about anything and everything, and he never raises his voice to me. I am grateful that my children finally have a role model for a solid relationship.

I wrote this poem for him:

I love the ways you think of me, every single day.
The things that show you care for me, in big and little ways.
My towel, hung, prepared for me, remembering the fan.
The trash and dishes emptied, helping every way you can.

All these things you do for me, illustrate your love.
Each act of yours, on my behalf, makes you rise above.
As I look toward our tomorrows, I see us hand in hand.
I know that I have found someone, the man who's my Good Man!

CHAPTER 42
Niki's Roller-Coaster
Sweet Sixteen

Niki is still an emotional light switch, hugging me one minute and cursing at me the next. Her Sweet Sixteen on June 7, 2019, was like a roller-coaster ride that aptly sums up the highs and lows I still experience daily in my family.

Niki had been trying to plan her Sweet Sixteen since she was about fourteen years old. She was enamored with the idea of a pretty dress and a big party. As the time grew closer, she and I planned almost all of the details—the invitations, the DJ, the decorations, the favors, the dress, and more. Richard went with us to Juliano's to see the room and taste the food. At this point, my relationship with her was very hot and cold. We could spend fun times together going to the movies or getting our nails done, with her telling me about the latest drama in her life. Other times, she cut me off and wouldn't speak to me, generally without provocation.

I knew there would be some kind of drama around Niki's Sweet Sixteen, but my crystal ball was a bit fuzzy as to what the details might be. In the days leading up to the party, the focus became clear: where Niki would have her hair and makeup done. Quite the first-world problem, but a problem, nonetheless. Thus began the up-and-down roller-coaster ride.

Since her party was on a Friday night, she had school during the day. We fought about her going to school, which I insisted on, since she was failing many of her classes. I spent time locating someone who would come to my house to do our hair and makeup.

Paulina was barely talking to me at the time, but I texted her about a week before, saying that if she wanted to come to my house, she could join us. I was in my new home, which she hadn't seen, just like she had never seen me in any of the places I'd lived since leaving my marital home. Although I was hopeful, I doubted that she would come, and as it turned out, she didn't.

Niki was supposed to come to my house straight from school, where the woman would be finishing working on me and would then do her. I had worked out a price for hair and makeup for both of us.

On the day of the Sweet Sixteen, Niki refused to come. Hurt and angry, I tried unsuccessfully to reason with her. Later I found out that Richard had his ex-girlfriend's daughter do Niki's hair and makeup, which infuriated me further! I tried to stay calm while the woman did my hair and makeup alone in my house. Thankfully, she didn't charge me for both of us, despite the last-minute notice.

I was the one who'd spent time arranging every detail, yet I was deprived of the joy of getting ready with my daughter on her special day. Worse still, the only task Richard had was arranging a photographer. He never bothered to tell me he'd arranged to have the photographer take pictures of Niki getting ready at his house before the party. Excluding me yet again! (Even worse was the fact that one of the few pictures I was part of in the photo album was more than halfway through the book, and I didn't even get a hard copy of it.)

Sebastian and I arrived at the event together, while Richard came with all of our kids. Being single at the time, he invited an old girlfriend and her kids to the event. It took ten minutes before we were able to turn into the parking lot, which we were only able to do when Richard nearly got hit by a car, standing in the middle of the street trying to stop traffic, to allow us to turn. It then took another ten minutes for the valet to take our car.

We got there just before everyone else and I quickly made sure everything was set up as it should be. The Ukrainian flag decorations were hung around the room and the water bottle favors were put out on a table.

As people started arriving and the DJ started playing, I happily greeted our family and Niki's friends. I introduced myself to the photographer and showed her our family, so she knew where to focus her attention. I asked all of my kids to pose for a picture with me, but Paulina refused. I even tried to get her to pose for a picture without me and just her siblings, but she would not, since I was the one who had asked. She made a display of fawning over Niki and posing for multiple pictures with her, while explicitly excluding me.

I had spoken to the DJ in advance and gave him a list of songs we had selected to be played as each family member made their grand entrance. I was very specific that I wanted to walk in separately from Richard and that it should be to "You Can't Lose Me" by Faith Hill. As we were about to walk in, the emcee instructed Richard and I to walk in together, first. When I reminded him that we were walking in separately, he said he didn't know, and it was too late. I was furious! I told him that was not what we'd discussed, and I would not walk in with Richard.

Paulina admonished me, telling me to stop making a fuss, which infuriated me all the more. The music was playing and it became one more time that I had to fight back tears, plaster a smile on my face, and go on with the show. I walked a few steps ahead of Richard, to some other song, then stood on the side applauding as the kids and Paulina made their entrances.

Finally, the star of the event, Niki herself, strutted into the room, her sparkly Sweet Sixteen crown held high on her head, her smile lighting up the room. I continued watching what should have been a beautiful moment, but instead, it was pierced with pain. With my phone videotaping, I watched the rehearsed father-daughter dance to a most apropos song, "Piece by Piece." I remained discarded, on the sidelines, while her father and siblings surrounded her.

The bar for the various simultaneous events at Juliano's was in a common area outside the room of the Sweet Sixteen party. When the song ended, I could feel the tears of hurt and anger welling up inside me. Though I had been fighting a cold, I pulled Sebastian out and went to get a drink. As I ordered, I told the bartender to make sure not to serve Paulina, as she was only twenty. He informed me that her father was already getting her drinks. Defeated again, we took our drinks to a nearby table outside the event to talk.

Sitting there, trying to process how many times I had been hurt just on this day alone, I burst into tears. With my beautifully done makeup now streaming down my face, Sebastian listened, as he always does, and tried to soothe me.

Suddenly, Paulina appeared and asked to speak with me. Really—now? I thought. She always knows how to get me when I'm at my most vulnerable, yet I still didn't want to refuse her attempt to connect with me.

I asked Sebastian to stay nearby and Paulina and I walked a few feet away, to a corridor outside the restrooms. She started with her usual sweet talk that she was so good at when she was either drunk or wanted something. I questioned her motives, not wanting to get sucked in yet again. I asked her if she was drunk and she assured me she wasn't. She said she was tired of fighting with me and suggested we go for lunch to discuss it.

"Really?" I asked, suspiciously.

"Yes," she confirmed.

Seizing the moment, I said, "Okay. How about tomorrow?"

"Fine. One o'clock?"

"Great. I'll pick you up."

Then she hugged me, a rare event, which made me cry again as I hugged her back.

"Don't cry," she said gently.

"Oh, Paulina!" was all I could say.

Then I repeated my request for a family photo and this time, she agreed. I cleaned up my face and when I went back inside, we took a quick selfie. As usual, it looked like a sweet, normal, mother-daughter picture. Only people who know us well had any inkling of what was behind it. When I asked for the family picture, she said she wanted to eat first and that we could take it afterwards.

We all got food and danced. I spent a bit of time with my sister and my nieces. My nephews and brother-in-law had stayed home. I met Niki's friends and took pictures with Sebastian, then my extended family and the kids. I got a few quick pics with me and Niki. Most of Niki's time and most of the professional pictures turned out to be with Niki and her girlfriend Lena. Theirs was a very troubled relationship, and though they mostly stayed together for about a year, they broke up soon after the Sweet Sixteen.

I chatted with my mother, who wondered why there were only Ukrainian flags, not American. I explained that Niki's heritage means a lot to her, and so the theme of the whole party was Ukraine. The color scheme, the flags, the water bottle favors—everything to honor her birth country, as she had wanted.

My mother briefly persisted, saying, "But she lives here now."

"Yes, but she left so much behind, and it's important to her."

There was no point in continuing to explain, so I went back to watching Niki having a great time dancing with her friends.

With another hour of the party to go, Eric told me that Paulina had left, and he was leaving too.

"What?" I asked incredulously. So much for the promised family picture!

I couldn't imagine what was suddenly more important than staying for their sister's party, but again, I had no say. Apparently, Olya, the nanny Richard employed, drove them each home.

Eventually, the party started wrapping up. I looked around for Richard, who was to tip everyone and take Niki and a few of her friends back to his house for a sleepover. He was nowhere to be found. Niki started getting upset, feeling like he'd abandoned her (and she already has huge abandonment issues). We both tried calling and texting and got nowhere. Even Richard's ex-girlfriend did not seem to know where he was.

I tried to put her at ease and assured her and her friends that Sebastian and I would drive them home.

"No!" Niki insisted. "I called Paulina and she said she will call me an Uber."

"Niki, that's silly. I will drive you and your friends home."

Back and forth we went, with Niki taking out her frustration on me once more, despite me trying to help. Finally, she relented, allowing me to drive her home.

We had the caterers wrap up the leftovers and made sure everyone took their party favors. I regretted not taking extra money, since Richard was supposed to handle the tips, and now he wasn't there to do so. I gave out what I had and apologized profusely to all of the people who worked at the party. I told them that Richard would send them something afterwards.

One of Niki's friends wasn't feeling well, so we had to deal with her getting sick, apparently from too much soda, on top of everything else.

Finally, we carried out the food and gifts and waited for the valet to bring my car.

Just as they brought it around, Richard showed back up. Without so much as a good-bye, Niki abruptly ran to his car and piled in with her friends. Furious, I tried to talk to him and see where the hell he had been. All I got in response was "Fuck you!" in front of the kids. Seriously? You disappear without a trace and rather than some explanation, I get cursed at?

Fuming once more, I got in my car with Sebastian and drove us back to my place.

Sadly, the next day wasn't much better.

At six a.m., Paulina texted me to cancel our lunch, probably because she'd gone out partying in the city the night before and was either still drunk or hungover. Next, I was supposed to see Niki that day, since it was her actual birthday, but she texted me saying, "I don't want you here." Ouch! Again, nothing new, but still super painful. Her father abandons her at her own Sweet Sixteen, I try to help, and I'm the one she lashes out at, for no reason!

Despite the crazy ups and downs of that event, what I treasured most were the speeches.

When it was time for us to say a few words, I made sure to go first, so as not to be upstaged by Richard. I gave a poignant speech about bringing Niki to the United States and how much I loved her, which the room listened to with rapt attention.

In part, I said, "While there are days that you challenge the hell out of me—"

Niki interrupted here, saying, "Mostly like every day!"

"Yes, mostly like every day," I continued, "pretty much for seven and a half years. But I do think that when I personally count my life's accomplishments, you are among them. One of the reasons I wanted to come in on the song 'Never Lose Me' is because no matter how you treat me, and no matter how our relationship has been, I want you to know that you will never lose me, because I am always here for you, including today, on your very special day. So, I thank you for coming into my life. You have made me the person I am, and I hope that I can help make you the person you will become."

As usual, Richard couldn't help but interrupt me—fourteen times (I later counted after watching the video I had Sabastian tape on my phone).

Richard then gave a speech, during which, of course, he cried.

Finally, Niki confidently took the mic and said, in part, "For my family, because they gave me a home and a shelter when

I didn't have any of that. I want to thank Mom. I know that I can be a raging bitch to you a lot, but I just wanted to say that through all the types of hell I put you through, that you never left my side, and I appreciate you for that, so thank you very much."

Makes it all worth it.

EPILOGUE

My story is not over. I've attempted to capture the highlights and lowlights of some of the major events of my adult life so far. My relationships with my ex-husband and my children continue to evolve, mostly for the better.

Below are updates in each of our relationships.

Richard

While my relationship with Richard will probably never be easy, we are in frequent contact. Most recently, he has been more open with me and has filled me in on what happens with the kids while they are with him. He sometimes seeks my input and support in dealing with the various crises that seem to arise regularly.

We live a few minutes away from each other and the kids go back and forth fairly easily. We both drop them off and pick them up and remain flexible about the time they spend with each of us. He still has not fulfilled many of the terms of our divorce decree, but keeps promising to.

I have tried to stay open to keeping things amicable. I have even invited him to family events, though he always declines. Our relationship will always have its ups and downs, but our mutual love for our children remains constant.

Paulina

Paulina continued not to speaking to me, though she was at least in college and had several waitressing jobs. Things took a turn for the worse on New Year's Day 2020, when she made the first of several attempts to kill herself by mixing alcohol and whatever pills she could find. Fortunately, each time, we were able to intervene, get her to a hospital and then to a short-term psychiatric treatment center. She has always turned to me when she has been most vulnerable, at least briefly. Sadly, visiting her in the psychiatric facilities were the longest and most meaningful conversations we have had in a long time.

After the first attempt, pre-COVID, I went to visit her nearly every day. I brought her clothes (with no drawstrings for safety), and sushi. We sat in the common room and chatted lightly about general topics. We did the best we could to celebrate her twenty-first birthday in the facility. They wouldn't let her keep the birthday-cake-flavored popcorn I found in a plastic champagne bottle, because it was made in a place that had nuts. Sadly, I carried it back home.

During her second attempt, Richard was in Paris with a new girlfriend, just as COVID started shutting things down, which meant Paulina was home alone. When she asked for our dog, Carmela, I knew she was depressed, so I went to go check on her one afternoon. When I told Niki she couldn't come with me, she fought me, nearly pushing me down the stairs and then running away. I called the police, who kindly brought her back and then offered to check on Paulina at Richard's house, when I told them I was concerned. Thank G-d they did, because they found her barely conscious, having taken pills again. I followed the ambulance to the hospital and stayed with her late into the night.

Returning the next day, Paulina got to see me advocate fiercely for her to go to what seemed to be a better facility than where they wanted to send her. Once there, she watched in amazement as I again firmly advocated for what she needed. Socks, a blanket, medicine for her psoriasis, books, and therapy. She got to see me in the role I've filled countless times for her siblings, but this time, it was just for her.

It continues to make me sad that Paulina has actively pushed away all I have to offer her as a mother. For this snapshot of time, she allowed it. For once, I could do something for her that no one else could. She recognized it and thanked me. We sat and talked, and she even showed me some of what she was working on at the facility. It was the first time I could recall her letting me in.

Upon her release, I picked her up and she actually came to see my house for the first time, and I'd been in this one for a year and a half. She actually continued texting with me for several weeks, which was also a new thing. Then, to my shock, she and her boyfriend joined us for dinner at my house a couple of weeks later. I kept trying to keep her engaged with light texts, which she sometimes responded to and sometimes ignored. Either way, this was more progress than we have made in years. Sadly, as of this writing, she is back to completely ignoring me and not answering texts I send her or even acknowledging a Christmas present I bought her.

She was seeing a therapist regularly at the time, who was beginning to help her learn to face her myriad issues. He strongly supported her trying to build a relationship with me, though we both recognize it will be a long bumpy road. I truly hope we can. There have been other therapists that have come and gone since then.

So many people have suggested I give up on Paulina, given how abusively she treats me. My answer is always the same: She is my daughter. She has been through a lot in her young life. Someday, I hope she finds a way to accept the love I have for her, that her biological mother was not able to provide. I don't excuse Paulina's behavior, but my arms remain open, hoping one day she'll warm to my embrace.

Eric

My relationship with Eric seems to have been mended and we have gone back to the solid foundation we had established when he was younger. I think the divorce rocked his trust in the sanctity of the world as he knew it. As the people around him influenced him to be suspicious of me, it must have been hard for his teenage brain to reconcile what he thought he knew to be true in our relationship with how I was being painted to him. With time, consistency, and therapy, he has matured in his understanding of what took place and has regained his trust in me and our relationship.

He now stays over regularly and I treasure our long talks on interesting subjects. He has impressive abilities both with technology and cooking, though he can't accept compliments for his expertise. I have come to rely on him as my in-house tech support, as have all members of our family. Hopefully, he will be able to apply his skills to a fulfilling career.

Eric continued to have issues, which most often manifested as school refusal. Sadly, he was in at least six different school programs, public and private, in seven years. His school refusal became so bad that we could not get him up and out of bed for any kind of program.

During the divorce, I begged Richard to explore residential programs for him, but he adamantly refused. Finally, after the divorce, I was able to convince Richard to hire educational consultant Donna Fegan from the Heller Agency. She is one of the only people I have known who has been able to get Richard to face reality.

After meeting with Eric for twenty minutes, Richard and I sat down with her. She looked at Richard and told him matter-of-factly, "You don't need to hire me. As long as you are okay with having Eric live out the rest of his life in your basement, continue doing what you are doing."

Her bluntness worked. She continued, validating what I had been saying for years. "He's seventeen. We can no longer just look at getting him through another year of school. We need to get him into a program that can prepare him to be a functioning adult."

Thank you! Finally, someone got what I had been saying, and was able to get the message through to Richard. We hired her, and ultimately, she found the Chamberlain School in Massachusetts, which has changed Eric's life and ours for the better.

Eric went from never going to class to going to all classes and doing his work. He has made friends at Chamberlain. He's learning how to be organized and productive (still a work in progress). It was the best thing we could have done for him.

Being home during COVID-19 was a setback in terms of his schooling, though I relished the time we had together. As soon as he returned to Chamberlain, Eric reengaged and was back to going to class and making progress. While it was hard not having him around, as always, I felt it was important to do what was in his best interests.

Eric graduated high school during the summer of 2021, having succeeded in getting a part-time job on campus and obtaining a 4.0 in the two college classes he took during his last year. He tried taking online classes at a community college, but it didn't work out. He's doing a small internship at my organization while we have him work on his executive functioning and organizational skills with a coach from Order Out Of Chaos. Hopefully, he'll be able to find a supportive program for work and/or school and be able to transition to independent living.

Niki

Niki and I still have a complicated, though much closer relationship. She continues to have difficulty managing her emotions and resents anyone in authority, including parents, teachers, and even the police. She was spending some time at my new home, but mostly stayed with Richard. When she was here, most of the time she was friendly and helpful. She helped make dinner, walk the dog, and keep her room clean. She'd put her arm around me and tell me about the latest issues with her and her friends. Most of the time, she tells me she loves me. I believe that she is learning to, and that our relationship will continue to grow stronger as she becomes an adult, though the bumps remain.

Niki still hasn't learned the meaning of friendship and continues to make poor choices in friendships and romantic relationships. She seems strangely comforted by chaos and seeks it out when things have been too calm, which is a characteristic of R.A.D. During COVID, she ran away many times, staying with friends and putting everyone at risk. Ultimately, the police helped get her to a facility where she got some of the support she desperately needed. Upon her return, she stayed with me more consistently and was initially respectful and friendly, going to therapy consistently, and calling or texting me to spend time together.

Unfortunately, as COVID wore on, her behavior worsened, and we felt we could no longer keep her safe. Ultimately, we hired a different educational consultant from the one we used with Eric, during her third stay at a psychiatric hospital, who helped us place her at a residential facility in Utah. When she turned eighteen and threatened to leave, we obtained guardianship of her, which caused her placement to discharge her.

We moved her to a young adult treatment center, where she received intensive support, including equine therapy, for her multitude of needs. In December of 2021, she had an incident there, where she shoved a staff member and ran. They called the Sheriff and collectively brought her back to the program and then to a psychiatric facility in Utah.

Ultimately, she was discharged from that facility and is now in a wilderness program. She seems to be making some progress there, and at least we found a place that has animals and practices Eye Movement Desensitization and Reprocessing (EMDR), which is one of the preferred treatments for complex post-traumatic stress disorder (C-PTSD) After that, we will need to find a fourth residential placement for her. Hopefully, she will learn how to process the multitude of traumas that have occurred in her life and how to regulate her emotions safely. I pray that this intensive treatment will give her time and tools to manage her life, so she can be happy and productive.

Charlie

Charlie remains my sweet, squishy, now six-foot-tall, seventeen-year-old, young man. He is still my "under-the-radar" kid who accepts the way life happens around him. He tolerates the challenges in our family and keeps on doing his own thing. Most of the time, he does his work, even remotely during COVID, when many others didn't. He helps around the house with chores and enjoys cooking, which he is really good at. I appreciate his intellect and creativity, and he seems to have a good head on his shoulders. It fills me with pride to see him grow up as a wonderful young man. He has applied to several colleges and next year will likely be living on campus, not too far from home.

Like many teens, most of his time is spent on his computer, though at least he socializes with others and watches some educational videos. I have always admired the creative way Charlie thinks about things, and we have great conversations. Though he hates going back and forth, he splits his time between my house and Richard's. He still lets me hug and kiss him and tolerates my mothering with just a hint of teenage annoyance. I remain grateful for Charlie as my only neurotypical child, as he is the barometer against which I measure some of the outrageous behaviors of his siblings.

Pets

I am happy to report that Richard and I now share our dog, Carmela. She generally comes here when the kids do. Thankfully, she is no longer pulled from my arms. She shows her appreciation by licking me and sleeping in my room. Sebastian and I also adopted a pug puppy we named Zelda, who licks Carmela's ears incessantly like a toy.

Sebastian

During COVID, Sabastian spent most of his time at my house and we got along better than ever. My children, friends and family all love him and appreciate his calm, responsible and kind manner. He has become a wonderful role model for my children. He doesn't try to take over being their father, yet they get to see the way a couple should interact – respectful, helpful and loving. During Chanukah of 2020, he gave me a promise ring, indicating his intention to propose to me. I am excited to marry him and spend the rest of our lives together.

Final Thoughts

People often ask me why we adopted if we were going to get divorced. I want to be clear that while we had a challenging marriage, we didn't plan to get divorced before the adoption. Many people stay in less-than-ideal relationships, and for us, adoption was the next step in our joint life plan.

Even with everything my daughters have gone through due to the divorce, when I look at the friends they left behind in Ukraine, many did not fare well. Even before the war, the fate of many orphans around the world can be bleak. I believe that despite their challenges, we have provided opportunities for them to have a better life than if they had stayed in Ukraine. I don't have a crystal ball. No one can know for sure. We have given them love, even if they still don't always accept it or quite understand what that means. Hopefully, in time, they will.

People also ask if I would have chosen not to adopt if I'd known what I would have to go through. Let me be exceedingly clear: Adopting my daughters remains one of the best things I have done in my life. I don't want anyone to come away from this book thinking they shouldn't adopt. It is not an easy road. Your life will change in ways you never could have imagined, both for better and for worse. Many people who adopt have challenges in their families. It doesn't matter whether they adopt babies or older children, domestically or internationally. Many parents have challenges with their biological children, as well. If you have the love, patience, and the means to support a child, I fully encourage you to do so!

Being a mother is still what I cherish the most. It is the role in life that challenges me more than any other. It is also the part of my life that brings me the deepest joy. When I hug my children, any of them, it warms me to my core. They know I like two-armed hugs that wrap all around me, and my body relaxes in their embrace. Even with the challenges of my divorce and its aftermath, the four best things that I wouldn't have had without it, are my children.

My boys split their time between me and their father. I love when they are with me and miss them when they are not. Now they are on the cusp of adulthood, and I know my time with them is limited. I cherish the quick, "Good morning, Mom", that I ask Charlie to tell me daily so I get to see him briefly before school. When I see the impressive meals and desserts they cook, I am grateful for their creativity, the time savings and the knowledge that I have done something to help them become self-sufficient. Raising children has been my challenge, my pleasure, and my goal. To advocate for my children's needs and teach them to do so for themselves, is what I strive for.

Most mornings, before I get out of bed, I think of things I am grateful for and set an intention for the day. In addition to being thankful for the big things, like my kids, Sebastian and still having my parents around, I think about things we may take for granted, like having heat and running water and being able to have food and supplies delivered. I know I am incredibly fortunate to have the level of financial security that I do.

My current home is the best house I have ever lived in. I look around and see the nook in my bedroom, next to my Peloton bike, where I can do meditation. I see the trees out my window and Sebastian lying next to me. I am grateful for my job, my health and my health insurance. It has supported the significant needs of my family and enabled me to be there through countless hours of phone calls, emails and appointments to get what was needed for my children.

Ultimately, I remain grateful for the new roots that have started to grow in my life. They ground me, so no matter what chaos appears, I know I will have the strength and support I need to keep climbing.

ACKNOWLEDGMENTS

Many people helped to bring this labor of love to fruition and deserve my appreciation.

For my children, who may not have liked that I wrote about my life, which included them, but they believed in me and gave me time and support to see this through.

My deepest love and gratitude to Sebastian, who helped me throughout my divorce and to rediscover what relationships and life partners should be. He was the first to read *Up-Rooted* and patiently listened to many revisions. This book would not be what it is without him.

To my parents who have always supported me and frequently let me know how proud they are of me. They are my role models as a parent.

To my life-long friends, who were with me every step of the way, through my relationships, building my family, my divorce and my new start in life. You always know when to make me laugh and when to lend a shoulder to cry on. I love each of you for that and always will!

To my therapist, Madeleine, who got me through some of the roughest times in my life.

Two people, who are not family members, have been among the biggest inspirations in my life. Speaker, Lori Palatnik, from Momentum, whose sage advice made me think deeply in Israel and at home. I appreciate the time she took to read an early draft and advise me so that this dream could become a reality. The inspiration from my favorite Peloton instructor, Christine D'Ercole, permeates my life, both on and off the bike.

I want to thank all the people who read early drafts of Up-Rooted, and provided valuable feedback to make this book the best it can be.

Finally, this endeavor would not be possible without the team assembled through When Words Count. Steve Eisner, Ben Tanzer, David LeGere and the team at Woodhall Press – thank you for believing in me!

ABOUT THE AUTHOR

T.J. Kyri is the author of articles on bullying from the playground to the workplace. Since 1992, she has been a leader in Appropriate Dispute Resolution (ADR). She has taught thousands of adults and students in organizations and schools, from elementary through graduate school. Her expertise includes conflict resolution, restorative practices, social emotional learning, cultural competency, mediation, communication and related skills, through a trauma-informed and resilience-focused lens. She is a facilitator, strategic planning expert, and a passionate defender of individuals with special needs.

As the divorced mother of four children, adopted and biological, she is no stranger to multiple sides of conflict. T.J. resides with some of her kids some of the time, her dogs and her boyfriend in Westchester, New York.

Contact her at www.TJEdTraining.com